Licensing for Conveyancers

Related titles by Law Society Publishing

A Guide to the National Conveyancing Protocol
The Law Society
1 85328 997 3

Business Tenancies: A Guide to the New Law
Jason Hunter
1 85328 956 6

Conveyancing Handbook, 12th edn (Autumn 2005)
General Editor: Frances Silverman
1 85328 928 0

Environmental Law Handbook, 6th edn (Autumn 2005)
Trevor Hellawell
1 85328 978 7

Planning and Compulsory Purchase Act 2004: A Guide to the New Law
Stephen Tromans, Martin Edwards, Richard Harwood and Justine Thornton
1 85328 925 6

Titles from Law Society Publishing can be ordered from all good bookshops or direct from our distributors, Marston Book Services (tel. 01235 465656 or email **law.society@marston.co.uk**). For further information or a catalogue, email our editorial and marketing office at **publishing@lawsociety.org.uk**.

LICENSING FOR CONVEYANCERS

A Practical Guide

Tim Hayden and Jane Hanney

The Law Society

ISBN 1–85328–966–3

Published in 2005 by Law Society
113 Chancery Lane, London WC2A 1PL

Typeset by J&L Composition, Filey, North Yorkshire
Printed by Antony Rowe Ltd, Chippenham, Wilts

Contents

Preface

Conveyancing transactions frequently involve 'licensed' premises of different types. This book aims to provide conveyancing lawyers with a basic understanding of licensing law in order to be able to advise clients effectively.

The Licensing Act 2003 introduces a radically different licensing regime from that which has been in existence for the past 175 years. In some ways it could be said that the new legislation will result in a less complex system: for instance, there is no longer a distinction between on-licences, off-licences and restaurant licences; a different type of licence is not required depending on the type of licensable activity that is to be carried out; the concept of a 'fit and proper' person is abolished; and exemptions to the general rules on licensing hours are no longer required. However, on the other hand, as the system itself is so totally different and as it is to be administered by the local authorities rather than the magistrates' courts, it could initially prove to be more complicated to administer in practice.

There is no evidence that the changes introduced by the new Act have been widely understood or absorbed by the trade. No doubt many current licensees understand the potential impact of the changes, but undoubtedly there are also many who do not. Consequently, conveyancers may well find themselves having to explain to existing or prospective licensees what steps are necessary now and over the next year as well as advising on compliance in accordance with the new provisions.

For these reasons, this book attempts to present conveyancers with a summary of the basic provisions of the 2003 Act together with some explanation of the rationale behind the Act in order to provide an understanding of the new law and how it will affect conveyancing transactions of licensed premises.

Please note that unless otherwise stated all references in Chapters 1–13 are to the Licensing Act 2003.

Abbreviations

2003 Act	Licensing Act 2003
AWP	amusement with prizes
BGLA 1963	Betting, Gaming and Lotteries Act 1963
Butchers' Shops Regulations	Food Safety (General Food Hygiene) (Butchers' Shops) (Amendment) Regulations 2000
DCMS	Department for Culture, Media and Sport
DPS	designated premises supervisor
Food Premises Regulations	Food Premises (Registration) Regulations 1991
the Guidance	*Guidance issued under section 182 of the Licensing Act 2003 and Guidance to Police Officers on the Operation of Closure Powers in Part 8 of the Licensing Act 2003*, issued by The Secretary of State for Culture, Media and Sport, July 2004
HACCP	hazard analysis and critical control points
Hearings Regulations	Licensing Act 2003 (Hearings) Regulations 2005
PL Regulations	Licensing Act 2003 (Personal Licences) Regulations 2005
PLCPC Regulations	Licensing Act 2003 (Premises Licences and Club Premises Certificates) Regulations 2005
TP Order	Licensing Act 2003 (Transitional Provisions) Order 2005

Table of statutes

Page numbers in **bold** indicate where the legislation has been set out in part or in full.

Table of statutory instruments & European legislation

Statutory instruments

European legislation

PART 1

Licensing Act 2003 issues

CHAPTER 1

Introduction

1.1 THE BACKGROUND TO THE PRE-2003 ACT LAW

In April 2000 the Government issued a White Paper entitled *Time for Reform: Proposals for the Modernisation of our Licensing Laws*. The gestation period of this reforming legislation was lengthy. Subsequent chapters of this book summarise the principal changes that are made by the Licensing Act 2003 to those in the trade and particularly to those lawyers whose workload includes the sale or purchase of licensed premises. The Licensing Act 2003 has been abbreviated to '2003 Act' throughout this book, and where references are made to a section number without an Act being cited, these references will be to sections of the 2003 Act. This chapter is accordingly a short reflection on how we have reached the new licensing framework.

Public opinion on the arrival of the Alehouse Act 1828 is difficult to gauge from this distance but that Act marks the start of 175 years of legislation regulating the sales of intoxicating liquor. For all of that period magistrates had responsibility for determining who are fit and proper persons to sell alcohol and authorising them to do so.

Control of licensed premises has never been limited to the judicial approval of those responsible for the sale of alcohol. The magistrates' courts have also had responsibility for ensuring that the quality of intoxicating liquor is maintained, i.e. that licensees cannot enrich themselves unjustly by serving adulterated or diluted drinks. Similarly, legislation has provided sanctions against licensees who permit their premises to be used by those whose drunken or immoral behaviour might threaten or corrupt other customers.

These controls were part of the pre-2003 Act law. Under s.174 of the Licensing Act 1964, licensees may refuse to admit or may expel 'any person who is drunken, violent, quarrelsome or disorderly'. Sections 172 and 173 prohibit licensees from permitting drunkenness or procuring drinks for a drunken person. Section 175 provides that the holder of a justices' licence must not knowingly allow the licensed premises to be the habitual resort or place of meeting of reputed prostitutes – although the section goes on to permit those individuals to remain in the premises long enough (but no longer) for the purpose of reasonable refreshment.

Apart from the perceived evils of prostitution and drunkenness, the first controls over licensed premises also regulated the admission of those of bad character and the unlawful playing of games. The control of gaming on such premises remains part of current legislation but see **Chapter 15**.

Restrictions on the hours when the sale of intoxicating liquor is permitted have also been ever present from 1828 to the regime prior to the 2003 Act. Those restrictions have reflected the social, economic and religious requirements of the time. As a result, Christmas Day, Good Friday and Sundays have had fewer permitted hours. Public houses cannot open between 11 a.m. and noon on Sundays under the old regime (although the desperate drinker can always slake a thirst between 10 a.m. and noon by means of an off-licence).

Until implementation of the 2003 Act, public houses still have to close at 10.30 p.m. on Sundays, rather than at 11 p.m. Logic perhaps suggests that this restriction was based more on economic grounds – an early night before the first working day of the week – than on any particular respect for the Sabbath. That observation cannot apply to Good Friday, which is similarly restricted to 10.30 p.m.

Many readers will recall the position prior to 1988 when licensed premises were allowed only two periods of permitted hours over lunchtime (11 a.m.–2 p.m.) and in the evening (6 p.m.–11 p.m.), although not on Sundays. The Licensing Act 1988 permitted all-day drinking in the form of a basic weekday entitlement of 12 hours from 11 a.m. to 11 p.m. The anticipated surge of drunkenness and disorder never arrived. However, in many rural areas the additional hours never arrived either. Economic factors precluded licensees from opening all day and many maintained (and still do) a pattern of lunchtime and evening hours wholly familiar to those who drafted the 1964 Act.

The trend to either derestrict or liberalise opening hours – which is wholly opened out by the Licensing Act 2003 – has also altered patterns for off-licensed premises. The Sunday hours for off-licences used to mirror those for public houses. It was not until the Licensing (Sunday Hours) Act 1995 that off-licences were permitted to open on Sunday mornings, from 10 a.m. onwards. Again, economic factors such as the number of customers and the cost of staff might preclude specialist off-licences from utilising the extra hours available but the major impact of these reforms has been seen by the supermarkets and convenience stores whose opening hours often exceed permitted hours in any event.

For many of these it was the Sunday Trading Act 1994 that limited trading rather than the Licensing Acts. Under that legislation, large retail premises are restricted to a maximum of six hours opening time on Sundays.

From 1840 onwards it has been possible to obtain a licence which restricts sales of alcohol to sales for consumption off the premises. These licences could only be granted to the true occupier of the premises, and occupation and control remained critical factors for licensing committees prior to the 2003 Act regime. Most required that at least one joint licensee should have day-to-day control of the premises. However this will often not amount to actual occupation, as many off-licences do not include residential accommodation. Committees generally sought to ensure that one licensee had 'hands on' responsibility for premises and staff in order to ensure compliance and prevent disorder. Absent licensees obviously have the same legal liabilities and accordingly risks if store staff ignore statutory requirements.

Space here does not permit full consideration of the liability of absent licensees for their staff but it is not always open to a licensee to hide behind either a lack of knowledge or the exercise of due diligence on his part to avoid the commission of an offence.

Control of gaming was first introduced in 1845. This legislation restricted the use of premises for billiards, particularly on days of religious significance. Extraordinarily these restrictions, which also applied to village halls and community centres, survived until 1987, when the right of police to enter such places to check for unauthorised billiard playing was removed. Constables retain the right to enter and check snooker halls which have the benefit of a liquor licence under s.186 of the Licensing Act 1964. Justices currently have the power to authorise some gaming under s.6 of the Gaming Act 1968 within licensed premises. This provision authorises the playing of dominoes or cribbage or other games specially authorised by the licensing justices.

The original controls over sales of alcohol to children could be viewed as either remarkably liberal or remarkably absent. In 1872 sales of spirits to children under the age of 16 was forbidden – or at least it was forbidden to those appearing to be under 16. In 1901 the Child Messengers Act prohibited the sale of intoxicating liquor to children under the age of 14 unless it was at least a reputed pint and corked and sealed. In 1923 restrictions were introduced on the sale of intoxicating liquor in a bar to those under 18 or the consumption of intoxicating liquor in a bar by those under 18. This remains the basic position to this date, subject to exceptions for 16 and 17 year olds, who are permitted to consume specified drink as an ancillary to a meal. This area was the subject of considerable interest and debate whilst the new legislation was consulted upon. It is discussed in more detail later, but, in simple terms, the Government has not seen fit to liberalise this area further.

The first licences for sales of intoxicating liquor did not involve scrutiny or approval of the premises from which sales would take place. Provided that licensees paid for the appropriate licence they could sell alcohol from their own dwelling houses for consumption on or off those premises. The Licensing Act 1872 required standard forms of application to license any houses for the sale of any type of intoxicating liquor, but it was not until 1902 that plans of the premises were required. The Licensing Act 1902 also gave licensing justices a complete discretion to refuse the grant of an off-licence. It also introduced controls very familiar to licensing practitioners today with the requirement that justices should approve any alterations to licensed premises or refuse consent for alterations which they thought inappropriate.

This legislation also prohibited the use of licensed premises for the holding of court proceedings or inquests. Since inquests 100 years ago often involved the examination of corpses, this legislation could be justified as much on grounds of hygiene as on the risk of miscarriages of justice.

The rules relating to renewal of licences were reviewed in 1910 (Licensing (Consolidation) Act 1910) to establish a system which has remained, up until the introduction of the new legislation.

Until 1910, renewals could be obtained in respect of any premises which had been previously licensed. After 1910 renewals could only be secured for premises which had held a similar licence at the time, or at the date of the preceding general annual licensing meeting. Subsequently a failure to renew at the general annual licensing meeting would lead to the licence expiring on 4 April following.

The application to renew could be pursued between the general annual licensing meeting and April *if* the licensee could demonstrate that failure to renew in time was not the result of mere inadvertence (unless that inadvertence was accompanied by some mitigating circumstances). The March sessions throughout the country have accordingly been illuminated by innovative and desperate excuses to secure renewals 'out of time' and to avoid the expense and delay of obtaining a new licence. Generally speaking, committees took a pragmatic approach to the oversights laid before them.

These renewals remained an annual event until the Licensing Act 1988, when a system of triennial renewals was implemented. Delays in the arrival of the Licensing Act 2003 meant a final round of renewals and a final round of imaginative excuses.

For the first 90 years or so there was no legislative control over the hours permitted for drinking. The Great War and the steps needed to prevent drunkenness in munitions factories resulted first in temporary controls and then permanent ones, under the Licensing Act 1920. The regime in 1920 comprised a permitted period of eight hours – nine hours in London – and then a total of five hours (everywhere) on Sunday.

Extensions to permitted hours were granted to restaurants, enabling them to secure an additional hour by way of what became known as 'supper hour certificates'. That additional facility was extended to all premises supplying table meals (provided that application was made under s.68 of the Licensing Act 1964). The certificate applied only in a part of the premises usually set aside for the service of such meals and to authorise sales of intoxicating liquor as an ancillary to such a meal.

Further extensions to permitted hours became available to premises supplying food and providing music and dance. Those reforms (extended from London to the whole of the jurisdiction in 1961) were covered by s.76

of the Licensing Act 1964. A 'special hours certificate' under that section permitted hours to be extended to 2 a.m. subject to times at which music and dance actually stops.

For premises without these additional hours the limitations remained in place until 1988. Many readers will recall the alternative views of outrage or relief expressed when the opportunity for pubs to remain open all day long arrived. The Licensing (Sunday Hours) Act 1995 subsequently extended all-day opening to Sundays. Nonetheless, Sunday hours (permitted by that legislation from noon to 10.30 p.m.) remained shorter than those permitted during the remainder of the week. Christmas Day became the only day where there was a mandatory break between lunchtime and evening hours – four hours from 3 p.m. onwards.

Reforms in relation to off-licences brought longer hours for those premises with off sales from 8 a.m. on weekdays and from 10 a.m. on Sundays.

Even against the backdrop of these extended hours, the arrangements for the Millennium Celebrations in 2000 represented a further evolution in deregulation. By bridging the period between 11 p.m. on 31 December and 11 a.m. on 1 January, the Government granted permitted hours for an entire 36-hour period. This arrangement has been repeated either by licensing committees or by way of statutory instrument on New Year's Eves since 2000 and in relation to the Queen's Jubilee celebrations in 2002.

Throughout these 175 years of legislative development, many fundamental reforms to the licensed trade have originated outside the Licensing Acts.

The most significant reform is the development of law relating to music and dancing – latterly public entertainment licences. Music, singing and dancing licences originated in 1890 under the Public Health Act (Amendment) Act. In the early 1980s the Local Government (Miscellaneous Provisions) Act 1982 removed control of such licences from justices to local authorities.

The popularity of musical entertainment in public houses meant that many licensees required a public entertainment licence to run in tandem with the liquor licence. For those premises seeking extended hours under a special hours certificate it was a prerequisite that a public entertainment licence should be held. The popularity of musical entertainment in public houses also meant that many licensees required public entertainment licences irrespective of the fact that their operation was entirely within hours permitted by the Licensing Acts.

To practitioners, the most significant changes to licensing practice since 1964 came in 1999 with the arrival of the Justices' Clerks' Society's Good Practice Guide. That Guide reflected many sensible approaches and principles to be found in the policies of licensing committees up and down the country.

It enabled licensing practitioners to argue consistency in front of committees whose approach had until 1999 been one of local concern. Most importantly – and under some protest – it effectively abolished the concept of 'need' in relation to applications for new licences.

Even in 1972 the Errol Committee (convened to advise on licensing reform) had indicated that the 'need' test was out of date. However, it survived in many justices' policy documents up to and even after 1999, as some committees clung to the notion that a new licence could only be granted if there were insufficient licensed premises in the area of their jurisdiction. The Good Practice Guide recommended that the issue of sufficiency of premises should carry little or no weight in determining applications for new licences and that the issue of need should be seen in the context of public safety and of protecting the public against nuisance and disorder.

Those principles reappear in the new legislation which represents the most significant legislative reform for 40 years and the first time that control of liquor licensing has been placed with local authorities.

1.2 COMMENCEMENT

The Licensing Act 2003 received Royal Assent on 10 July 2003.

The Guidance to licensing authorities and police on the discharge of their functions under the 2003 Act was issued by the Secretary of State on 7 July 2004.

The commencement order announcing the 'first appointed day' as 7 February 2005 came into force on 1 August 2004. This date marks the beginning of the transitional period. The 'second appointed day' was announced on 8 June 2005 and is 24 November 2005.

During the transitional period the old and new systems will run in parallel to a certain extent. Any applications for renewals, variations, transfers, etc. to existing licences, or any applications for new licences, that are to take effect before the end of the transitional period will need to be made under the 1964 legislation.

Within the first six months of the transititional period (referred to in this book as the 'conversion period'), holders of existing licences can convert their licences to the new licences. All new licences will take effect from the second appointed day and this will signify the end of the old licensing regime.

CHAPTER 2

The pre-2003 Act regime

2.1 INTRODUCTION

In view of the fact that this book is due to be published during the transitional period between the first and second appointed days, the pre-2003 Act regime is a topic which is not yet of merely academic interest. Until the second appointed day (24 November 2005), the law relating to licensed premises is that which was set out within the framework of the Licensing Act 1964 and which, of course, has been subject to countless amendments over the last 40 years or so. Some of those amendments will be referred to in other chapters but what follows here is a brief summary of the pre-2003 Act regime and some practical advice covering the acquisition or transfer of licensed premises until such time as the new system is in force.

The second appointed day has been set as 24 November 2005. There has been a slow start to the process of converting existing licences into the new system. This has placed huge pressure on the local authorities and most applications have been submitted during the latter half of the transitional period. With a period of just three and a half months between the end of the transitional period and the second appointed day, it appears possible that not all of the applications will be processed by the second appointed day.

It might have been assumed that the imminent arrival of a new system would have slowed down activity within the current licensing committees, but that does not appear to be the case. Many licensees, particularly multiples, are taking these final opportunities to place additional licensees on to existing justices' licences. Operators who for years have resisted overtures to place two or three licensees on off-licensed premises – for example – have now placed five or six on to licences of that type. There are two possible reasons for this enthusiasm. One is the suspicion of the new system and in particular the extent to which political considerations will influence its operation. The second possible reason is that holders of justices' licences prior to August 2005 will (subject to police objections) secure personal licences under the new system without the need to undergo the training specified in the Regulations published under the 2003 Act.

Clearly, there will be many sales or acquisitions between the two dates in any event. The industry is scarcely likely to shut down over a period of this length. Retirements, business failures, new business opportunities and the wish to make further investments will keep licensing justices occupied until their jurisdiction is taken from them.

The following sections accordingly set out the existing and continuing requirements for those opening new premises, transferring existing ones, or wishing to extend current licences during the period prior to the second appointed day.

2.2 NEW LICENCES

In order to make retail sales of intoxicating liquor, the seller must be the holder of a justices' licence.

The definition of intoxicating liquor includes spirits, wines, beers and ciders together with any other fermented, distilled or spirituous liquor. Excluded from the definition is liquor which contains not more than 0.5% alcohol by volume and various other 'alcoholic' substances such as perfumes or medicines (Licensing Act 1964, s.201(1)).

The fact that a licence is required for retail sales suggests, of course, that non-retail sales can be made without the seller being licensed. As a result, sales to those within the licensed trade do not require a licence. Additionally, sales in large quantities are also excluded (Licensing Act 1964, s.201(1)). The quantities are one case (or 9 litres) for spirits or wine, and two cases (20 litres) for beer or cider. These sales are to be made from the vendor's own premises for consumption off the premises. This has been a very useful provision for many years for wine shippers (selling by the case only) or producers of cider (selling from the farms) and also for garage proprietors prevented by the 1964 legislation from holding a justices' licence but able to sell in bulk from the forecourt. The definition of sale by retail under the 2003 Act incidentally removes the exception based on the quantity sold and limits wholesale trading to sales or supplies made to other traders or licensees.

The types of licences that can be granted by licensing justices are set out by statute as follows.

Justices' on-licence (Licensing Act 1964, s.1(3)(a)):

- intoxicating liquor of all descriptions;
- beer, cider and wine only;
- beer and cider only; or
- wine only.

Justices' off-licence (Licensing Act 1964, s.1(3)(b)):

- intoxicating liquor of all descriptions; or
- beer, wine and cider only.

Committees are not permitted to grant licences which do not fall into the statutory list. Nor can they create a licence which differs from those above by imposing conditions which limit the type of intoxicating liquor which can be sold.

The grant of a justices' licence can be made to any person considered by the licensing committee to be fit and proper (Licensing Act 1964, s.3(1)). It follows that any person can apply (subject to the disqualifications specified in s.9) for a licence and that the justices have an unfettered discretion as to whether the licence should be granted. This position can be contrasted with the 2003 Act in relation to premises licences, where the categories of applicant are restricted, as are the grounds on which the licence can be refused.

The initial advice required from a practitioner for a client who seeks to obtain the new justices' licence is likely to relate to the suitability of the proposed premises and the suitability of the applicant(s). That applicant needs to be 'fit and proper'. In 1999, the Justices' Clerks' Society published a Good Practice Guide to establish common principles to be applied in licensing applications, and this Guide has been reviewed regularly since its inception. It recognises the general acceptance that new entrants to the trade should undergo training – generally speaking the training courses which result in the grant of the National Licensees Certificate. Although policies still vary from committee to committee, most will not grant a licence to a new applicant (by way of new grant or transfer) unless the applicant either has held a licence within the previous three years, or is the holder of the National Licensee's Certificate.

The general experience and training of the applicant is only the first part of whether that individual is a fit and proper person. The second part relates to his character and in particular whether there are previous convictions which could mark him out as unsuitable. The police will make their own assessment of suitability and will check to find details of previous convictions. Although spent convictions should rarely be relevant, the police often tender them to licensing committees as a matter of routine. The police also look at the aspect of effective control and objections are still maintained from time to time where the ability to exercise control is doubted in view of the antecedent history of the applicant's spouse or partner, rather than their own previous history.

In addition to a suitable licensee, the premises must also be suitable. Justices are directed (save for temporary premises) not to grant a new justices' licence unless the premises are structurally adapted to the class of licence required (Licensing Act 1964, s.64). The justices and the police will be concerned to ensure that the layout of the premises enables proper supervision, and also that the location of the premises is appropriate. Many aspects of suitability, however, are legislated for outside the Licensing Acts. Jurisdiction for planning issues or environmental matters will lie with the local authorities rather than with the licensing justices.

The Good Practice Guide lists areas which should be considered by licensing committees in relation to premises:

- nature, size, character and location;
- safety of users;
- security of premises;
- supervision of licensed areas (also gardens and car parks);
- condition and standard of maintenance of premises.

2.3 NEED

Licensing practitioners with a long period of experience will recall that previously most of the evidence on new applications related to whether additional premises were needed in a particular locality. The recommendation in the Good Practice Guide, however, is that when considering the question of need or demand committees should not attach much, if any, weight to the threat from competition and should not consider trade protection as being a matter which is relevant when exercising their discretion. Although committees' discretion in these matters remains unfettered, most committees have adopted the recommendations of the Guide and opposition from competitors has become rare.

The only caveat to this principle is that committees will look at the number of premises in a particular area for the purpose of determining whether premises are becoming so numerous in the locality as to lead to problems of noise and disturbance or disorder.

2.4 PROVISIONAL GRANTS (LICENSING ACT 1964, S.6)

There will be occasions when practitioners are approached by clients who wish either to construct new licensed premises or to convert premises to make them suitable for such use. The same overriding principle – namely that an applicant should know before he makes his investment whether a licence would be granted – applies in both the new and the old licensing systems, although the new system does not provide the same degree of certainty as in the system it will replace. The current timescale for full implementation of the new legislation, however, means that there will be very few new applications to justices for provisional licences. The practitioner is now more likely to encounter applicants who already hold provisional licences and are seeking a final grant.

The effect of a provisional grant is to approve licensed premises on the basis of the plans submitted by the applicant showing the proposed development. When those premises have been completed a final grant will be made by the licensing committee (the committee has no discretion) provided that it is satisfied that the premises have been completed in accordance with the approved plans (Licensing Act 1964, s.6(4)). The committee could decline to make a final grant if it is not satisfied that the applicant is a fit and proper person, although this will normally have been dealt with at the provisional stage. The provisional grant procedure has been re-enacted under the 2003 Act but in the form of provisional statements and in such a way that it is possible that the provisional approval could be rejected on the basis of objections raised for the first time once the premises have been completed. This area is covered in detail at **para.7.10**.

Procedural requirements for these applications (new licences, provisional grants and final grants) are set out in Sched.2 to the 1964 Act. Twenty-one clear days' notice of the application must be given in writing to:

- the chief executive to the licensing justices;
- the chief officer of police; and
- the proper local authority.

In England but outside Greater London, the local authority will be the district council. In Greater London, the local authority will be the appropriate London borough council. If the premises are in Wales then service should be on the proper officer of the county council or county borough council. Where the premises to be licensed are in a parish, the proper officer of the parish council should be served, or in the absence of a parish council, the chairman of the parish meeting. Where there is a town council, rather than a parish council, the proper officer of the town council should receive a notice. Finally, if there is a community council, the notice should be directed to the proper officer of that council. In all cases involving new licences, the fire authority must be served as well.

2.5 SERVICE OF NOTICES

It is necessary to keep in mind at all times that the periods specified in Sched. 2 to the Licensing Act 1964 are not optional or discretionary. The failure to abide by the procedural requirements may cause delays in the completion of a transaction or a delay of the time at which the purchaser can start trading. Both could result in financial losses, and the possibility of claims being made against the solicitor responsible.

The following general propositions may be of assistance:

1. Where a statute authorises the service of a document by post, service shall be deemed to be effected by properly addressing, pre-paying and posting the letter containing the document. Unless the contrary is proved, service will have been effected at the time when the letter would have been delivered in the ordinary course of post.
2. Section 197 of the Licensing Act 1964 authorises the service of any notice or document by post. This is not a mandatory requirement and therefore does not exclude personal service which may be necessary where time is very short.
3. Delivery of a letter sent by first class mail will be presumed to take place on the second day after posting with no account being taken of Sunday. Accordingly, a letter posted on Monday will be presumed to be delivered on Wednesday, and one posted on Friday may be presumed to have been delivered on the following Monday. Acknowledgements provided by recipients may of course (assuming that first class post is generally more efficient than the presumption) demonstrate that the service was actually effected on the day after posting.
4. There is no requirement for the service of notices by any service which provides recorded delivery. Whilst such a service will provide independent evidence of the posting, pre-payment and correct addressing of an envelope, it will not prove the contents of that envelope. To cover both aspects, the most frequent proof of service is by way of the certificate from the person who posted the document dealing with the particulars of the posting and also exhibiting a copy of the notice.
5. When it is convenient to do so, or when time is of the essence (so much of the essence in fact that service by post may not be feasible) then service can be made in person. It will be necessary to ensure that the recipient receives the document on the date of service. It will not be sufficient for an envelope containing the notice to simply be left in a post box or for collection. The certificate provided in these circumstances should specify the date and time that service was effected and the identity of the person who received the document.
6. Schedule 2 provides that notices of application for justices' licences shall be served on recipients 'not less than' 21 days before the date of the licensing sessions. This means 21 'clear' days and as a result the day of actual service and the date on which the transfer sessions occur are both excluded from the calculation. If a transfer session is held on Thursday 23 May, then notices to be effected would have to be served at the latest by Wednesday 1 May. Bearing in mind the comments above concerning postal service, any service effected by post would have to take place no later than Monday 29 April.
7. Care needs to be taken to check the identity of the appropriate recipient and that the notice is being sent to the correct address for that recipient.
8. The first enquiry should be to the office of the clerk to the licensing

committee. In that way the practitioner can determine any particular requirements which the committee may have set out in its statement of policy. Some committees for example require that notices should be sent not only to the chief executive of the local authority, but also to the chief environmental health officer, chief planning officer and head of building control. Further to that, the clerk will be able to confirm the local authorities with the responsibility for the area of the premises and provide names and addresses for the proper officers. Finally, the clerk will be able to inform the practitioner of any particular requirements relating to notices prior to the hearing, e.g. that all certificates should be lodged with the court in order to prove service of notice, etc. a certain number of days prior to the sessions themselves.

In addition to the statutory requirements set out in Sched.2, it has become accepted practice for a questionnaire to be supplied by the police covering matters which relate to the fitness of the applicant to hold a licence. The questionnaire is set out at Appendix 4 to the Good Practice Guide. Most committees will also require the completion of a questionnaire (at Appendix 7 to the Guide) relating to the suitability of the premises.

There are also set out in Sched.2 requirements to advertise on the premises and in a local newspaper. The requirement for a notice on the premises is that it should be in place for a period of seven days, and located where it can conveniently be read by the public on or near the premises to be licensed. The period must fall within the 28 days prior to the licensing sessions. Where the application is for a provisional grant, posting on or near the proposed site will suffice.

The newspaper advertisement is to be placed not more than 28 and not less than 14 days before the licensing sessions. Notice of application must be placed in a newspaper circulating in the place where the premises to be licensed are situated. This is again a situation where practitioners should seek the advice of the clerk to the licensing justices. Within their policy statements the committees will generally designate newspapers which are approved for the purposes of service.

The importance of early contact with the clerk's office cannot be overestimated. Apart from such basic details as obtaining details of the next and following transfer sessions, the responsibility of a licensing committee for a particular premises or areas will often need to be checked. Historical peculiarities abound in licensing practice and the author knows of two sets of premises within the jurisdiction of Somerset committees which are respectively (according to the ordnance survey sheet) in Devon and Dorset!

Finally on the procedural requirements, para.3 of Sched.2 requires that a plan shall be deposited for the grant of a new justices' on-licence. In practice, committees will always require a plan for a new application (off-licences as well as on-licences) and the policy statement will cover the scale of the plan (generally 1:100) and the colouring which the justices require.

There is no requirement for advertisement of an application to transfer a licence either on the premises or in a newspaper.

2.6 PART IV LICENCES

Part IV of the Licensing Act 1964 regulates licences for restaurants and hotels. These licences are subject to statutory conditions which restrict the sale or supply of intoxicating liquor to particular categories of customer. The licences covered by Part IV are restaurant licences, residential licences or a licence combining those two uses (Licensing Act 1964, s.93). Provided that no conditions (other than the statutory ones) are applied to these licences then the premises will be defined as holding a Part IV licence with fixed conditions, differing hours (other than in the case of a purely residential licence) and limited grounds for refusal.

Licensing committees will grant a restaurant licence if they are satisfied that the premises are structurally adapted and intended to be used for habitually providing a customary main meal at lunchtime or in the evening (or both) for those attending the premises. Such a licence is subject to the condition that intoxicating liquor shall not be sold or supplied on the premises otherwise than to persons taking table meals there and for consumption by such a person as an ancillary to his meal (Licensing Act 1964, s.94(1)).

A residential licence will be granted for premises used or intended to be used for the purpose of habitually providing for reward board and lodging including breakfast and one other at least of the customary main meals. This licence is subject to the condition that intoxicating liquor shall not be sold or supplied on the premises otherwise than to persons residing there and for consumption by such a person either on the premises or with a meal supplied at but to be consumed off the premises (Licensing Act 1964, s.94(2)). In addition, supplies of alcohol can be made to private friends of those residing there, but these supplies must be at the expense of the residents.

A residential and restaurant licence will be granted to premises which satisfy both of the above requirements and is subject to a condition that intoxicating liquor shall not sold or supplied otherwise than as permitted by the conditions which apply to a restaurant licence or to a residential licence (Licensing Act 1964, s.94(3)).

In addition to these conditions, there is a further condition (described in the statute as implied) that suitable non-alcoholic beverages will be available for consumption with or otherwise as an ancillary to meals served on the licensed premises (Licensing Act 1964, s.94(5)). Additionally there is a requirement for residential premises that, in the absence of good reason, there should be made available to residents a seating area which is not used for sleeping accommodation, for the service of substantial refreshment or for the supply or consumption of intoxicating liquor (Licensing Act 1964, s.96).

Once an applicant has demonstrated as part of his application that he can comply with the requirements of such a licence, then the powers of the committee to refuse the grant are limited. This of course contrasts with the position of the committee on an application for a full justices' licence where their discretion is unlimited.

The grounds of refusal can be summarised as follows (Licensing Act 1964, s.98).

1. That the applicant is under the age of 18 or is not fit and proper.
2. That the premises are not suitable or convenient in view of the use proposed.
3. That in the 12 months prior (clearly this must relate to a grant on renewal or transfer) the licence has been forfeited or the premises ill-conducted.
4. That the licensee has failed to provide table meals of a kind to which the consumption of intoxicating liquor might be ancillary.
5. That service is by way of self service which is undesirable.
6. That large numbers of persons resorting to the premises (restaurant or residential) are under 18s who are unaccompanied by adults.
7. That there has been a failure by the applicant to permit inspection of the facilities by the statutory authorities.

Where either a restaurant licence is held or a restaurant and residential licence, then the provisions of s.68 of the Licensing Act 1964 are automatically applied. Such premises therefore have an automatic supper hour certificate permitting sales of intoxicating liquor for one hour after normal permitted hours, i.e. until 12 midnight from Monday to Saturday and until 11.30 p.m. on Sundays. Such sales or supplies however must of course be ancillary to a meal being provided under the terms of the licence.

2.7 CONDITIONAL LICENCES

The licensing justices are enabled by s.4 of the Licensing Act 1964 to place conditions on the grant of any on-licence. The section empowers the justices to impose such conditions as they think proper in the interests of the public.

From the outset of any transaction, practitioners will need to establish whether conditions have been imposed on any licence and whether the conditions have been complied with. Although the licence must specify the conditions imposed, very often those conditions are endorsed on the back of the licence and may not be photocopied when a copy of the licence is obtained. Specific enquiry will need to be made.

There are a small number of removable conditions, for example on six-day or early-closing licences, which are imposed at the request of the original applicant and which can be removed on request.

The vast majority of conditions however are imposed by the licensing justices on a discretionary basis. These are permanent conditions which can only be removed by an application for the grant of a new licence free of the conditions originally imposed. The old licence would be surrendered as part of the same process.

Many conditions on older licences were placed there with the encouragement of the original applicant. When need was a factor in determining whether a new licence would be granted, applicants would often offer conditions to appease objectors and to encourage licensing justices to make the grant, albeit on a limited basis. As a result, licences still include conditions preventing such things as off-sales or the ability to obtain occasional licences. Such conditions would now be unlawful. It has been held that the following types of condition cannot be imposed by justices.

1. A condition which alters the types of alcohol which can be sold or supplied under a justices' on-licence. The categories are prescribed by statute and committees are not at liberty to create new categories by the imposition of conditions which either add to or subtract from the types of intoxicating liquor which can be sold or supplied.
2. A condition that off-sales cannot be made – such sales are a fundamental part of a justices' on-licence.
3. Conditions which prevent a licensee from exercising a lawful right to make further applications. This would cover a condition which prevented an application to extend permitted hours and could equally apply to a condition precluding an application for an occasional licence.

In view of the fact that conditions can only be imposed on a justices' on-licence, a parallel system has developed in relation to off-licences. Rather than the imposition of conditions, committees have obtained undertakings or assurances from the licensee when an off-licence has been granted. These undertakings are endorsed on the licence in exactly the same way as conditions. Whilst a breach of an undertaking would not be an offence, it is something that could result in a refusal to renew a licence, or provide the basis of an application to revoke.

2.8 STRUCTURAL ALTERATIONS

Applications for new licences will inevitably diminish, but in anticipation of applications to convert to the new system, there is and will be a stream of applications to alter licensed premises.

Where licensees are considering alterations to their premises, different considerations apply dependent on whether those premises are on-licensed or off-licensed. Off-licences have never been subject to a statutory requirement that a plan should be lodged for approval when the licence is granted. Many off-licensed premises do not have plans setting out the licensed areas. Whilst it has been accepted practice to file plans for off-licences as well as on-licences, most committees will grant the licence for the whole of the retail area, rather than limiting the licensed area to the (often small) area utilised for the display and sale of intoxicating liquor.

In these circumstances, licensees can move, diminish or enlarge those areas as they wish. The only area of caution is that substantial enlargement of premises is likely to result in the requirement to seek a new licence for premises which have been changed to such an extent that they no longer represent the same premises as those for which the licence was originally granted. As a matter of practice, minor enlargements or alterations are dealt with by simply depositing an amended plan with the clerk to the relevant committee.

For on-licensed premises similar considerations apply where there is a major enlargement. Most licensing policies have a section detailing the percentage increase in the licensed area which will normally require the submission of an application for a new licence rather than an application for approval of structural alterations.

For the practitioner dealing with a sale or purchase of licensed premises, it will not be prospective structural alterations which will first require his attention. Consideration of whether structural alterations have taken place at the premises will be the matter of primary concern. Frequently licensees will alter premises without prior approval from the licensing committee. By the time that they have secured planning permission or building regulation consent, many overlook the separate requirement to obtain consent from the licensing justices.

There are three areas of alteration which require approval (Licensing Act 1964, s.20).

1. An alteration which gives increased facilities for drinking in a public or common part of the premises.
2. An alteration which conceals from observation a public or common part of the premises used for drinking.
3. An alteration which affects the communication between the public part of the premises where intoxicating liquor is sold and the remainder of the premises or any street or other public way.

Approval cannot be given retrospectively. Contravention of these provisions (on a complaint) can result in forfeiture of the licence or an order that the premises be restored to their original condition (Licensing Act 1964, s.20(3)). In practice the practitioner should advise a licensee who has carried out unauthorised alterations that the new area of the premises should be taken out of commission and that the licensee should immediately apply for a new licence to encompass the revised layout. The risks to the purchaser are obvious. The power of the magistrates to forfeit the licence or to require the restoration of the original premises is not limited to the period whilst the premises are in the occupation of the licensee who carried out the unauthorised work.

For prospective applications, the procedural requirements are as follows.

1. Check that the proposed alterations are of a type which require approval, and if in doubt seek a preliminary view from the committee.
2. Check the licensing policy of the relevant committee as to the requirements for service. There are no statutory requirements but the policy will normally require plans to be deposited at least 21 days prior to a transfer session date and will require service of the plans on the police, fire authority and the local authority. The policy will also generally include directions as to how the alterations are to be identified on the plans which must be served.

Apart from altering the premises themselves, licensees or prospective licensees may well wish to secure additional facilities, in terms of extended hours for the service of intoxicating liquor, for their premises or for the premises which they are seeking to acquire. The two variations from standard permitted hours most frequently encountered are by way of s.68 of the Licensing Act 1964, commonly known as a 'supper hour certificate', and s.77 of the Licensing Act 1964 by way of a 'special hours certificate'. There is also a facility under s.70 of the Licensing Act 1964 for extended hours in restaurants which provide entertainment but such orders are rarely found in practice.

2.9 SUPPER HOUR CERTIFICATES

When the 1964 legislation was enacted, and for a substantial period afterwards, there was a lengthy break between the licensing hours at lunchtime and those in the evening. On Sundays, for example, public houses closed at 2 p.m. and reopened at 7 p.m.

Section 68 of the Licensing Act 1964 enabled licensees of premises providing table meals to apply for a certificate which permitted them to serve alcohol – subject to the conditions below – during the break between the first and second parts of the permitted hours. This provision (due to the gradual extension of licensing hours) is now only relevant on Christmas Day, that being the only day where there is a compulsory break between lunchtime and evening hours. That break is between 3 p.m. and 7 p.m.

Of wider relevance, however, is the second opportunity provided by this section, namely, to add an hour at the end of the evening to those which are generally permitted. Accordingly a certificate obtained under s.68(1)(b) will permit the service of intoxicating liquor until midnight from Monday to Saturday and until 11.30 p.m. on Sundays.

As the name of the certificate suggests, the extension of permitted hours in this manner is for the purpose of supplying intoxicating liquors to diners rather than to the general public. Sale or supply is therefore limited to the sale or supply to persons taking table meals and the consumption of intoxicating liquor must take place in a part of the premises set apart for the service to those persons and it must take place as an ancillary to the meal.

'Table meal' is defined in s.201(1) of the Licensing Act 1964 and the definition is not limited to tables. It includes for example a counter. Whatever the structure, however, the diner must be seated.

'Set apart' does not mean a separate or isolated part of the premises. It will be a question of fact as to whether the area qualifies, but put simply it should be an area reserved for customers taking table meals. Apart from legal difficulties ensuring that an area shared by diners and other customers is actually 'set apart', the licensee is likely to run into practical difficulties if he seeks to operate the certificate in an area where non-diners are present. If he wrongly determines which customers are subject to extended facilities, then he will risk prosecution.

The word 'ancillary' also requires some explanation. It has been defined as not being limited to drinks taken with the meal itself. An aperitif before the meal and/or a digestif afterwards appear to fall within the definition of ancillary. Both, however, would have to be served in an area set apart. The consumption of several pints of beer after the meal would not be likely to be regarded as ancillary. In the unlikely event of a dispute on this issue, the justices would be required to determine as a matter of fact whether drinks after a meal remain ancillary to it.

As for the procedural requirements, notice of an application for a supper hour certificate must be served on the chief officer of police and on the clerk to the licensing justices at least seven days before the licensing sessions. The justices will need to be satisfied that the premises are structurally adapted and intended to be used for the purpose of providing substantial refreshment to which the sale of intoxicating liquor is ancillary. Substantial refreshment is again a matter of fact. It need not be a 'main meal' but it should be a meal rather than provision of a snack.

The certificate applies to the premises as a whole. There is no legal reason why the area 'set apart' should not differ according to the licensee's requirements. However, it is clearly envisaged in the Good Practice Guide that specified areas should be set out on a plan and that a plan should be submitted with the application.

2.10 SPECIAL HOURS CERTIFICATES

Just as those providing table meals have a facility to extend the hours permitted for sale of intoxicating liquor, so do those providing either gaming facilities or music and dancing. The provisions relating to gaming are discussed at **Chapter 15** and so this section looks briefly at the current requirements to extend trading hours for premises which provide facilities for music and dancing. As with supper hour certificates, there is an overriding principle that the sale of intoxicating liquor should be ancillary to the dominant use of the premises. The dominant use here is that the premises should be structurally adapted and used (or intended to be used) for the purpose of providing music and dancing and substantial refreshment to which the sale of intoxicating liquor is ancillary.

If a special hours certificate is granted, then it has the effect of extending permitted hours until 2 a.m. on weekdays, except in the following situations.

1. When music and dancing is not provided after midnight, permitted hours will end at midnight.
2. If music and dancing ends between midnight and 2 a.m., permitted hours will end at that time.
3. If there is a condition imposed specifying a terminal hour for the certificate, permitted hours will end at that time.

For parts of London (see the Licensing Act 1964, s.76(3)) the basic extended hour from Monday to Saturday is until 3 a.m. On Sundays the effect of the certificate will be to extend permitted hours until 12.30 a.m., but there are similar exceptions to those set out above in relation to weekdays. Where the Sunday concerned immediately precedes a bank holiday (for example, Easter Sunday) then the extended hour will be until 2 a.m. or 3 a.m. for parts of London.

Whilst special hours certificates were previously the domain of nightclubs, many licensees running public houses applied to extend their permitted hours by providing music and dancing together with substantial refreshment, and then seeking to satisfy licensing committees that sales of intoxicating liquor in their premises would be ancillary to those facilities.

Many licensees believe that there is a licence available on application known as a 'late night licence'. Many do not realise that where a special hours certificate has been obtained, the sale of intoxicating liquor must be 'ancillary' during the whole of the hours during which the premises operate and not just during those hours that have been added on after standard permitted hours have ended.

Practitioners will need to check the terms of the special hours certificate and that it has been complied with. The following general propositions may be of assistance.

1. A public entertainments licence must be in force for the premises and the certificate can only be granted for parts of premises which are covered by that licence. If the public entertainments licence lapses (or is revoked), then the special hours certificate lapses at the same time.
2. There is no requirement that each customer should either take substantial refreshment or that they should dance, but clearly if neither of those facilities is used then it will be difficult for a licensee to demonstrate that sale of intoxicating liquor is ancillary to those uses.

3. The justices will look at the overall use of the premises over the whole period of hours permitted. It will accordingly satisfy the requirements of the section if there is a dominant food use in the afternoon and a dominant music and dancing use in the evening so long as the sales of intoxicating liquor throughout can be said to be ancillary.
4. On viewing the overall use of the premises it is open to committees to impose a commencement as well as a terminal hour.
5. Particular attention on applications will be given to the use of the premises during the additional hours provided by such a certificate.
6. There is specific provision for the police to apply for revocation of a special hours certificate on the basis that it is being used primarily for the sale or supply of intoxicating liquor rather than for an appropriate purpose (in this context music and dancing and/or substantial refreshment).

2.11 TRANSFERS (LICENSING ACT 1964, S.8)

The previous sections dealt with new licences and licences extended either physically or by way of a certificate which permits longer trading hours. The vast majority of transactions under the pre-2003 Act licensing regime, however, will be made up of transfers of existing licences. These will result either from new ownership or from the departure of employed licensees from the premises where they have been working.

The conveyancer's role in a transaction involving licensed premises is complicated by the fact that the normal conveyancing procedures and safeguards must be implemented within a framework which secures continuity of trading.

The vendor and the purchaser cannot both hold the liquor licence at the same time. The purchaser will not want to enter a binding agreement to purchase the business until he knows that the licence will be transferred to him. The vendor cannot permit the transfer of the licence until such time as his own trading period comes to an end. The conveyancer must avoid a situation arising where the selling party is prevented from trading whilst he is in possession or the acquiring party is prevented from trading when the business has been transferred.

The problem is compounded by the fact that licensing committees only meet on a limited number of dates each year. It might be possible, but hardly practicable, to arrange completions for transfer session dates but long before that stage a prospective purchaser will be seeking an assurance – as best he can – that the licence will be transferred to him. The mechanism which will enable both vendor and purchaser to be authorised to make sales during this period is a protection order.

2.12 PROTECTION ORDERS

The provisions relating to protection orders are set out in ss.10 and 11 of the Licensing Act 1964. These orders are granted by justices sitting in petty sessions and most benches will deal with applications of this sort on a weekly basis.

In order to grant a protection order the justices will need to be satisfied that the applicant is an eligible person to whom the licensing justices might grant a transfer of the licence. The first issue is therefore whether the applicant is a fit and proper person. Assuming in the conveyancer's view that the client will clear that hurdle, then the next issue is whether a transfer is likely to be granted.

There are six categories of persons to whom licensing justices may grant a transfer set out in s.8 of the Act. One of those categories (s.8(1)(d)) is where the holder of the licence has given up or is about to give up, or his representatives have given up or are about to give up, occupation of the premises to the tenant or occupier of the premises, or the person to whom the representatives or assigns have by sale or otherwise *bona fide* conveyed or made over the interest in the premises.

The other circumstances where a protection order may be granted cover such matters as incapacity, bankruptcy, failure to renew (on the part of the tenant) or application by the owner of the premises where the licensee has been disqualified or ordered to forfeit. Where a licensee has died, his personal representatives are automatically in the same position as the holder of a protection order.

The effect of a protection order is to confer the same authority and responsibilities as if the holder of the order was the holder of the licence. The duration of the order is until the conclusion of the second transfer session after the order has been granted. At that stage it will lapse unless it is renewed. From the prospective purchaser's point of view the protection order serves two purposes. First, it will enable him to trade for several weeks at a time when the licensee is also able (under the authority of the licence) to make sales. Secondly, its grant provides an assurance, although not a guaranteed one, that the licence will eventually – and almost invariably after completion – be transferred to him.

The procedural requirements of a protection order are that seven days' notice (i.e. seven clear days) should be given to the court and the police. In cases of urgency, the justices are permitted to shorten the notice period. Urgency usually arises from the unexpected departure of a licensee rather than events in the course of sale. The conveyancer will wish to manage the process in order to give the police as much time as possible to make their enquiries.

If the police have made all their checks and have confirmed that there is no objection to the applicant, the grant of a protection order will provide a very secure assurance that the transfer will go through without difficulty. If, on the other hand, the police have had insufficient time to make enquiries and have reserved their position until the transfer application is made, then the element of risk is very much increased.

Apart from matters covered by police enquiries, the justices will also look at the previous experience of an applicant within the licensed trade and the training undertaken. If an applicant does not hold the National Licensee's Certificate or something comparable, then the court will consider whether such a qualification is necessary before a transfer would be granted. Where applicants have recent and extensive experience in the trade, qualification of that nature is generally not required. If the court determines that a National Licensee's Certificate is a requirement before a transfer will be approved, normal practice is to grant the protection order but making it clear that the training will have to be undertaken between the order and the transfer. Again, if it is possible to arrange for the applicant to undertake the course in advance, that removes the element of uncertainty as to whether the eventual transfer will be granted.

The Good Practice Guide identifies the factors to which the justices will have regard at the protection order stage as follows:

- age and experience;
- character and health;
- knowledge of licensing law;
- knowledge and conditions of undertakings on the licence;
- ability to communicate effectively; and
- ability to control and supervise the premises.

Where the police views are known at the protection order stage and the justices are entirely satisfied with the fitness of the applicant, the court may release the protection order holder from attending on the subsequent transfer application. If this is achieved, the only matters which would prevent the transfer being approved in due course are either a failure to deal with the procedural requirements on transfer or if the applicant's fitness is compromised in the intervening period.

Since the protection order lasts until the conclusion of the second sessions following its grant, careful consideration should be given to the timing of the application. An application one day prior to a transfer sessions would give the protection order a duration of just over four weeks for a typical licensing committee. If the conveyancer can wait until one day after the sessions, that duration may be extended to a period of just under eight weeks. It is critical that the practitioner should ensure that the application for the transfer is in the list for one of the two sessions which are available for that purpose. It may be necessary to adjourn the transfer if there are delays in the conveyancing process, but provided that the application for transfer is in the list at the second sessions (at latest) then the protection order will continue until the transfer application has been determined.

2.13 TRANSFER APPLICATIONS

The procedural requirements which apply to applications for new licences also apply to transfers, subject to the following variations:

1. There is no need to advertise the application on the premises.
2. There is no need to advertise the application in a newspaper.
3. There is no need to serve a copy of the notice on the fire authority.
4. There is a requirement to serve the existing licensee.

The notices must therefore be served 21 clear days before the relevant transfer sessions and if there is a failure to do this the application is likely to go to the next sessions. In order to protect the protection order holder from prosecution during that period, it will be necessary to apply for a further protection order. The only alternative is a 'slip clause' under para.7 of Sched.2 to the 1964 Act which provides that where an applicant has failed to comply with the requirements of the schedule by inadvertence or misadventure then the justices may postpone consideration of the application, on terms that they think appropriate, and then deal with it as if the applicant had complied with the requirements.

The notice must be signed by the applicant or his agent and must give details of the applicant's full name and address and occupation during the preceding six months. It must also specify the situation of the licensed premises.

It is good practice to obtain an acknowledgement of service from the outgoing licensee and to ask that individual to confirm when he acknowledges receipt that he consents to the transfer. The only necessity in relation to the outgoing licensee is to prove effective service but the indication of consent is a useful assurance for the prospective purchaser.

Finally, if the application to transfer is overlooked then the purchaser – generally in occupation and trading at this stage – can only sell intoxicating liquor until the date of the second transfer sessions after the grant of his protection order. Once that order lapses, the only person entitled to sell from the premises will be the vendor – now perhaps happily in retirement elsewhere. Until such time as the new protection order can be obtained, the only legitimate sales that could be made would be by another licensee selling his own liquor under the terms of an occasional licence, which can be obtained from magistrates normally within 24 hours' notice.

As this pre-2003 Act regime comes to a close, it is worth mentioning the impact of applications during the transitional period on the conversion of licences under the 2003 Act. The only licences which can be converted are those which were in existence on 7 February 2005, but the fact that the licence has been altered or extended after that date will not affect the ability of the licensee to use the conversion process. Licences which come into existence after 7 February 2005 cannot be converted. Those who for commercial reasons need a new licence during the transitional period will accordingly have to apply for a new premises licence under the 2003 Act.

CHAPTER 3
Overview of new law

3.1 NEW SYSTEM

The Licensing Act 2003 is intended to modernise the outdated existing licensing laws. The Act introduces a single integrated scheme for licensing premises which sell alcohol, provide regulated entertainment, or provide late night refreshment. This is achieved by amalgamating the six existing licensing regimes which govern alcohol, public entertainment, cinemas, theatres, late night refreshment houses and night cafés.

By replacing the system of separate licences for different activities with a single licence (the premises licence), the new legislation is intended to reduce bureaucracy, thus simplifying and streamlining the licensing system and making it more efficient.

The 2003 Act is also designed to be deregulatory, although not for everyone. In general terms the activities covered by the new licensing regime are broadly in line with those covered by the old licensing regimes. However, a number of areas which were not covered under the old licensing regime are now brought into the system. Most notably, for the first time 'takeaways' outside London serving hot food between 11 p.m. and 5 a.m. will be required to hold a premises licence.

The licensable activities covered by the 2003 Act (s.1(1)) are:

- the sale by retail of alcohol;
- the supply of alcohol by clubs;
- the provision of regulated entertainment; and
- provision of late night refreshment.

Thus one premises licence could cover an establishment for the provision of alcohol, regulated entertainment and late night refreshment.

At the same time, a new system of personal licences will be introduced. These will be portable, allowing the licence holder to move from one licensed premises to another without any procedural requirements (other than notifying change of address when necessary).

Club premises certificates will be required in place of the current club registration certificates and temporary event notices will replace the existing system of occasional permissions and occasional licences.

3.2 LICENSING OBJECTIVES

The legislation focuses on the promotion of four fundamental statutory licensing objectives (s.4(2)). These are:

- the prevention of crime and disorder;
- public safety;
- the prevention of public nuisance; and
- the protection of children from harm.

These objectives establish the criteria to be used by the licensing authorities in determining or reviewing licence applications.

A key element of the 2003 Act is to recognise the rights of individuals to carry on legitimate businesses and for those individuals to accept that this also brings responsibilities. Thus the purpose behind the new licensing laws is to strike a balance between the needs of all those who have an interest in the operation of licensed premises. This will include those who run licensed premises as a business, those who use them as consumers, those who live nearby licensed premises and those who have the responsibility of enforcing the law and keeping the peace.

The new legislation also supports a number of other key government aims and objectives. These include:

- greater freedom and flexibility for businesses in order to allow them to meet customer expectation and increase competitiveness;
- further development of the tourism, retail, hospitality and leisure industries;
- increased consumer choice;
- an increase in the number of 'family friendly' premises;
- more opportunities for culture and live music, dancing and theatre in rural areas and towns and cities;
- regeneration of areas that need the increased investment and employment opportunities that a thriving and safe night-time economy can bring; and
- protection of local residents.

The 2003 Act is also a key part of the Government's policy for combating alcohol-related crime and disorder and anti-social behaviour. It is anticipated that the introduction of flexible opening hours, even with the potential for up to 24-hour opening, seven days a week, will actually decrease public disorder. This is on the basis that the disorder associated with fixed closing times will be reduced by staggering the times when consumers leave the various licensed premises. At the same time, other provisions of the legislation enable local residents and businesses and other interested parties to make formal objections to licence applications, and also ensure that the impact of any licensable activity on local residents and businesses is taken into account.

It is hoped that the increased flexibility in relation to opening hours will also benefit the tourist industry by improving the basis on which cities in England and Wales can compete with European cities.

It should be noted that the 2003 Act does not address public health issues. The Government's position is that it is inappropriate to deal with such topics under the Act. It is not within the remit of the licensing regime to manage smoking or health issues related to drinking, as these are better dealt with by health-related bodies.

3.3 SECRETARY OF STATE'S GUIDANCE

The 2003 Act (s.182) provides that the Secretary of State must issue national guidance to the licensing authorities detailing how the 2003 Act will work and how the licensing authorities should carry out their functions in this respect. This guidance was issued on 7 July 2004 (the 'Guidance').

The Guidance is used by the licensing authorities in the preparation of their licensing policy statements (see below) and is intended to ensure use of best practice and consistency across the country in the application of the new law.

3.4 ADMINISTRATION OF NEW SYSTEM

The 2003 Act provides for local decision making, so that determinations reflect local circumstances and take into account local discretion. Thus the responsibility for alcohol licensing will transfer under the new law from the magistrates' courts to local authorities, who are already responsible for public entertainment licensing.

The licensing functions will be delegated to licensing committees consisting of between 10 and 15 members and which will be set up specifically for this purpose (s.6(1)). Sub-committees consisting of three members of the full committee may also be established and powers may then be delegated to those sub-committees (s.9). Powers may also be delegated to council officers (s.10(1)(b)). However, council officers cannot make decisions on applications where objections have been made (s.10(4)) by interested parties, relevant authorities or the police. It is therefore anticipated that only uncontested, uncontroversial applications will be determined under delegated authority by council officers. Thus, if there are no police objections to an application for a personal licence, or no relevant representations made to an application for a premises licence or club premises certificate, or no police objections to a temporary event notice, these decisions are likely to be made by a council officer.

Each authority will also have to maintain a register (s.81) recording all personal licences, premises licences and club premises certificates issued, and all temporary event notices received by the authority. This register will be available for public inspection free of charge.

The role of the magistrates will be limited to certain rights of appeal (Sched.5). This includes both appeals by applicants who are aggrieved by decisions made by the licensing authorities to reject or amend their applications, and appeals by those who have made representations against an application and feel it should not have been granted.

3.5 STATEMENT OF LICENSING POLICY

Under the 2003 Act (s.5(1)), each licensing authority is required to determine and publish a statement of its licensing policy every three years, which must be kept under review and revised when necessary.

This policy will set out the basis upon which the authority will make its licence application decisions. Although all licensing authorities must have regard to the Secretary of State's Guidance in preparing their statements of licensing policy, there will be differences between the different statements. When applying for licences it will therefore be necessary to consider the licensing policy for the licensing authority in whose area the premises are situated, particularly in relation to any special policies that may have been adopted.

The purpose of the licensing policy statement is to set out the criteria which will be used in determining licence applications and provide transparency so that all those involved in a licence application, such as licensing committee members, applicants, local residents and businesses, are aware of these criteria. The policy statement may also be used in any court case where a decision by the licensing authorities is being challenged.

3.6 ENFORCEMENT

Enforcement under the new legislation is also intended to be more focused and more proportionate, concentrating on those premises which are causing problems within the community, whilst ensuring that there is less interference with those which are benefiting and enhancing the community.

The 2003 Act also introduces a review procedure which enables certain parties to request that the licensing authority reviews the licence of a particular premises as a result of a matter arising at the premises concerned.

A number of new offences are also introduced and the powers of the enforcement authorities are extended so that proceedings for any offences may be instituted by the licensing authority as well as the Director of Public Prosecutions and, in certain circumstances, by trading standards officers. Police powers are also increased to include the provision to close licensed premises within a specified geographical area in cases of actual or likely disorder.

3.7 OPENING TIMES

In contrast to the old law, the 2003 Act does not prescribe the days or the opening hours when alcohol may be sold by retail for consumption on or off premises. Nor does it specify when other licensable activities may be carried on. Instead, applicants for a premises licence or a club premises certificate will be able to choose the days and the hours during which they wish to be authorised to carry on licensable activities at the premises for which a licence is sought. In fact the Guidance stresses that with regard to alcohol, longer licensing hours are important in order to stagger the times at which customers leave premises. This, presumably, would not mean universally longer licensing hours which would be unlikely to deliver the reductions of disorder which are being sought.

Whilst this does provide the potential for premises to provide 24-hour opening on a daily basis, this is unlikely to be required by the vast majority of premises. Primary inhibitors would be the impact on local residents and economic factors. For example, the cost of employing staff to work around the clock may well not be covered by the amount of business which could be attracted during the quieter periods.

Government guidance recommends that shops, stores and supermarkets selling alcohol should usually be permitted to match their hours to their normal trading hours during which sales take place, unless there are exceptional reasons relating to disorder or disturbance. Consequently, if a shop is legally permitted to open 24 hours per day, the licensing authority should generally permit the sale of alcohol during those hours.

Zoning policies, in other words, the setting of fixed trading hours within a specified area, should not be adopted by licensing authorities, although it is accepted that stricter conditions on noise control may be needed in highly residential areas.

3.8 CUMULATIVE IMPACT

A licensing policy statement may contain a special policy with a presumption against granting new licences within a particular area because this area is already saturated with certain types of premises. However, the authority would have to justify why such a policy had been adopted and provide evidence in support of the policy. In addition, the merits of each individual application would still need to be considered and, where grant of a licence would be unlikely to add significantly to the cumulative impact of licensed premises on the promotion of the licensing objectives, the licence should be granted.

3.9 FEES

Fees are set centrally by the Secretary of State for Culture, Media and Sport. This will avoid the problem of the regional differences currently encountered with public entertainment licences, where the fees are set by the individual local authorities.

Fees are payable to the licensing authority in respect of:

- applications for new premises licences;
- applications to vary premises licences;
- applications for club premises certificates;
- applications to vary club premises certificates;
- applications to convert licences;
- annual fees for premises licences and club premises certificates;
- applications for the grant and renewal of personal licences;
- giving a temporary event notice; and
- replacement of lost or stolen licences.

3.9.1 Personal licence

The fee for a personal licence is currently £37.

3.9.2 Premises licence

Premises will be allocated to fee bands depending on the non-domestic rateable value of the premises. Fees will be payable for applications for licences and there will also be an annual charge payable by those holding licences as follows:

Band	A	B	C	D	E
Rateable value	£0–£4,300	£4,301–£33,000	£33,001–£87,000	£87,001–£125,000	£125,001 and over
Application Fee	£100	£190	£315	£450	£635
Annual Fee	£70	£180	£295	£320	£350

There is also a multiplier for city/town centre premises in Bands D (×2) and E (×3) where the premises are exclusively or primarily in the business of selling alcohol.

Application fees for club premises certificates, variations (excluding changes of name and address or changes to designated premises supervisor) and conversion of existing licences are set at the same levels as applications for premises licences.

The application fee for a premises licence or club premises certificate is the same regardless of whether it authorises one or a number of licensable activities.

There is an additional fee for those premises that supply alcohol and wish to vary their licence at the same time as conversion of the existing licence as follows:

Band	**A**	**B**	**C**	**D**	**E**
Fee payable	£20	£60	£80	£100	£120

Other fees and charges are as follows:

Event	**Fee**
Supply of copies of information contained in register	Set by relevant local authority
Application for copy of licence or summary on loss/theft of premises licence or summary	£10.50
Notification of change of name or address (holder of premises licence)	£10.50
Application to vary to specify individual as premises supervisor	£23.00
Application to transfer premises licence	£23.00
Interim authority notice	£23.00
Application for provisional statement	£315.00
Application for copy of certificate or summary on theft/loss of club premises certificate or summary	£10.50
Notification of change of name or alteration of club rules	£10.50
Changes of relevant registered address of club	£10.50
Temporary event notices	£21.00
Application for copy of notice on theft/loss of temporary event notice	£10.50
Application for copy of licence on theft/loss of personal licence	£10.50
Notification of change of name or address (personal licence)	£10.50
Notice of interest in any premises	£21.00

CHAPTER 4

Personal licences

4.1 WHAT IS A PERSONAL LICENCE?

One of the major changes made by the 2003 Act is the introduction of personal licences which will be issued to individuals to sell, supply or authorise the supply of alcohol (2003 Act, Part 6). These licences are separate from the licence which authorises the premises to be used for the sale/supply of alcohol and their introduction brings to an end the regime whereby licence holders were tied by the licence relating to the premises where they worked. Their introduction also brings to an end the 'fit and proper' test required under the old system.

Separation of the licensing of individuals and premises means that personal licences are portable and permit the holder to move from one premises to another without the need for formal licence applications, thereby simplifying job transfers and improving employment opportunities.

A personal licence authorises the holder to sell or supply alcohol or to authorise the sale or supply of alcohol for consumption on or off the premises for which a premises licence is in force (s.111). It should be noted that a personal licence relates only to the sale/supply of alcohol under a premises licence (s.111(b)). It does not permit the holder to sell/supply alcohol from any venue, only from establishments operating under a premises licence or at temporary events.

There is no requirement for every person selling alcohol at premises licensed for that purpose to hold a personal licence, but every sale or supply of alcohol under a premises licence must be at least *authorised* by a personal licence holder (s.19(3)).

A personal licence is not required for other licensable activities such as the provision of regulated entertainment or late night refreshment or for the sale/supply of alcohol under a club premises certificate or a temporary event notice (although personal licence holders can hold many more temporary events than those who do not hold a licence).

Individuals can only hold one personal licence at any one time. Any licence granted to someone who already holds a licence would not be valid (s.118). Only one current application is permitted to be directed to the licensing authority where the applicant ordinarily resides.

4.2 VALIDITY

The licence is valid for 10 years initially, unless it is surrendered by the holder, revoked by the licensing authority, or forfeited or suspended by the court (see **para.4.10**) (s.115).

At the end of the 10-year period, the holder may apply for renewal of the licence and it may be renewed at 10-yearly intervals thereafter (s.115(1)(b)).

4.3 REQUIREMENTS FOR A PERSONAL LICENCE

Under the 2003 Act, the applicant must fulfil the following qualifying criteria in order to obtain a personal licence (s.120(2)):

- the applicant must be aged 18 or over;
- the applicant must be in possession of a recognised licensing qualification, or be a person of a prescribed description;
- the applicant must not have had his personal licence revoked in the previous five years; and
- the applicant must not have been convicted of any relevant offence or foreign offence.

Provided that the above four criteria are all met, the licensing authority must grant the licence (s.120(2)). If any of the first three conditions are not met, the application must be rejected (s.120(3)). If the first three conditions are met, but the applicant has an unspent relevant conviction, the application will need to be considered by the police (s.120(4)) (see **para.4.7**).

An applicant does not have to be employed by or have any association with a licensed trade in order to apply for a personal licence. Thus the licensing authority cannot take such matters into account when considering an application. The only factors that may be considered are the four listed above.

The 'fit and proper' test associated with the old liquor licensing regime is abolished and the only involvement of the police is if the applicant has any unspent previous relevant or foreign convictions (see **para.4.7**). The police will need to consider any such conviction in the context of the crime prevention objective. Furthermore, as long as the applicant has a relevant qualification and no relevant previous convictions, the licensing authority is not required to make any other determination of knowledge or character.

Once a personal licence is granted, the holder is required to notify the licensing authority of any change in name or address. Failure to do so is an offence under the 2003 Act attracting a fine at level 2 on conviction (s.127). When notifying the licensing authority of such changes, the licence holder must send the personal licence and the appropriate fee with the notice.

4.4 RECOGNISED QUALIFICATION

Applicants for a personal licence will need to hold a licensing qualification which has been accredited by the Secretary of State and has been awarded by similarly accredited bodies (s.120(8)).

A syllabus for the licensing qualification for a personal licence has been published by the Department for Culture, Media and Sport (DCMS) and includes the following topics:

- personal licences;
- licensing authorities;
- alcohol;
- unauthorised licensable activities;
- police powers;
- duties of the personal licence holder;
- premises licences;
- operating schedules;
- permitted temporary activities;
- disorderly conduct on licensed premises;
- protection of children;
- rights of entry; and
- prohibitions.

Persons of 'prescribed description' as mentioned above are described in the Licensing Act 2003 (Personal Licences) Regulations 2005, SI 2005/41 (the PL Regulations), reg.4. Such applicants will not need to possess the licensing qualification, but will be required to show proof that they comply with the requirements of the PL Regulations to the licensing authority when making an application for a personal licence.

4.5 RELEVANT OFFENCES

Relevant offences are listed in Sched.4 to the 2003 Act, which is reproduced at **Appendix A3**. They include:

- offences created by the Licensing Act 2003;
- offences under previous licensing regimes;
- offences related to firearms;
- offences under a number of provisions of the Theft Acts 1968 and 1978;
- offences involving drugs;
- offences involving serious crime;
- certain sexual offences;
- false trade description of alcohol-related products;
- road traffic offences involving alcohol;

- certain offences under the Food Safety Act 1990 where the food is or includes alcohol; and
- operating without a licence under the Private Security Industry Act 2001.

Comparable offences to those described in the 2003 Act, which have been committed in places outside England and Wales, including Scotland and Ireland, where English law is not applicable are termed 'foreign offences'.

4.6 APPLICATION PROCESS

Applications can only be made by individuals. An applicant for a personal licence must submit the appropriate application form (PL Regulations, Sched.1) to the relevant licensing authority. If the applicant is ordinarily resident in the area of a licensing authority, then the application should be made to that licensing authority. If this is not the case, then the application may be made to any licensing authority. The application form must be signed by the applicant himself, not by a representative.

The application form must be accompanied by (PL Regulations, reg.7):

1. Two photographs – (dimensions 45mm × 35mm) one of which must be endorsed as a true likeness by a solicitor, notary, person of standing in the community or someone with a professional qualification.
2. Either:
   (a) a criminal conviction certificate issued under s.112 of the Police Act 1997,
   (b) a criminal record certificate issued under s.113A of the Police Act 1977, or
   (c) the results of a subject access search under the Data Protection Act 1998 of the police national computer by the National Identification Service.
3. Disclosure of criminal convictions and declaration form (PL Regulations, Sched.3).
4. Proof of licensing qualification.
5. Fee (currently £37).

In order to demonstrate that they have not been convicted of any relevant offence or foreign offence, applicants must submit one of the police documents listed above to the licensing authority. In addition, a declaration must be made by applicants (PL Regulations, Sched.3) that either they have not been convicted of a relevant or foreign offence or that they have been convicted of such an offence together with details of the nature and date of any conviction and any sentence imposed in respect of it.

Details of spent convictions for relevant or foreign offences are not required (see **para.4.7** for the definition of spent convictions).

The application form includes a declaration at the end that 'the information is correct to the best of my knowledge and belief' making it clear that making a false statement is a criminal offence liable to prosecution, and conviction could lead to a fine of up to £5,000.

As noted above, provided that the four requirements in **para.4.3** are met, the licence will be granted. If the applicant fails to meet any of the first three requirements, the licence will not be granted.

4.7 POLICE OBJECTIONS

If the first three requirements are met, but the applicant has an unspent conviction (see definition below) for a relevant or foreign offence, the licensing authority must notify the police to that effect (s.120(4)). If the police consider that, as a result of the conviction, the granting of the licence would undermine the crime prevention objective, they should object to the application by issuing an objection notice within 14 days (s.120(5)). In these circumstances the applicant is entitled to a hearing before the licensing authority (s.120(7)(a)). The hearing must be held within 20 days of the end of the police objection period (Licensing Act 2003 (Hearings) Regulations 2005, SI 2005/44 (Hearings Regulations), reg.5 and Sched.1).

Under the Rehabilitation of Offenders Act 1974, after a certain period of time all convictions (except those involving prison sentences over 30 months) are deemed to have been 'spent', i.e. they are no longer required to be disclosed. The length of the rehabilitation period depends on the sentence and runs from the date of conviction. The rehabilitation periods for various sentences are given in **Appendix A4**.

If a conviction is a spent conviction under the Rehabilitation of Offenders Act 1974, it must be disregarded as a consideration during the process of determining an application for a personal licence (s.114). Prior to the Licensing Act 2003, licensing committees had (and still have to the end of the transitional period) a discretion to consider spent convictions.

The Guidance recommends that, if the police object to an application, the licensing authority should normally reject the application, unless there are, in the opinion of the licensing authority, exceptional and compelling circumstances which justify the application being granted.

If the applicant has unspent previous relevant or foreign convictions but the police fail to issue an objection notice during the required 14-day period, the licensing authority must grant the licence provided that it otherwise meets the requirements of the 2003 Act (s.120(6)). This is the case even if the authority believes that the applicant is not suitable. However, if a police objection is received outside the 14-day period, it may be that in order to comply with its overriding duty to promote the licensing objectives (s.4(1)), the licensing authority must also hold a hearing as described above to consider the objection.

4.8 RENEWALS

Personal licences are valid for 10 years and may then be renewed for further 10-year periods. Applications for renewal must be made during the two-month period commencing three months before the licence is due to expire (s.117(6)).

Considering that licences are valid for 10 years, a renewal period of only two months would appear to be a very narrow timescale. It would seem likely that a number of licensees will fall foul of this provision when the time comes for renewal, necessitating applications for new licences and an inevitable hiatus whilst those applications are processed.

Application for renewal is made to the licensing authority which originally granted the licence (the 'relevant licensing authority') even though the individual may have moved out of the area (s.119(3)).

Applications for renewal should be made using the form set out at Sched.2 of the PL Regulations and be accompanied by the following.

1. Current personal licence.
2. Two photographs, one of which must be endorsed as to true likeness.
3. Criminal conviction certificate or criminal record certificate or the results of a subject access search of the police national computer by the National Identification Service.
4. Disclosure of criminal convictions and declaration form (PL Regulations, Sched.3.
5. The appropriate fee (currently £37).

If the renewal is not determined prior to the expiry of the licence, the licence will remain effective until a decision is made, provided that it was submitted in accordance with the prescribed timescale (s.119).

Renewal of the licence must be granted, unless the applicant has been convicted of a relevant or foreign offence since the original grant. If this is the case, the police will be notified (s.121(2)) and they may object to the renewal on crime prevention grounds. If this occurs the applicant is entitled to a hearing before the licensing authority. If the police do not issue an objection notice within the 14-day period following notification by the licensing authority, the licensing authority must grant a renewal (s.121(5)).

4.9 CONVICTIONS DURING APPLICATION PERIOD

If an applicant is convicted of any relevant or foreign offence during the application period for the licence, the applicant must notify the relevant licensing authority as soon as is reasonably practicable (s.123(1)). If this requirement is not complied with, this will be an offence attracting a level 4 fine (s.123(2)).

If an applicant is convicted of a relevant or foreign offence during the period between making the application and its determination, but the conviction does not come to the attention of the licensing authority until after the grant of the licence, the authority must notify the police (s.124(2)). If the police consider that continuation of the licence may undermine the crime prevention objective, they must issue an objection notice within 14 days of being notified by the licensing authority (s.124(3)). A hearing will then be held to consider the objection notice (s.124(4)) and the licensing authority may revoke the licence if the authority considers this to be necessary in order to promote the crime prevention objective (s.124(5)).

4.10 FORFEITURE OR SUSPENSION OF LICENCE

If a personal licence holder is charged with a relevant offence, he must produce the licence to the court before or at his first appearance at court (s.128(1)). If an applicant is granted a personal licence after being charged, he must produce it to the court at his next appearance in court (s.128(3)).

In addition to producing his licence to the court, if a personal licence holder is charged with a relevant offence, he also has a duty to notify the court if he makes or withdraws any application for renewal of his licence, or of any surrender, renewal or revocation of the licence (s.128(4)). Failure to disclose his licence or notify the court in the above circumstances will mean that the licence holder commits a further offence which is punishable on conviction with a fine not exceeding level 2 on the standard scale (s.128(6) and (7)).

If a personal licence holder is convicted of a relevant offence, the court may order the forfeiture of the licence or suspend it for up to six months. The court is specifically permitted to take account of previous convictions. Pending any appeal against conviction or sentence the court may suspend the order to forfeit or suspend the licence, which will permit the licence to continue to continue in force until the appeal has been determined (s.129).

The court must also notify the relevant licensing authority of a conviction for any relevant offence and of any decision to order that the personal licence be suspended or declared forfeit (s.131(2)(a)). If the licensing authority does not have the licence then the authority will contact the licence holder and require the production of that licence so that the necessary action can be taken. The holder must produce his licence to the authority within 14 days (s.134(4)). The licensing authority will then place details of the conviction and any period of suspension in its records and endorse the licence accordingly (s.134(1)) before returning it to the holder. If the court has ordered that licence is declared forfeit, the licence will be retained by the licensing authority.

The licence holder also has a duty to notify the licensing authority of any convictions for relevant or foreign offences where the courts are not aware of the existence of the licence (s.132(2)(a)). Failure to comply with this requirement is an offence (s.132(4)). The licence holder is also required to produce his licence to the licensing authority at the same time that this notice is given (s.132(3)).

These provisions relating to convictions and possible forfeiture of licence are very relevant to employers of licensees. As explained at **para.5.11**, it is a mandatory condition of a premises licence that alcohol cannot be supplied from a premises where there is no current licensed designated premises supervisor (DPS). Thus, if a personal licence holder who is also the DPS is convicted of a relevant offence and the court orders the forfeiture of his licence as a result of a conviction, the establishment in which he works must cease selling alcohol immediately. It is therefore advisable for employment contracts in such areas of work to contain provisions stipulating that an employee must advise the employer if he is facing prosecution. The employer can then make arrangements to appoint another DPS if necessary.

4.11 APPEALS

There is provision for an applicant to appeal against a refusal by a licensing authority to grant or to renew his licence (Sched.5, para.17(1)).

The chief officer of police may also appeal against the decision of the licensing authority to grant or renew a licence despite police objection to the application (Sched.5, para.17(2) and (3)).

Where convictions for relevant offences have come to the attention of the licensing authority after the grant or renewal of a personal licence and the authority has decided to revoke the licence, the holder may appeal against this revocation decision (Sched.5, para.17(4)).

In addition, under similar circumstances, where the licensing authority has decided not to revoke the licence, the police may appeal against the decision not to revoke (Sched.5, para.17(5)).

Appeals are made to the relevant magistrates' court and must be made within 21 days of notification of the decision appealed against (Sched.5, para.17(6) and (7)).

4.12 PRODUCTION OF LICENCE

The holder of a personal licence who is selling/supplying/authorising the sale of alcohol in accordance with a premises licence is under a duty to produce his personal licence when requested to do so by a constable or authorised person (s.135(2)). Failure to produce the licence is an offence under the 2003 Act and a person guilty of such offence is liable to a fine not exceeding level 2 (s.135(4) and (5)).

4.13 DESIGNATED PREMISES SUPERVISOR (DPS)

Where the premises licence specifies the provision of alcohol, there must be a DPS (s.15) on the premises and that person must be in possession of a personal licence (s.19(2)) and be named on the premises licence (s.17(4)(e)). Details of the role of the DPS are given at **para.5.11**.

CHAPTER 5

Premises licences

5.1 WHAT IS A PREMISES LICENCE?

A premises licence authorises the holder to use the premises to which the licence relates for one or more licensable activities (s.11) (see **Appendix A1**). Separate licences will no longer be required for different activities and the operators of an establishment will be able to apply for a single premises licence to permit any or all the licensable activities that they wish to carry on. For example, a premises licence could permit the provision of alcohol as well as the provision of regulated entertainment and late night refreshment. The premises licence will specify the nature of the licensable activities permitted and any applicable conditions. The detailed rules governing premises licences are set out in the Licensing Act 2003 (Premises Licences and Club Premises Certificates) Regulations 2005, SI 2005/42 (the PLCPC Regulations).

The majority of conveyancing transactions involve premises where a licence is already in existence. Under the old system, the steps involved in the application for a new licence were rarely of importance to a conveyancer unless either the licence had lapsed, or the premises had been subject to unauthorised alterations. However, under the new system, for the reasons given below, conveyancers will need to know when and how a premises licence should be pursued.

First, the process involved in an application to vary the licence is very similar to the procedure required when seeking a new licence. Many new owners and occupiers will wish to vary the operations on site and accordingly will need either to vary the licence or to secure a new one. Variations are dealt with in detail in **Chapter 7**.

Secondly, as can also be seen from **Chapter 7**, where the premises themselves are being extended or altered, the most appropriate approach may be to apply for a new premises licence.

Thirdly, there will be occasions when extensions of hours will require that a time limited premises licence is obtained (that is to say, a new licence of limited duration) rather than the usual practice for extensions which will be to seek a temporary event notice.

5.2 LICENSABLE ACTIVITIES

Licensable activities are defined in the 2003 Act (s.1(1)) as:

- the sale by retail of alcohol;
- the supply of alcohol by clubs;
- the provision of regulated entertainment; and
- the provision of late night refreshment.

(For further details of licensable activities requiring a premises licence, see **Chapter 6**.)

5.3 WHO CAN APPLY?

Under the 1964 legislation, anyone considered by the justices to be a 'fit and proper' person would be granted a justices' licence. This concept of 'fit and proper' does not exist under the 2003 Act and the licensing authority does not as a result have a broad discretion based on its view of the suitability of the applicant. However, whilst committees need no longer grapple with the concept of fitness (or indeed the fitness of the applicant's spouse or partner) the eligibility criteria are nevertheless more restrictive than the old regime.

An application for a premises licence can be made by anyone who is carrying on, or proposes to carry on, a business that involves licensable activities on the premises (s.16(1)(a)). This would include individuals over the age of 18 (s.16(2)), companies, partnerships, etc., provided that they were engaged in a business which involves the use of the premises for licensable activities.

In addition, certain other categories of eligible applicants are also specified (s.16(1)(b)–(i)), including:

- a registered club;
- a charity;
- a health service body;
- a chief officer of police; and
- 'a person of such other description as may be prescribed'.

Where companies operate tenanted estates, either the operating company or the tenant would generally be eligible to apply for and be granted a premises licence. Each could demonstrate that they proposed to carry on a business involving licensable activities. However, in the circumstances of a managed public house, the manager, as an employee, would generally not be eligible to apply for the premises licence and thus the operating company would have to do so.

Joint applications for a premises licence are possible provided both applicants are carrying on a business that involves licensable activities on the premises. Thus, if a husband and wife or other similar partnership own or hold the joint tenancy of a public house, they would be able to make a joint application for the licence if they are both actively involved in the running of the business.

However, such a joint application might not be so straightforward if it involves two businesses, e.g. where a public house is owned by a company and run by its tenant. Both would be eligible to apply and the Guidance makes it clear that it is not for the licensing authority to decide which is the most appropriate licensee. The advice goes on to emphasise that joint applications by two separate businesses will be discouraged. The Secretary of State has made it clear that it is preferable that the premises licence be held by a single business to ensure that lines of responsibility and accountability are clear.

The Guidance indicates that it is possible for there to be more than one premises licence relating to a particular premises. The example cited suggests that an application for a premises licence authorising regulated entertainment could be made by one individual in respect of premises or part of a premises for which an authorisation to sell alcohol was already held by a different individual. It is difficult to see where this would be of relevance in the majority of conveyancing transactions. However, in the case of a large stadium where there are several bars and restaurants operating independently, it would be sensible for each to have its own premises licence.

5.4 LICENSING OBJECTIVES

As noted in **Chapter 3**, the new legislation is aimed at promoting the four statutory licensing objectives (s.4(2)): the prevention of crime and disorder; public safety; the prevention of public nuisance; and the protection of children from harm. Thus these are:

- the issues which the applicant must address in making an application for a premises licence;
- the only matters which a licensing authority may take into account in determining the grant of a licence;
- the only grounds on which an objection may be made to the grant of a premises licence; and
- the only grounds on which a licensing authority will be able to refuse a premises licence or impose conditions on it.

5.5 APPLICATION PROCESS

Applications are made to the licensing authority in whose area the premises are situated or mainly situated (ss.17(1), 12(2) and 12(3)(a)). If the premises are situated across two or more areas equally, the applicant can nominate one of the authorities as the relevant licensing authority (s.12(3)(b)).

The applicant must complete the relevant application form (PLCPC Regulations, Sched.2) and this must be accompanied by (s.17(3) and PLCPC Regulations, reg.10):

- an operating schedule (see below for details);
- a plan of the premises (see below for details);
- the appropriate fee (see **Chapter 3**);
- if the premises are to be used for the supply of alcohol, the name of the designated premises supervisor (DPS);
- if the premises are to be used for the supply of alcohol, the written consent of the individual to be specified as the DPS (PLCPC Regulations, Sched.11, Part A).

5.6 OPERATING SCHEDULE

The operating schedule, which is in fact incorporated into the application form, sets out the details of how the applicant proposes to operate the premises when carrying out the licensable activities. It is therefore the applicant who initially determines the extent and the limitations of the licence being applied for. The concept of the operating schedule is a radical departure from the way in which the old licensing regime used to operate.

The operating schedule must include the following details (s.17(4)):

- the licensable activities to be carried out;
- the proposed hours when the relevant licensable activities are to take place, including the times during each day of the week, during particular holiday periods, or seasons if these are likely to be different;
- any other times when the premises are to be open to the public;
- the duration of the licence (if it is to have a fixed term);
- details of the DPS, if the licensable activities include the supply of alcohol;
- whether alcohol is to be supplied, and if so whether the alcohol will be supplied for consumption on or off the premises or both;
- a statement of the steps that the applicant proposes to take to promote the licensing objectives;
- such other matters as may be prescribed.

If the application for the premises licence is approved, the operating schedule will be incorporated into the licence itself and prescribes the activities that will be permitted and any limitations on them. The information to be included in the operating schedule must, therefore, be considered carefully. The operating schedule also provides the information which will be used by any responsible authority or interested party to assess whether the steps taken to promote the licensing objectives are satisfactory and will therefore influence whether or not they make relevant representations (see **para.5.14** onwards).

Although the matters listed above are the only matters prescribed by the 2003 Act, the Guidance also specifies certain other details which would be expected to be included in the schedule to enable the licensing authority, the police and the various other responsible authorities and interested parties to assess whether the steps taken to promote the licensing objectives are sufficient. These include:

- a general description of the nature and character of the business;
- where alcohol is sold for consumption on the premises, the extent of seating provided;
- the type of activities available on the premises, whether licensable under the 2003 Act or not;
- where dancing is to take place, the type of dancing;
- where music is provided, the type of music.

In preparing operating schedules, the Guidance advises that applicants should consult the relevant licensing authority's statement of licensing policy. This is of particular relevance where a licensing authority specifies additional areas that it would expect to see addressed within an applicant's operating schedule – for example, matters relating to instruction, training and supervision of staff.

With regard to the steps necessary for meeting the licensing objectives, applicants are expected to conduct a thorough risk assessment and it may thus be expedient to liaise with the local police and other responsible authorities as to their expectations regarding the steps necessary for promoting the licensing objectives.

5.7 'DRINKING UP TIME'

When the new premises licences come into force, the familiar concept of 'drinking up time' will disappear (subject to the comments in **Chapter 12**, see **para.12.4**). As the 2003 Act does not make any provision for 'drinking up time', the operating schedule relating to an application for the sale/supply of alcohol should specify the times when the sale of alcohol will take place, together with the times that the premises will be open for other than licensable activities, which will include 'drinking up time'.

Consumption of alcohol is not a licensable activity. It is therefore possible to allow drinking of alcohol outside the hours permitted in the licence for the sale or supply of alcohol. Again, this is an area which may be specifically addressed in a licensing authority's statement of licensing policy.

5.8 SPECIAL OCCASIONS/EXTENSIONS

The new legislation does not make any provision for extending hours of operation for special events. The hours of operation are set in the operating schedule. It will therefore be necessary to make provision in the schedule for any anticipated special events, or apply for a temporary event notice (see **Chapter 8**) when an extension is required.

With regard to regular special occasions such as bank holidays, St Patrick's Day, etc. it should normally be quite simple to anticipate when extended opening hours may be required and to incorporate these in the operating schedule when making an application for the premises licence. With other special events which are not anticipated, it will generally be necessary to apply for a temporary event notice to vary the hours for these occasions, subject to the numbers involved (see **para.5.9**).

In order to reduce the need for repeated service of temporary event notices for this purpose, some licensing authorities are encouraging applicants to include in their operating schedules provision for extending their operating hours by up to three hours beyond the normal terminal hour on 24 occasions per calendar year. In these circumstances, applicants should also specify in their operating schedule that written notice of any such proposed late opening will be served on the licensing authority and the police at least 14 days in advance of the event.

Where exceptional events of local, national or international significance arise, it is possible for the Secretary of State to make a licensing order which will allow premises with a premises licence or a club premises certificate to open for extended hours on these special occasions (s.17(2)). This will be broadly similar to the way in which licensing hours were extended generally for the Millennium celebrations and subsequently for the Queen's Golden Jubilee and over the New Year holiday.

5.9 TIME LIMITED LICENCES

As will be seen in **Chapter 8**, temporary event notices are limited to events where fewer than 500 people will be attending. Consequently, if it is anticipated that more than 500 people will attend the event, it will be necessary to apply for a premises licence which is of a specified duration (s.26(1)(b)). This could be for just one day.

Similarly, if premises are covered by a licence authorising the sale of alcohol only and an event including regulated entertainment is planned and it is anticipated that more than 500 people will attend, it is possible to apply for a premises licence authorising regulated entertainment for a specified time.

5.10 PLANS

All applications for a premises licence must be accompanied by a plan of the premises (s.17(3)(b) and PLCPC Regulations, reg.23(1)). Plans must normally be on a scale of 1mm:100mm (PLCPC Regulations, regs.2(1) and 23(2)). However, it may be possible to agree a different scale with the licensing authority.

The following information must be shown on the plan (PLCPC Regulations, reg.23(3)):

- the extent of the boundary of the building, if relevant, and any external and internal walls of the building and, if different, the perimeter of the premises;
- the location of points of access to and egress from the premises;
- if different from above, the location of escape routes from the premises;
- in a case where the premises is used for more than one existing licensable activity, the area within the premises used for each activity;
- fixed structures (including furniture) or similar objects temporarily in a fixed location (but not furniture) which may impact on the ability of individuals on the premises to use exits or escape routes without impediment;
- in a case where the premises includes a stage or raised area, the location and height of each stage or area relative to the floor;
- in a case where the premises includes any steps, stairs, elevators or lifts, the location of the steps, stairs, elevators or lifts;
- in a case where the premises includes any room or rooms containing public conveniences, the location of the room or rooms;
- the location and type of any fire safety and any other safety equipment;
- the location of a kitchen, if any, on the premises.

The licensing authority may also list other information which it believes will expedite the application, and this may be added to the plans if the applicant wishes.

5.11 DESIGNATED PREMISES SUPERVISOR (DPS)

The designated premises supervisor (DPS) is the person identified in the operating schedule of the premises licence as the premises supervisor for those particular premises (s.15(1)). Only one DPS may be specified in a single premises licence.

Where the premises licence specifies the provision of alcohol, there must be a DPS on the premises and the DPS must be in possession of a personal licence and be named on the premises licence (s.17(4)(e)).

The exact role and responsibilities of the DPS are not entirely clear as yet, but the Guidance envisages that the main purpose of having a DPS will be to ensure that there will be a specified individual who can be readily identified at the premises. It is anticipated that the DPS will be the point of contact for the licensing authorities, or for the police or fire services if problems occur at the premises.

It is likely therefore that the DPS will play an important role in the management and supervision of the premises. The DPS will most appropriately be the person with the day-to-day responsibility for running the premises. Some statements of policy suggest that the premises licence holder should be *required* to give day-to-day responsibility for running the premises to the DPS.

The DPS does not necessarily have to be the same as the premises licence holder, but there is nothing to prevent an individual who holds a premises licence from also being specified in the licence as the DPS (s.15(2)).

The DPS does not have to be present on the premises at all times, but it is important that the DPS should be contactable should problems arise and it is expected that the DPS will spend a significant amount of time on the premises. However, provided these requirements are fulfilled, it is possible for an individual to be the DPS for more than one premises.

5.12 ADVERTISING AND NOTIFICATION OF APPLICATIONS

All applications must be advertised (s.17(5)(a) and PLCPC Regulations, reg.25) by displaying a notice at the premises concerned and placing an advert in a local newspaper.

The notice to be displayed at the premises must be (PLCPC Regulations, reg.25(a)):

- A4 size or larger;
- pale blue;
- printed or typed in black ink in font size 16 or larger;
- placed on the premises the day after the day on which the application was given to the licensing authority;
- placed prominently on the premises concerned so it can easily be read from outside;
- if the premises is larger than 50m square in area, further notices must be placed every 50m along the external wall adjoining any highway;
- displayed for at least 28 days (period during which representations can be made).

A copy of the notice must be sent to the licensing authority. Applicants must also publish a notice in a locally circulating newspaper or, if there is none, in a local newsletter, circular or similar publication circulating in the vicinity of the premises. The newspaper notice must be published at least once within the 10-day period starting on the day after the day on which the application was given to the licensing authority. (PLCPC Regulations, reg.25(b)). A copy of the newspaper containing the advertisement should be sent to the licensing authority.

The premises and newspaper notices should contain the following information (PLCPC Regulations, reg.26):

- name of applicant;
- postal address;
- brief summary of the application;
- proposed licensable activities;
- where the full application may be viewed;
- the date by which representations (i.e. objections) may be made;
- that such a representation should be made in writing;
- that it is an offence knowingly or recklessly to make a false statement in connection with an application and the maximum fine for such an offence.

An example notice is appended at **Appendix C5**.

Licensing authorities may also include details of applications on their websites.

A copy of the application together with all accompanying documents should also be submitted to each responsible authority on the same day as the application is made (s.17(5)(b) and PLCPC Regulations, reg.27).

'Responsible authorities' (s.13(4)) are defined as the following in relation to the area in which the premises are situated:

- the chief officer of police;
- the fire authority;
- the health and safety authority;
- the local planning authority;
- the environmental health authority;
- the local weights and measures authority;
- the body recognised as being responsible for protection of children from harm;
- any licensing authority other than the relevant licensing authority.

Many licensing authorities provide a list of the relevant responsible authorities and their contact details in their licensing policy statements.

5.13 DETERMINATION OF APPLICATION

The Secretary of State's Guidance highlights that, in determining applications for new and major variations of premises licences, licensing authorities need to consider the five main policy aims that underpin the 2003 Act. These are as follows.

1. The main purpose of the licensing regime is to promote the licensing objectives.
2. Applicants are expected to conduct a comprehensive risk assessment with regard to the licensing objectives when preparing their applications.
3. Operating schedules should be reviewed by the relevant professional experts.
4. Local residents and businesses are free to raise relevant objections to the applications.
5. The role of the licensing authority is primarily to resolve disputes when they arise.

Provided that the application has been lawfully made and properly advertised according to the Regulations and there have been no objections (i.e. relevant representations, see **para.5.14**) from responsible authorities (see **para.5.12**) or interested parties (see **para.5.14** below), the application *must* be granted (s.18(1) and (2)).

The conditions attached to the licence will be consistent with those listed by the applicant in the operating schedule, together with the mandatory conditions (s.18(2)(a) and (b)) (see **para.5.18**).

5.14 WHO CAN OBJECT?

As noted above, all applications for premises licences must be advertised and responsible authorities notified. This is so that the responsible authorities and other interested parties can make objections (termed 'relevant representations' in the 2003 Act) relating to the application if they wish to do so (s.18(6)).

Relevant representations may only be made by responsible authorities (see **para.5.12**) and interested parties and must be made within 28 days of the application being made (s.18(7) and PLCPC Regulations, reg.22).

'Interested parties' (s.13(3)) are defined as any of the following:

- a person living in the vicinity of the premises;
- a body representing persons who live in that vicinity;
- a person involved in a business in the vicinity of the premises; and
- a body representing persons involved in such businesses.

Thus, residents, residents' associations, businesses and business associations are all given the opportunity to make representations to the licensing authority regarding an application. Representations do not have to be objections, although obviously some of the representations made may be objections. Other comments may also be made, either neutral or in favour of the application. The Guidance emphasises that the views of vocal minorities should not be allowed to predominate over the general interests of the community.

'Vicinity' is not defined in the 2003 Act. However, in their statements of licensing policy, some licensing authorities give an indication of how they will interpret the term. Frequently, the starting point will be to consider whether the objector's home or business is within 100m of the premises for which a licence is sought.

5.15 GROUNDS OF OBJECTION

For a representation to be relevant (s.18(6) and (7)), it must:

- relate to the effect of the grant of the licence on the promotion of the licensing objectives;
- be made by an interested party or a responsible authority within the required period;
- not have been withdrawn;
- if made by an interested party, not be frivolous or vexatious;
- if it concerns the identity of the DPS, be made by a chief officer of police and include a statement explaining the reasons for the objection.

All representations made by responsible authorities are relevant if they concern the effect of the grant of the application on the licensing objectives.

It should be noted that only the police can object to the designation of a new DPS. This is anticipated to be only in exceptional circumstances where they consider that the appointment would undermine the crime prevention objective.

Where a representation is made by an interested party, the licensing authority must first decide whether it is relevant. This will involve determining whether it relates to a licensing objective, and whether it has in fact been made by an interested party, in addition to ensuring that it is not frivolous or vexatious.

With regard to whether a representation is 'frivolous' or 'vexatious' the test is whether the licensing authority is of the opinion that it is frivolous or vexatious (s.18(7)(c)), with those words being given their ordinary meaning. The relevant licensing authority must, therefore, form a view as to whether a reasonable person would consider the representation to be frivolous or vexatious.

If relevant representations are made, the licensing authority must hold a hearing in order to consider the representations, unless all parties agree that a hearing is not necessary (s.18(3)). The hearing must start within 20 working days following the end of the period during which relevant representations can be made (Hearings Regulations, reg.5 and Sched.1) and at least 10 working days' notice must be given before the hearing is due to commence (Licensing Act 2003 (Hearings) (Amendment) Regulations 2005, SI 2005/78, reg.2) (see **Figure 5.1**).

Figure 5.1 Applications for premises licence – time line

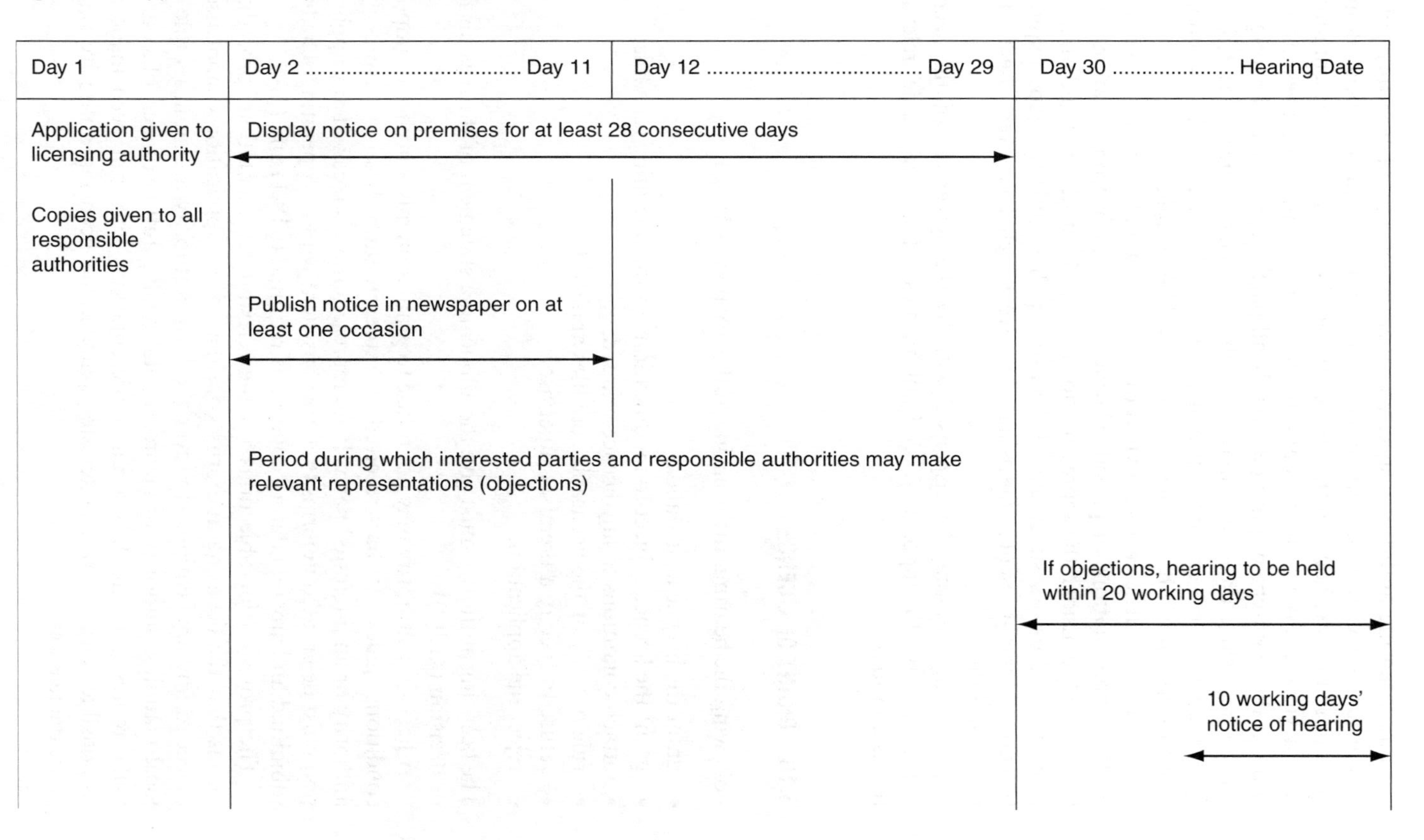

Some licensing authorities specify in their statements of licensing policy that where relevant representations are received a council officer should attempt to mediate between the applicant and those making representations, with a view to taking steps to ensure that the licensing objectives are met without the requirement for a hearing. If all parties agree that a hearing will not be necessary, the officer may issue the premises licence subject to the agreed amendments to the terms and conditions of the licence. If a suitable compromise cannot be reached, a hearing will be arranged.

All relevant parties will be invited to the hearing and allowed to comment on the representations or provide clarification of their representations. The hearing will consider the representations in the light of the Guidance, the licensing authority's statement of licensing policy and the steps required to support the particular licensing objective which has given rise to the representation(s).

A hearing may only be dispensed with by the agreement of the licensing authority, the applicant, and all parties who have made relevant representations.

5.16 GRANT OF LICENCE

Following the hearing, the licensing authority may (s.18(4)):

- grant the licence as it stands;
- grant the licence subject to modifications to the operating schedule;
- attach conditions to any licence granted;
- rule out any of the licensable activities applied for;
- refuse to specify a premises supervisor;
- reject the application.

The licensing authority must give the applicant a statement of the reasons for its decision (s.23(2)).

A licensing authority may not refuse to grant a premises licence or impose conditions unless it has received a representation from a responsible authority or an interested party. If no representation is received any application must be granted in terms that are consistent with the operating schedule submitted and any mandatory conditions required (s.18(1) and (2)).

The provision for objections via the relevant representations procedure means that the licensing authority considering the application cannot itself object to any application. However the local authority acting in its role as local planning authority or environmental health authority can, of course, make representations. If relevant representations have not been made by responsible authorities or interested parties, the licensing authority must grant the licence.

Furthermore, in the absence of relevant representations, the licensing authority cannot attach any conditions other than those consistent with the operating schedule and any mandatory conditions required (s.18(2)(a) and (b)).

5.17 DISCRETIONARY CONDITIONS ATTACHED TO A PREMISES LICENCE

If, following the consideration of relevant representations, the licensing authority decides to impose conditions on the premises licence, these must be shown to be necessary for the promotion of the licensing objectives in any individual case. In theory this means that licensing committees should not impose conditions (other than the mandatory ones) unless they have come to the view that the application would be refused unless those conditions were in place.

In contrast to the previous licensing regime which used standardised conditions, one of the key concepts underscoring the 2003 Act is that any conditions should be tailored to the individual style and characteristics of the premises and the events concerned. The Guidance stresses that any conditions applied should be proportionate and appropriate to the business, organisation or individual concerned. However, some local authorities are specifying that there must be at least one personal licence holder on the premises at all times. In the absence of any relevant representations during the application process this is not something they can require by law but, if relevant representations are made, this requirement could be added as a condition.

A pool of model conditions relating to each of the licensing objectives is listed in the Guidance and is reproduced at **Appendices B2–B5**. These may be drawn upon by licensing authorities where necessary and appropriate. Conditions should not duplicate areas covered by other legislation and should also not duplicate licensing offences.

5.18 MANDATORY CONDITIONS

Some conditions are mandatory for certain licensable activities and must therefore be attached to the relevant licence as follows:

- Where a licence authorises the supply of alcohol (s.19):
  - there must be a DPS who is the holder of a valid personal licence; and
  - any supply of alcohol must be made by a personal licence holder or someone authorised by a personal licence holder.
- Where a licence authorises the exhibition of a film (s.20):
  - admission of children must be restricted in accordance with the recommendations of the relevant film classification authority.

- Where the provision of door supervision is a requirement of the licence (s.21):
  - anyone carrying out such a security function must be licensed by the Security Industry Authority.
- Where a licence authorises the performance of a play:
  - licensing authorities cannot attach conditions relating to the nature of the play performed or the manner of its performance, unless they are justified in doing so to ensure public safety (s.22).

5.19 VALIDITY OF LICENCE

A premises licence will have effect until the licence is revoked (s.26(1)(a)), or it is surrendered (s.28), or it lapses, but otherwise it will not be time limited unless the applicant requests a licence for a limited period only (s.26(1)(b)). The licence will, therefore, be valid for the life of the business.

However, note that a premises licence lapses on the death, mental incapacity or insolvency of the licence holder (s.27).

5.20 DUTIES RELATING TO LICENCE

The holder of a premises licence must notify the licensing authority of any change of name or address of the licence holder or of the DPS (s.33(1)).

The licence holder must ensure that the premises licence, or a certified copy of the licence, is kept on the premises to which the licence relates and that this is kept either in his custody or under his control or under the custody or control of a nominated person (s.57(2)). In addition, a summary of the licence or a certified copy of the summary must be prominently displayed at the premises (s.57(3)).

Failure to comply with any of these duties is an offence under the 2003 Act attracting a level 2 fine (s.57(8)).

5.21 APPEALS

Appeals may be made to the magistrates' courts against decisions made by the licensing authority in relation to premises licences (Sched.5, Part 1) by any party involved in the decision (i.e. applicants, responsible authorities and interested parties) in the following circumstances.

- An applicant may appeal against the decision by the licensing authority to reject the application for a premises licence (Sched.5, para.1).

- Where a licence is granted, the licence holder may appeal against the imposition of conditions on the licence, the exclusion of a licensable activity, or the refusal to specify the nominated person as DPS (Sched.5, para.2).
- Those who made relevant representations may appeal against the decision to grant the licence (Sched.5, para.3(a)).
- Where a licence is granted, those who made relevant representations may appeal on the grounds that different or additional conditions should have been imposed, or that a particular licensable activity should have been excluded (Sched.5, para.3(b)).
- The chief officer of police who gave a notice may appeal against the grant of an application to specify an individual as a premises supervisor.

Appeals are made to the relevant magistrates' court in the area where the premises concerned are situated and must be made within 21 days of notification of the decision appealed against.

There is no right of appeal, however, for an interested party who wishes to make representations but who is refused the opportunity to do so by the licensing authority on the basis that those representations are irrelevant, frivolous or vexatious. The only way to challenge the local authority's view would be by way of judicial review.

5.22 REGISTER OF INTERESTS

People or businesses with a property interest in a premises may register their interest with the licensing authority in order to be notified of licensing matters affecting those premises (s.178). This is not a legal requirement and is entirely the choice of the individual/company concerned. However, it will be of particular interest to companies who operate tenanted estates, as it will ensure that they will be informed of any changes affecting their properties.

Similarly, conveyancers acting on acquisitions should advise their clients of the opportunity to register if it is not intended that the purchaser will be the holder of the premises licence.

To register an interest, notice must be given using the form set out in Sched.1 to the PLCPC Regulations and should be accompanied by the prescribed fee (s.178(1)). The notice will have effect for 12 months (s.178(2)) and during that time the person or business will be notified of any changes made to the licensing register relating to the property concerned, and of their right to request a copy of the information contained in any entry in the register (s.178(3)). The notice may be renewed each year for a fee.

Those with a property interest include a freeholder, leaseholder, mortgagee, occupier and those with a prescribed interest (s.178(4)).

CHAPTER 6

Licensable activities

6.1 WHEN WILL I NEED A PREMISES LICENCE?

A premises licence (or a temporary event notice – see **Chapter 8**) will be required for any premises where licensable activities are being carried out (s.11). As already noted in **Chapter 3**, licensable activities comprise the sale or supply of alcohol, the provision of regulated entertainment and the provision of late night refreshment.

6.2 SALE/SUPPLY OF ALCOHOL

The licensable activities related to alcohol are relatively straightforward. They include the direct sale by retail of alcohol, i.e. sale in pubs, restaurants, hotels, where previously an on-licence was required, and sales of alcohol from off-licences, supermarkets, local stores, etc., where previously an off-licence was required.

Until the 2003 Act, the supply of alcohol in clubs was accepted as not constituting a sale by retail. The 2003 Act treats the supply of alcohol by or on behalf of a club to, or to the order of, a member of the club as a separate licensable activity (s.1(1)(b)).

The definition of alcohol remains the same as in the pre-2003 legislation. Alcohol means spirits, wine, beer, cider or any other fermented, distilled or spirituous liquor with a strength of more than 0.5% alcohol by volume. The sale of liqueur confectionery is not licensable (s.191).

A club will also require a premises licence (in addition to a club premises certificate (see **Chapter 9**)) where it wishes to sell alcohol to non-members/non-guests (s.1(3)).

6.2.1 Wholesale

Until the Licensing Act 2003, the sale of alcohol in defined wholesale quantities to the general public was not licensable. This changes under the 2003 Act. Although wholesale quantity is not defined in the 2003 Act, all sales by retail come under the Act (s.1(1)(a) and s.192) unless they are business-to-business sales, as outlined below. Consequently, wholesalers will require a premises licence to sell alcohol to members of the public, whatever the quantities involved.

Business-to-business sales are excluded from the scope of the new legislation (s.192(2)). Thus sales of alcohol made to a trader for trade purposes, to a club which holds a club premises certificate, to a personal licence holder for the purpose of making sales authorised by a premises licence, to a premises licence holder or to a premises user with a temporary event notice for purposes permitted by those certificates, licences or notices, are not licensable activities and do not require a premises licence.

6.2.2 Internet/mail order sales

Retail of alcohol involving internet or mail order sales also requires a premises licence. Where there is a separate call centre and storage facility, a premises licence is required for the premises where the alcohol is selected and despatched to the purchaser, i.e. usually the storage warehouse.

6.3 REGULATED ENTERTAINMENT

A separate licence to provide public entertainment is not required under the 2003 Act. Anyone wishing to provide entertainment should apply for a premises licence authorising the provision of regulated entertainment and any other licensable activity that they wish to provide.

The activities covered by regulated entertainment are basically in line with those covered under the current 'public entertainment' law, except there is no requirement for the music and dancing to be 'public'. Thus, under the new legislation it is not just public entertainment which is licensable, but also private entertainment if it is provided for 'consideration and with a view to profit'.

Under the Licensing Act 1964, where up to two performers were singing or playing music at a premises where a justices' licence was in force, there was no requirement for a public entertainment licence. This was known as the 'two in a bar' rule, but it is abolished under the 2003 Act (Sched.8, para.1(2)(a)). Where regulated entertainment is provided, a premises licence will be required regardless of the number of performers.

The definition of regulated entertainment is given in Sched.1 to the 2003 Act (Sched.1, para.1; see **Appendix A2**). As can be seen, this definition is somewhat longwinded and complicated. Put as simply as possible, to constitute regulated entertainment, four criteria must be satisfied, as follows.

1. There must be the provision of entertainment (see **para.6.3.1**) or entertainment facilities (see **para.6.3.2**).

2. The entertainment or entertainment facilities must be provided:
   (a) solely or partly for members of the public; or
   (b) exclusively for club members and their guests; or
   (c) for private entertainment for which a charge (see **para.6.3.4**) is made, with a view to profit; and
   (d) the premises on which the entertainment or entertainment facilities are provided are made available for the purpose of enabling the entertainment concerned to take place.
3. None of the exemptions listed in Sched.1, Part 2 of the 2003 Act must apply (see **para.6.3.3**).

6.3.1 What is defined as 'entertainment'?

The descriptions of entertainment given in the 2003 Act are (Sched.1, para.2):

- the performance of a play (including a rehearsal if the public are admitted);
- an exhibition of a film;
- an indoor sporting event;
- boxing or wrestling entertainment (indoor and outdoor);
- a performance of live music;
- any playing of recorded music;
- a performance of dance;
- entertainment similar to live music, recorded music or dance;

where the entertainment described takes place in the presence of an audience and is provided in order to entertain the audience.

6.3.2 Entertainment facilities

Entertainment facilities are described (Sched.1, para.3) as facilities for enabling people to take part in entertainment consisting of:

- making music (vocal or instrumental or both);
- dancing;
- entertainment similar to making music or dancing;

where the facilities are provided for the purpose of being entertained.

6.3.3 Exemptions

A number of exemptions to the definition of regulated entertainment are given including (Sched.1, Part 2):

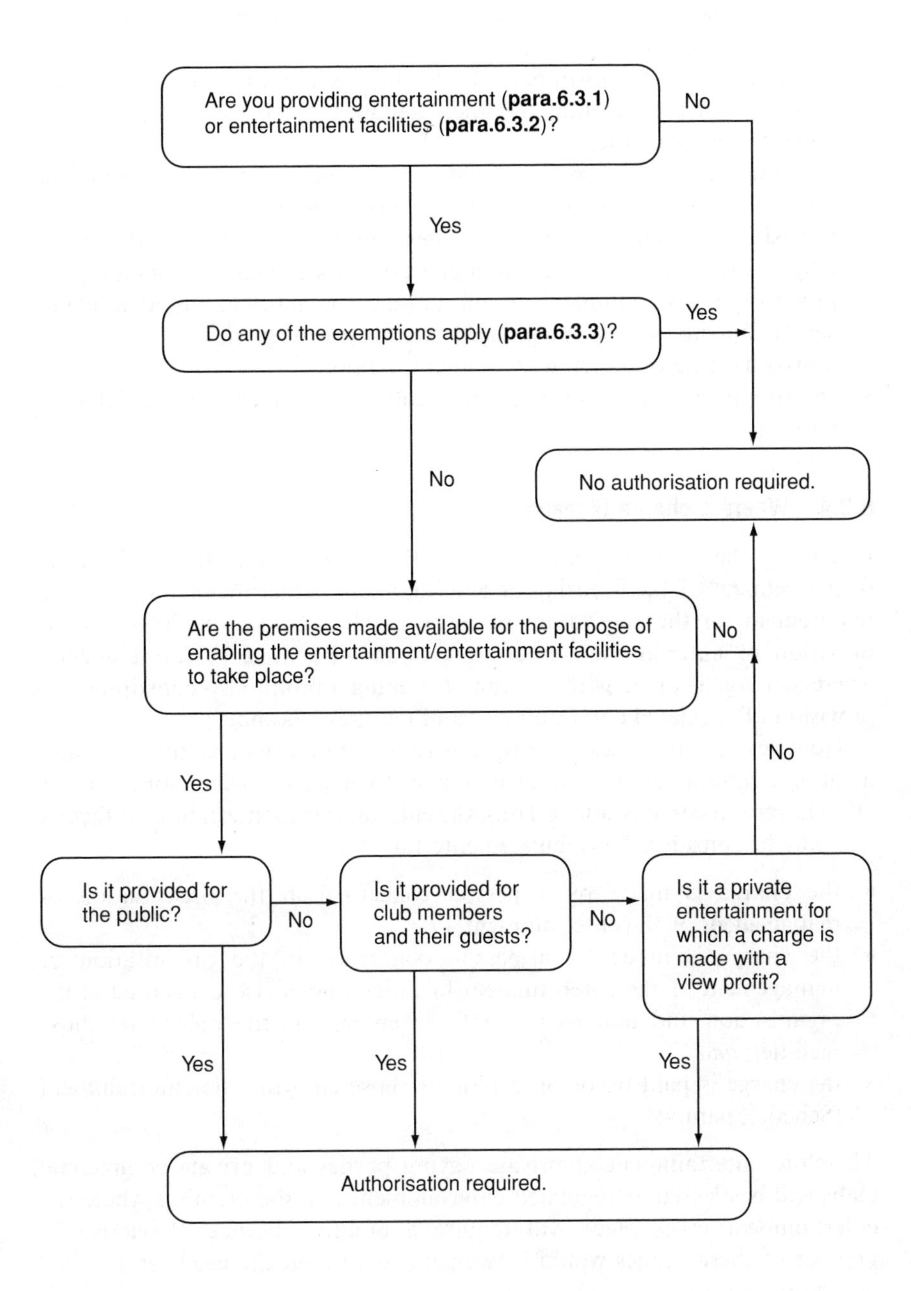

Figure 6.1 Are you providing regulated entertainment?

- film exhibitions where the main purpose is product demonstration, advertisement, education or instruction;
- film exhibitions that form part of an exhibit at a museum or art gallery;
- music which is incidental to other activities which themselves are not regulated entertainment;
- showing live TV or radio broadcasts to an audience (however, the replaying of pre-recorded broadcasts is not exempt);
- provision of entertainment or entertainment facilities incidental to religious services or provided at a place of public religious worship;
- provision of entertainment or entertainment facilities at a garden fete or similar function unless the proceeds are for private gain;
- morris dancing or dancing of a similar nature;
- entertainment or entertainment facilities provided on vehicles in motion.

6.3.4 Where a charge is made

Essentially the main difference between the 1964 Act and the 2003 Act in their treatment of the licensing of entertainment is that there is no longer a requirement for the entertainment to be 'public'. Under the 2003 Act the provision of entertainment/entertainment facilities to a private audience, where a charge is made with the aim of making a profit, also constitutes the provision of regulated entertainment and requires a licence.

However, this provision is tempered to a certain extent as the entertainment or entertainment facilities will only be treated as provided for consideration in certain circumstances. Thus, the entertainment/entertainment facility will only be considered as regulated entertainment if:

- the charge is made by a person concerned in the organisation or management of the entertainment; *or*
- the charge is made by a person concerned in the organisation or management of the entertainment facilities who is also concerned in the organisation and management of the entertainment enabled by those facilities; *and*
- the charge is paid by or on behalf of those enjoying the entertainment (Sched.1, para.4).

Therefore entertainment at private paying parties and private commercial clubs will be classed as regulated entertainment and the premises where the entertainment takes place will require a premises licence. Previously, a number of these venues would have operated without the need for a public entertainment licence.

However, the Guidance admits that private houses such as historic houses which are let out for private functions where a dance floor is available will only require a premises licence if the owner of the house also provides the entertainment.

Furthermore, those playing or performing live or recorded music, such as a musician or DJ, will not be considered as being involved in the organisation or management of the entertainment where their only involvement is to choose the music, or to decide how it is to be performed, or provide their own instrument or equipment (Sched.1, para.6).

Entertainment will not be considered to be 'regulated' and require a premises licence in the following circumstances:

- if regulated entertainment is made to a private audience and a charge is made to cover costs; or
- if regulated entertainment is made to a private audience but members of the audience are free to make a voluntary donation to a charity of their own choice.

According to the Department for Culture, Media and Sport (DCMS), the reasoning behind this distinction between profit-making and non-profit-making private events is that the desire to maximise profits can lead organisers to economise in areas of public safety or the protection of children. By ensuring that a licence is required, it is envisaged that such matters will have to be addressed before a licence is granted.

6.3.5 Guidance from the DCMS

The definitions and in particular the scope of exemptions are likely to be the subject of many appeals early in the life of the new legislation. In the meantime, some guidance is available from the DCMS including the following:

1. Provision of a juke box is not an entertainment facility, whereas provision of a karaoke machine for the use by and entertainment of customers is an entertainment facility.
2. Provision of a juke box in a pub may, however, be entertainment, or may be considered to be incidental to other activities, depending on the volume levels.
3. Provision of a dance floor for use by the public in a nightclub is an entertainment facility.
4. Provision of amplifiers, pianos, etc. for use by the public would be the provision of entertainment facilities.
5. Pub games which take place in the presence of an audience and are provided to entertain the audience would come under the definition of an indoor sport and therefore be a licensable activity.

6. A sporting event that takes place at a venue which has a roof which can be opened or closed would not constitute an indoor event, even if the roof were closed.
7. As sport and sporting events are defined in terms of physical skill and physical recreation, a publicly contested chess game or similar activity would not be considered to be an indoor sporting event. Pub quiz events would appear to escape regulation on the same basis.
8. Entertainment/entertainment facilities provided at private events would not be regulated entertainment unless a charge was made and with a view to profit.

As can be seen from the examples above, the permutations here are so wide that it is not possible to cover every eventuality through the Guidance. The Secretary of State exhorts 'the simple application of common sense' to these issues.

6.3.6 Small scale music events

There is also a form of exemption for dancing and live music for premises which have a permitted capacity of not more than 200 people and which are used primarily for the supply of alcohol for consumption on the premises (s.177(1) and (2)). In these circumstances, where a premises licence or club premises certificate is in place authorising the supply of alcohol and the provision of music entertainment (i.e. live music or dancing or facilities for such) the only conditions that may be applied to that musical entertainment, apart from those submitted in the operating schedule, are those relating to either crime and disorder or public safety. This means that conditions relating to protection of children from harm or public nuisance do not apply to the musical entertainment. However, if there is a review of the licence (see **Chapter 10**), the exempted conditions can be applied.

It should be noted that this exemption only applies to 'live' music. Thus a disco plus dancing would not be exempt under this provision as it is not 'live' music, whereas if the music was provided by a live band playing musical instruments it would be exempt.

A similar additional exemption is available (s.177(3) and (4)) for premises which have a permitted capacity of 200 or less and which hold a premises licence or club premises certificate authorising the provision of musical entertainment. In such premises, where there is a performance of live unamplified music during the hours between 8 a.m. and midnight, but no other form of regulated entertainment is provided, then no licence conditions other than those described in the operating schedule may be applied to the licence in relation to the musical entertainment. Again, if there is a review of the licence, the exempted conditions can be applied.

6.3.7 Non-licensable activities/exempt premises

Non-licensable locations

Certain activities which otherwise would be 'licensable activities' are non-licensable if they are carried on in certain locations, e.g. on aircraft, hovercraft, trains, aboard a vessel on an international journey (s.173).

Raffles and tombolas

Minor raffles and tombolas involving prizes of alcohol are not treated as licensable (s.175) if they fulfil the following conditions:

- the lottery is promoted as incidental to an exempt entertainment;
- after deduction of all relevant expenses, none of the proceeds are used for private gain;
- the alcohol is in a sealed container;
- none of the prizes are money prizes;
- the tickets or chances are sold or issued and the results of the draw are announced at the time of, and in the same place as, the entertainment.

Village halls, etc.

Village halls, parish halls, community halls, church halls, chapel halls or other similar premises will require a premises licence for the provision of regulated entertainment, but they will be exempt from having to pay the associated fee. However, if the licence also authorises the provision of alcohol or late night refreshment, a fee will be required for those activities.

6.3.8 Garages

With regard to the sale of alcohol at motorway service areas and garage forecourts, the new legislation generally maintains the position which existed under the Licensing Act 1964. This means there is a general prohibition on the sale or supply of alcohol from service areas and from premises that are used primarily as a garage, i.e. for the retailing of petrol or derv, or the sale or maintenance of motor vehicles (s.176).

However, it is expected that licensing committees will follow the approach that the courts have taken in assessing applications made under s.9(4A) of the Licensing Act 1964. In determining the primary use of garage premises, courts have considered such factors as the intensity of use by customers and the net turnover of income from the various parts of businesses which include the garage premises. Therefore in rural areas if the garage shop is used more intensely and/or more profitably for the purchase of non-garage goods, it may be appropriate to apply for a premises licence to sell alcohol. A combination of the reduction in numbers of village shops (other than garages) and low profit returns on fuel, means that in recent years these applications have been granted by licensing justices on a more regular basis.

6.4 LATE NIGHT REFRESHMENT

6.4.1 The new regime

Prior to the 2003 Act there were two separate regimes controlling the provision of late night refreshment. One covered the Greater London area and required licences for premises that provided hot food and drink for consumption either on or off the premises. The other covered the rest of England and Wales and only required licences for those premises providing late night refreshment for consumption on the premises.

Under the 2003 Act late night refreshment is provided if, between the hours of 11 p.m. and 5 a.m., hot food or hot drink:

- is supplied to the public for consumption on or off the premises; or
- is supplied to any people on or from premises to which the public has access (Sched.2, para.1(1)).

Food or drink is 'hot' if it is heated on the premises or elsewhere before it is supplied, or can be heated on the premises after it has been supplied, so that it can be consumed at a temperature above the ambient air temperature (Sched.2, para.2).

These provisions regulating late night refreshment are similar to those that already existed in most of London, and are now extended to cover the whole of England and Wales. They are intended to address the problems of disorder and disturbance which can be associated with premises serving hot food and drink late at night.

In practice this means that, for the first time outside London, takeaway food stores and night cafés will require a licence to provide their services. In addition, supermarkets or shops selling hot food and drink or providing facilities for heating food and drink, will require a premises licence authorising the provision of late night refreshment. Similarly, garages that provide a microwave for heating food will also require a premises licence authorising this.

Mobile food vendors serving hot food or drink between 11 p.m. and 5 a.m. will also need a premises licence. In fact, they will need a separate premises licence for each location they operate from (s.189).

Restaurants providing food between 11 p.m. and 5 a.m. will also require authorisation for the provision of late night refreshment. However, as most restaurants will also be serving alcohol, they will only need to apply for one premises licence to authorise both the sale of alcohol and provision of late night refreshment. Restaurant owners will need to specify in the operating schedule that they wish to provide both alcohol and late night refreshment and will be required to detail the hours during which each licensable activity is proposed.

Similarly, where late night refreshment is provided as a secondary activity from public houses, nightclubs, cinemas, etc., a single premises licence will cover all the licensable activities specified in the operating schedule. In such situations it is unlikely that conditions specific to the provision of late night refreshment will be required, as any relevant conditions such as those relating to crime and disorder or public nuisance are already likely to have been covered by the conditions attached to the other licensable activities.

6.4.2 Exemptions

There are a number of situations where a premises licence is not required for the provision of late night refreshment. These include circumstances where the public are not admitted to the premises involved and the supply of hot food or drink is to:

- guests of hotels or similar premises, the main purpose of which is to provide overnight accommodation;
- members of a recognised club;
- an employee of a particular employer, e.g. a staff canteen;
- a person who is engaged in a particular trade, or is a member of a particular profession or follows a particular vocation, e.g. a tradesman carrying out work at a particular premises;
- guests of any of the above;
- premises already licensed under certain other Acts (Sched.2, para.3(2)).

The following are also exempt and do not require authorisation for the provision of late night refreshment (Sched. 2, para.5(1)):

- the supply of hot drink which consists of or contains alcohol (although authorisation for the provision of alcohol will be required);
- the supply of hot drink by means of a vending machine where the payment is inserted into the machine and the hot drink is supplied directly by the machine to a member of the public;
- the supply of hot food or drink free of charge, provided there is also no charge for admission to the premises or for some other item in order to be able to obtain the hot food or drink;
- the supply of hot food or drink by a registered charity;
- the supply of hot food and drink from a vehicle, unless it is permanently or temporarily parked.

The exemption for vending machines only covers the supply of hot drink. If hot food is supplied by a vending machine, even where there is direct payment to and supply from the machine, the premises on which the vending machine is situated will require a licence authorising late night refreshment, provided that the food is supplied between the relevant hours.

CHAPTER 7

Licence changes

7.1 CAN A PREMISES LICENCE BE VARIED?

The holder of a premises licences may apply to vary the licence (s.34(1)). Variations may include altering conditions attaching to the licence, or changes to the hours of operation, or changes to the authorised licensable activities. An application to vary the actual premises may also be made, provided the change is only minor.

The 2003 Act also specifically provides that a licensing authority may vary a licence so that it has effect subject to different conditions in respect of different parts of the premises concerned or different licensable activities (s.36(7)).

The only limitation specified in the 2003 Act as to what may be varied is that it is not possible to vary a time limited licence to extend the time for which the licence has effect; nor is it possible to make a substantial variation to the premises to which the licence relates (s.36(6)). 'Substantial' is not defined in the Act and it will be for the licensing authority to interpret its meaning. Substantial alterations to premises will require an application for a new licence rather than variation of the existing one.

There are separate procedures to notify change of name and address and to change the DPS (see **paras.7.4** to **7.6**).

7.2 PROCEDURE FOR APPLICATION TO VARY

The procedure for an application to vary is essentially the same as for the original grant of a licence. Applications are made to the licensing authority which granted the original licence (s.35(1)).

The application must be made using the form set out at Sched.4 to the PLCPC Regulations and must be accompanied by the premises licence to be varied unless this is impracticable, in which case a statement explaining why must be provided. If relevant, a revised operating schedule may also be required. The appropriate fee must also be included.

As with the application for the original licence, applications to vary must be advertised and notice of the application also given to each responsible authority, and to such other persons as may be prescribed, within the prescribed period. The requirements for advertising and notification are the same as those described at **para.5.12**.

Responsible authorities and interested parties may make objections in the form of relevant representations relating to any of the variations applied for. The requirements for a representation to be relevant are the same as those described in **Chapter 5** in relation to new licences.

If no relevant representations are received by the licensing authority, it must grant the variation as applied for, provided it has been validly made, subject only to conditions which are consistent with the operating schedule and any mandatory conditions (s.35(1) and (2)). Again, the licensing authority itself has no discretion to object to any variation in the absence of relevant representations.

If the licensing authority receives any relevant representations, it must hold a hearing within 20 working days in order to consider the representations (Hearings Regulations, reg.5 and Sched.1), although such a hearing can be dispensed with if all relevant parties agree (s.35(3)(a)). Following the hearing, and if it considers it necessary for the promotion of the licensing objectives, the licensing authority will either modify the conditions of the licence, or reject the whole or part of the application (s.35(4)). In determining the application, the licensing authority may vary the licence to impose different conditions on different parts of the premises or impose different conditions in relation to different licensable activities (s.36(7)).

If the licensing authority does not consider it necessary to modify the licence or reject the application, it will grant the variation in the terms sought.

If the licence is modified or rejected, the licensing authority must give a statement of the reasons for its decision to the applicant (s.36(2)).

7.3 APPEALS RELATING TO APPLICATIONS TO VARY

Appeals may be made to the magistrates' courts against decisions made by the licensing authority in relation to applications to vary premises licences by any party involved in the decision – applicants, responsible authorities and interested parties.

Applicants may, thus, appeal against the rejection of an application to vary (Sched.5, para.1(6)), or where the licensing authority has modified the conditions of the licence before granting a variation, the applicant may appeal against the modification (Sched.5, para.4(2)).

Those who made relevant representations in relation to an application to vary can appeal against the decision to vary, or against any modification imposed, or that a different modification should have been made (Sched.5, para.4(3)).

Appeals must be made within 21 days of notification of the decision appealed against (Sched.5, para.9(2)).

7.4 CHANGE OF NAME OR ADDRESS

A premises licence holder must notify the licensing authority that issued the licence of any change of name or address (s.33(1)). The notification must be accompanied by the appropriate fee and the premises licence to be amended.

Failure by a premises licence holder to notify the licensing authority of a change of name or address is an offence under the 2003 Act attracting a fine on conviction not exceeding level 2 (s.33(6) and (7)).

7.5 VARIATION OF DESIGNATED PREMISES SUPERVISOR (DPS)

There is a separate procedure if the premises licence holder wishes to vary the licence by applying to name a person in the licence as the DPS or substitute a different person for the person currently named in the licence (s.37(1)).

As detailed in **Chapter 5**, where the premises licence authorises the provision of alcohol, there must be a DPS. If this person leaves the premises, or for any other reason the licence holder wishes to change the person designated, an application must be made to the licensing authority to vary the licence to change the name of the designated premises supervisor specified in the licence.

In addition, where an application to vary the licence to add the provision of alcohol as an authorised licensable activity is submitted, it will be necessary to make a separate application to specify the individual named in the application as the designated premises supervisor.

Such applications must be made using the form set out in Sched.5 to the PLCPC Regulations (PLCPC Regulations, reg.13) and be accompanied by (s.37(3)):

- the premises licence or the relevant part of the licence (or a statement explaining why the licence cannot be submitted);
- form of consent by the proposed new DPS (PLCPC Regulations, Sched.11, Part A); and
- the appropriate fee.

Notification of such an application must be given to the chief officer of police for the area in which the premises is situated and to the current DPS, if there is one, by sending them copies of the application together with accompanying documents on the same day as the application is made (s.37(4) and PLCPC Regulations, reg.28(a)).

The chief officer of police may object to the variation if he believes that due to the exceptional circumstances of the case, granting the variation would undermine the crime prevention objective (s.37(5)); however, this is likely to be rare. Any objection by the police must be made within 14 days and they must give reasons for the decision (s.37(6)).

It is not possible for other responsible authorities or interested parties to make relevant representations.

An application to vary the licence to name a different DPS may also request that the variation take immediate effect, i.e. from the time when the application is received by the licensing authority (s.38). This will be relevant where the existing DPS leaves suddenly, or is injured or ill and unable to work, so that the holder of the premises licence will be able to continue the provision of alcohol while the application is being determined.

The licensing authority will grant the application to vary the DPS (s.39(2)) unless the police have objected, in which case a hearing will be held within 20 working days (s.39(3), Hearings Regulations, reg.5 and Sched.1). Following the hearing, the licensing authority may either grant or reject the application.

If the variation is granted, the licence holder has a duty to notify the person who has been replaced as DPS. If the variation is not granted, the proposed DPS must be notified of the decision. If the licence holder fails to notify as specified he will be committing an offence (s.40).

Applicants may appeal against the decision to reject an application for a variation of a DPS (Sched.5, para.1(c)). The police may also appeal if following their objection to a specified individual, the licensing authority decides to grant the application to vary (para.5).

7.6 REQUEST TO BE REMOVED AS DPS

If a DPS wishes to cease acting as such, he must notify the licensing authority (s.41(1)). If the DPS is also the premises licence holder, he must also send the premises licence or the appropriate part of the licence to the licensing authority (s.41(3)). If he is not also the licence holder, he must notify the licence holder within 48 hours of his intentions and request the licence holder to send the licence or appropriate part to the licensing authority (s.41(4)).

Provided that the correct procedure is followed, the DPS will cease to act as such from the time the licensing authority receives the notice or a later date if one is specified in the notice (s.41(7)).

It is important that purchasers of premises licensed for the sale of alcohol should be aware not only that the supply is conditional on the existence of a DPS for those premises but also that it is open to the DPS to resign with immediate effect from that position.

7.7 TRANSFER OF PREMISES LICENCE

Where a business that involves a licensable activity is sold to a new owner, or the person who holds the premises licence is to change for some other reason (for example where the tenant of a tenanted estate holds the licence and there is a change of tenancy) it will be necessary to transfer the premises licence.

The new legislation provides that any person or company that is eligible to apply for a premises licence may apply to have a premises licence transferred to them (s.42(1)). Such a transfer will only change the identity of the licence holder and will not alter the licence in any other way.

An application for transfer should be made to the licensing authority that granted the premises licence using the form set out in Sched.6 to the PLCPC Regulations (PLCPC Regulations, reg.14) and should be accompanied by:

- the premises licence (or a statement of reasons why it has not been submitted) (s.42(4));
- the consent of the current licence holder (s.44(4) and (6), PLCPC Regulations, reg.24(2) and Sched.11, Part B);
- the appropriate fee.

An application to transfer must be notified to the chief officer of police (s.42(5)) by sending a copy of the application together with accompanying documents on the same day that the application to transfer is made to the licensing authority (PLCPC Regulations, reg.28(b)). In exceptional circumstances where the police believe that the transfer may undermine the crime prevention objective, they may object to the application, but this is expected to be rare. Such objection, if made, must be given within 14 days of receiving the notice. Objections to a transfer cannot be made by other responsible authorities or interested parties.

If no objections are received from the police, the licensing authority must transfer the licence in accordance with the application, provided it has been duly made and the following requirements are complied with (s.44(2) and (4)):

- the existing licence holder has agreed to the transfer; or
- an application for transfer with immediate effect has been made (see below); or
- the requirement for the existing licence holder's consent has been waived.

In the majority of cases a transfer will be a simple administrative process that will be handled by a council officer.

If the police have objected to the transfer, then a hearing will be held, unless all relevant parties have agreed a hearing is not necessary (s.44(5)). Any hearing must be held within 20 working days of the end of the police objection period (Hearings Regulations, reg.5 and Sched.1).

The applicant for the transfer of a premises licence which includes a request that the transfer have immediate effect must notify the DPS, if one is specified in the licence, that the application is being made (s.46(2)). In addition, if a transfer is granted, the applicant must also notify the DPS of this fact (s.46(3)). Failure to do so is an offence.

Applicants may appeal to the local magistrates' court against the decision by the licensing authority to reject their application for a transfer of a licence (Sched.5, para.1(d)). The chief officer of police may also appeal if the application to transfer was granted despite their objection (Sched.5, para.6).

7.8 TRANSFER WITH IMMEDIATE EFFECT

Until recently, when buying a licensed premises it was usual to apply for a protection order or interim authority which would have effect on the completion date or shortly beforehand, in order to be able to carry on business at the premises as soon as the purchase was finalised. An application for transfer would then be made at a later stage.

Under the 2003 Act there is no provision that specifically replaces either a protection order or an interim authority in these circumstances (but see **para.7.11** for interim authorities on the death, mental incapacity or insolvency of the licence holder). However, in order to enable continuity and ensure there is no interruption to business at the premises during determination of the transfer, it is possible to request that the application for transfer be given immediate effect, i.e. from when it is received by the licensing authority until it is formally determined or withdrawn (s.43(1)).

An application for transfer with immediate effect will normally require the consent of the current licence holder (s.43(3)). However, this may be waived if the applicant can demonstrate that he has taken all reasonable steps to obtain the consent and can show that he is in a position to use the premises immediately for the licensable activities authorised by the licence (s.43(5)).

To avoid any problems with respect to obtaining the consent of the holder of the premises licence to an immediate transfer, it may be sensible for the contract for sale to include the agreement of the licence holder to the buyer making an application for transfer with immediate effect (s.43) on or before the completion date.

7.9 CONSTRUCTION, EXTENSION OR ALTERATION OF PREMISES

Under the Licensing Act 1964, where premises which were intended to be used for the sale/supply of alcohol were being constructed, extended or altered, it was possible to apply for the provisional grant of a justices' licence, prior to construction being started and this would be followed by an application for a final grant once the building works had been completed. The licensing justices could only refuse to declare final a provisional grant where the works had not been completed in accordance with the deposited plans, or where the provisional licence holder had been disqualified or was deemed not to be a 'fit and proper' person.

Thus the provisional licence gave investors in a project assurance that a justices' licence would be granted provided the building work was completed satisfactorily.

Under the new legislation, provisional grants have been replaced by provisional statements, but their method of operation is somewhat different. The provisional statement does not provide an assurance that the full licence will be granted once the building work has been completed. It merely describes the likely effect of the intended licensable activities on the licensing objectives and gives an indication of the prospects of any future application for a premises licence.

However, according to the Guidance, there is nothing to prevent an application being made for a full premises licence before new premises are constructed or existing premises are extended or changed. The proviso is that the applicant is eligible in that he engages in or proposes to carry on a business that involves licensable activities on the premises.

Of course an application for a full licence for such premises could only be made if all the relevant information outlined in **Chapter 5** was available. This would mean there must be detailed plans of the proposed structure together with sufficient information to formulate an operating schedule including:

- licensable activities to be carried out;
- proposed hours of operation of licensable activities;
- any other times when the premises are to be open to the public;
- the duration of the licence (if it is to have a fixed term);
- details of the DPS, if the licensable activities will include the supply of alcohol;
- whether alcohol is to be supplied, and if so whether the alcohol will be supplied for consumption on or off the premises or both;
- a statement of the steps the applicant proposes to take to promote the licensing objectives.

The procedure for determination would be as described in **Chapter 5**, the only difference being that if the licence was granted it would not have immediate effect, but the date when it would become effective would be included in the licence.

7.10 PROVISIONAL STATEMENT

An application for a provisional statement may, therefore, only need to be made when provision of the above information is not possible. In these circumstances such an application may be made by any individual over the age of 18 or any company/organisation with an interest in the premises to be constructed, extended or altered (s.29(2)). The applicant could, therefore, be a developer, firm of architects or investor, as well as those who would be eligible to apply for a premises licence. In case law decided under s.6(1) of the Licensing Act 1964 the word 'interest' was construed broadly and was not limited to legal, equitable or contractual interests.

In deciding whether to make an application for a provisional statement or a full time-delayed premises licence, one important factor to consider is that the class of applicants for provisional statements is much broader than those who are eligible to apply for a premises licence.

Applications for a provisional statement should be made to the licensing authority in whose area the premises are or are proposed to be situated or mainly situated and should be made using the form set out in Sched.3 to the PLCPC Regulations (PLCPC Regulations, reg.11) and accompanied by a schedule of works and the appropriate fee (s.29(5)).

The schedule of works is a statement made by the applicants which should include (s.29(6)):

- particulars of the premises;
- proposed licensable activities;
- plans of the work to be done;
- description of the work to be carried out.

Applications for provisional statements must be advertised in the same manner as for applications for premises licences (s.30 and PLCPC Regulations, regs.25 and 26). The information to be contained in the notices is the same as for applications for premises licences (see **para.5.12**), but in addition a statement is required that representations are restricted after the issue of a provisional statement. Details of proposed licensable activities need only be included if known.

The application must be notified to responsible authorities by sending them a copy of the application together with all accompanying documents on the same day that the application is given to the licensing authority (PLCPC Regulations, reg.27).

Both responsible authorities and interested parties have the right to make relevant representations (as defined in **Chapter 5**) in the same way as for an application for a premises licence. If no relevant representations are made, the licensing authority must issue a provisional statement stating that no relevant representations were received (s.31(2)).

If objections are made, a hearing must be arranged within 20 working days of the end of the period for making representations (Hearings Regulations, reg.5 and Sched.1) for the licensing authority to consider the representations unless all parties agree a hearing is not necessary. The licensing authority must then decide if, when the proposed work is completed and if an application were made for a premises licence, it would be necessary for the promotion of the licensing objectives to attach conditions to the licence, or to exclude any of the proposed licensable activities, or to refuse to accept the nominated person as premises supervisor, or to reject the application (s.31(3)).

A provisional statement outlining the authority's deliberations and the reasons for its decisions will then be issued to the applicant (s.31(3)(c)). A copy of the provisional statement will also be provided to each person who made relevant representations, if any, and to the chief officer of police for the area (s.31(4)).

Such a provisional statement would thus give an indication to the applicant of the prospects of any future application for a premises licence. In contrast to the provisions under the 1964 Act, where the provisional licence would be declared final provided the specified work was satisfactorily completed and the applicant was a fit and proper person to hold a justices' licence, it can be seen that the provisional statement gives no such certainty as to obtaining a premises licence in due course.

However, following the issue of a provisional statement there are restrictions on making representations against a later application for a full premises licence for the same premises (s.32). Where:

- the application for the premises licence is in the same form as the licence described in the provisional statement; and
- the work described in the schedule of works has been satisfactorily completed (which means substantial compliance (s.29(7));

representations made by responsible authorities and interested parties will be *excluded* in the following circumstances:

- where the same or substantially the same representation could have been made at the time of the provisional statement application; *and*
- there has been no material change in the circumstances relating to the premises or to the vicinity of the premises since the provisional statement was made.

The above restriction will not apply if the person wishing to make a representation has a reasonable excuse for not having made the representation at the time of the application for the provisional statement.

Changes to the immediate neighbourhood of the premises may accordingly permit further objections and leave open the possibility of refusal after the premises have been completed.

The applicant for a provisional statement or anyone who made a relevant representation may appeal against the terms of the statement issued (Sched.5, para.3). It should be noted that there is no right of appeal for the applicant against the refusal of an application for a provisional statement, because the licensing authority cannot refuse to issue a provisional statement.

7.11 INTERIM AUTHORITIES

A premises licence lapses on the death, mental incapacity or insolvency of the licence holder (s.27). As there may be a delay before a new premises licence holder can be appointed, for example, the time taken for probate and other legal matters in dealing with the deceased's estate, or appointment of an administrative receiver, there are provisions under the new legislation to permit the continuation of the authorisations under a premises licence until a formal transfer can occur. This arrangement is called an 'interim authority' and allows the licensable activities to continue until such formal transfer.

In order to have the benefit of an interim authority, those with a prescribed interest in the relevant premises or those connected to the licence holder must submit an interim authority notice (PLCPC Regulations, reg.15 and Sched.7) to the relevant licensing authority within seven days of the lapse of a premises licence due to the death, the mental incapacity or the insolvency of a premises licence holder (s.47(2)). A copy of the notice together with accompanying documents must also be sent to the chief officer of police on the same day that the notice is given to the licensing authority (s.47(7)(a) and PLCPC Regulations, reg.28(b)). The DPS, if any, should also be notified that an interim authority notice has been made.

Only those with a prescribed interest, i.e. those with a legal interest in the premises as freeholder or leaseholder (PLCPC Regulations, reg.8), and those connected to the licence holder by virtue of being the licence holder's personal representative, having an enduring power of attorney in respect of that person, or acting as the licence holder's insolvency practitioner, may give an interim authority notice (s.47(5)).

The effect of giving an interim authority notice is to reinstate the premises licence from the time the licensing authority received the notice and for the person giving the notice to become the licence holder (s.47(6)).

The maximum period for which an interim authority notice may have effect is two months (s.47(10)). An application for transfer to a new licence holder must, therefore, be made within this time period.

Having received a copy of the interim authority notice, the police can object within 48 hours of being notified (s.48(2)). However, they can only object where they believe that the exceptional circumstances of the case would result in the undermining of the crime prevention objective if the interim authority notice were not cancelled (s.48(1)(c)). If the police do object, then the licensing authority must hold a hearing within five working days (Hearings Regulations, reg.5 and Sched.1) to decide whether or not to cancel the notice, unless all parties agree that a hearing can be dispensed with. If the licensing authority agrees with the police objection and cancels the interim authority notice, the premises licence will again lapse (s.48(6)).

Where a licensing authority decides to cancel an interim authority notice following a notice from the chief officer of police, the person who gave the interim authority notice may appeal against the decision (Sched.5, para.7(2)).

Where the licensing authority does not cancel the interim authority notice following a notice from the police, the chief officer of police may appeal against this decision (para.7(3)).

7.12 TRANSFER ON DEATH, ETC. OF LICENCE HOLDER

Where a premises licence has lapsed due to the death, incapacity or insolvency of the holder, or where it has been surrendered by the holder, it is also possible for anyone who is eligible to apply for a premises licence to apply for a transfer of the licence with immediate effect as described in **para.7.8** (s.50).

Such an application for transfer with immediate effect must be made within seven days of the lapse of the licence (s.50(3)(a)) but cannot be made if an interim authority notice is already in force (s.50(1)(a)). The effect of this application will be to reinstate the premises licence from the time the application was received by the licensing authority and it will continue until determination of the application (s.50(5)).

The process and procedure for an application of this type is exactly as described in **para.7.8** except there is no requirement to obtain the previous licence holder's consent (s.50(4)).

CHAPTER 8

Permitted temporary activities

8.1 WHAT ARE PERMITTED TEMPORARY ACTIVITIES?

Part 5 of the Licensing Act 2003 introduces a system of permitted temporary activities which provides for the temporary provision of licensable activities at premises which are not authorised by either a premises licence or a club premises certificate. This replaces the old arrangement for obtaining occasional permissions, occasional licences or temporary entertainment licences.

Under the old regime, conveyancers would rarely be involved in circumstances which required authorisation for permitted temporary activities. However, as will be seen below (**para.8.10**), the system of permitted temporary activities may also be necessary in certain circumstances where a premises licence is already in existence, but an extension of hours is required.

Under this scheme the event organiser (the 'premises user') is allowed to carry out licensable activities on a temporary basis, subject to various conditions and limits (see **para.8.2**) relating to the number of people attending and the number of events which may be permitted.

The method of operation of this system is entirely different from the system it is replacing. It is not necessary to obtain a prior approval for permitted temporary events. Instead, the system involves notification, by submitting notice (s.100) of an event to the licensing authority and the police. Providing that certain conditions are satisfied and that there are no police objections, the event can proceed on the basis of that notification.

This system is intended to reduce bureaucracy as the licensing authority can only intervene if the specified conditions are not met. Generally, unless there are police objections, the only role that the licensing authority will play will be to acknowledge the notification.

There is no provision for responsible authorities, other than the police, nor for interested parties to object to temporary event notices.

8.2 WHAT ARE THE LIMITATIONS?

The conditions which apply to permitted temporary activities relate to:

- the number of people allowed;
- the length of the event;
- the number of temporary events permitted per year;
- the number of temporary events permitted per premises;
- the interval between temporary events;
- the maximum aggregate duration of temporary events for any premises.

The limitations are that:

- the event must be attended by fewer than 500 people (i.e. the maximum number allowed is 499) (s.100(5)(d));
- the event must last for no longer than 96 hours (s.100(1));
- a personal licence holder may hold up to 50 temporary events per year (s.107(2));
- premises users who are not personal licence holders may hold up to five temporary events per year (s.107(3));
- no premises may be used more than 12 times in any one calendar year for temporary events (s.107(4));
- there is an overall maximum of 15 days in any one year on which temporary events may take place at a particular premises (s.107(5));
- there must be at least 24 hours between individual temporary events in respect of the same premises (s.101(1)).

If a temporary event does not satisfy the above conditions, a full premises licence or club premises certificate will be required. A year is defined by the 2003 Act to be a calendar year.

The requirement for at least 24 hours to pass before another event may be held is designed to prevent a premises user holding several consecutive temporary events as a means of circumventing the requirement for a premises licence. In this respect, any temporary event notice issued by another person who is related to, associated with, or in business with a premises user will be treated as having been made by that premises user (s.101(2)(b) and (c)). A temporary event notice will be void if it is found that there is less than a 24-hour period between events notified by the premises user in respect of the same premises. Furthermore, if any temporary event is proposed to take place on premises that are included within or include other premises where another temporary event takes place, then the two events are deemed to take place on the same premises (s.101(2)(d)).

8.3 WHO CAN HOLD PERMITTED TEMPORARY ACTIVITIES?

Any person aged 18 years or over can submit a temporary event notice in order to hold a temporary event (s.100(3)). There is no requirement that the premises user must hold a personal licence. However, as noted above, the holder of a personal licence is able to give 50 temporary event notices a year. A maximum of five is permitted to a premises user who is not a personal licence holder.

8.4 WHERE CAN PERMITTED TEMPORARY ACTIVITIES BE HELD?

Temporary events can be held either indoors or outdoors. 'Premises' is defined in the 2003 Act as any place, and this includes a vehicle, vessel or moveable structure (s.193).

8.5 PROCEDURE

The person proposing to hold a temporary event, i.e. the premises user (s.100(2)), must submit a temporary event notice to the relevant licensing authority detailing the proposal for the temporary event. The relevant authority is the one in whose area the temporary event will take place. If the premises where the proposed event is to take place are situated across more than one licensing authority, then the temporary event notice must be given to each authority (s.99).

The temporary event notice must be in the prescribed form (at the time of writing regulations prescribing the form had not been made). It must be made in duplicate and submitted at least 10 working days before the proposed temporary event is to take place, accompanied by the appropriate fee (s.100(7)).

'Working day' is defined as any day other than a Saturday, Sunday, Christmas Day, Good Friday, or a day which is a bank holiday. Ten working days means 10 working days exclusive of the day on which the event is to start.

A copy of the notice must also be submitted to the police no later than 10 working days before the proposed event is to take place (s.104(1)).

Although the 2003 Act specifies 10 working days' notice, most licensing authorities recommend a longer period of notice in their statements of licensing policy. The majority recommend a minimum notice period of one month prior to the date of the event taking place. Some licensing authorities also state a preferred maximum notice period in advance of the proposed event.

There are clear risks for the event holder if notification is left too late. The decision of the licensing authority to permit or refuse must be made no later than 24 hours before the date of the event. This may, of course, be far too late to notify ticket holders of a cancellation. At the other end of the process, it can only be hoped that licensing authorities give sufficient time (in stipulating the maximum length of time that notification can be given prior to an event) for appropriate planning and marketing to take place.

Details that need to be included in the notice include (s.100(4) and (5)):

- the licensable activities to be carried out;
- the total length of the event (which must not exceed 96 hours);
- the times during which the licensable activities are to be carried out;
- the maximum number of people to be allowed on the premises (which must be less than 500);
- if the licensable activities include the supply of alcohol, whether this is to be for consumption on or off the premises;
- if the licensable activities include the sale of alcohol, a condition must be included in the notice that all supplies will be made by, or under the authority of, the premises user; and
- other matters as may be prescribed.

The temporary event notice must also be accompanied by the appropriate fee, currently £21 (s.100(7)(b) and Licensing Act 2003 (Fees) Regulations 2005, SI 2005/79, Sched.6).

The licensing authority must acknowledge receipt of the temporary event notice. This is done by returning the duplicate copy of the notice to the premises user by the end of the working day following the day on which it was received (or before the end of the second working day if it was not received on a working day) (s.102).

8.6 COUNTER NOTICE WHERE PERMITTED LIMITS EXCEEDED

However, acknowledgement will not be made if the licensing authority determines that any of the following permitted limits have been exceeded:

- the premises user is a personal licence holder and has already given at least 50 temporary event notices within the same calendar year;
- the premises user does not hold a personal licence, but has already given five temporary event notices in that year;
- twelve temporary event notices have already been given in respect of the same premises in that year; or
- temporary event notices have already been given for the same premises and in aggregate they amount to 15 days within the calendar year.

If any of the above limits have been exceeded, the licensing authority will issue a 'counter notice' to the premises user, which means that the temporary event will not be allowed to proceed (s.107(1)). A counter notice must be issued at least 24 hours before the proposed event is to start (s.107(8)).

In addition, when determining the number of temporary event notices, the licensing authority will examine whether notices relating to the same premises have been made by business associates or family members of a premises user. If the authority determines that this is the case, the authority will treat the notices as having been made by the premises user (s.107(10)).

Apart from the situation outlined above, the licensing authority cannot intervene in any other way, for example by attempting to attach any conditions or limitations to the carrying on of licensable activities at permitted temporary events.

8.7 POLICE OBJECTIONS

The police can only object to a temporary event taking place if, in their view, allowing the event to proceed would undermine the licensing objective of preventing crime and disorder.

If the police consider this to be the case, they must issue an 'objection notice' to both the premises user and the licensing authority explaining the reasons for their objection (s.104(2)). This objection notice must be sent out within 48 hours of the police receiving the temporary event notice (s.104(3)).

On receipt of an objection notice, the licensing authority will hold a hearing within seven working days (Hearings Regulations, reg.5 and Sched.1), unless all parties agree that it is not necessary (s.105(2)(a)). Consideration of the objection by the licensing authority is confined to factors relating to the crime prevention objective. The licensing authority cannot uphold a police objection on other grounds, such as public nuisance.

If the licensing authority accepts the police objection it will issue a counter notice to the premises user together with a notice giving the reasons for its decision (s.105(2)(b) and (3)(b)). A copy of both notices will also be given to the police (s.105(2)(b) and (3)(b)). If a counter notice is issued, the event will not be able to proceed.

If the authority does not accept the police objection, the premises user will be notified of the decision and will be able to go ahead with the temporary event (s.105(3)(a)).

Any decision or counter notice must be issued to the premises user at least 24 hours before the event is to take place (s.105(4)). Failure to do so will mean that the premises user will be able to continue with the event as planned.

Where the police have issued an objection notice, the premises user may agree to modify the temporary event notice so that it no longer undermines the promotion of the crime prevention objective. Such agreement may take place at any time before a hearing is held. When this occurs, the police objection is withdrawn and the modified temporary event notice has effect (s.106).

8.8 DUTIES

The premises user must ensure that a copy of the temporary event notice is prominently displayed at the premises where the temporary event is being carried out (s.109(2)) or is kept at the premises under his control (s.109(3)(a)(i)) or the control of someone else nominated by him (s.109(3)(a)(ii)). In the latter situation, a notice with details of the nominated person must be displayed at the premises (s.109(3)(b)).

It is an offence to fail to comply with the above requirement (s.109(4)). It is also an offence if the premises user or nominated person does not produce the temporary event notice to a constable or an officer of the licensing authority when requested to do so (s.109(5)). If convicted of these offences, the premises user is liable to a fine not exceeding level 2 (s.109(9)).

8.9 RIGHT OF ENTRY

The police or an authorised officer have the right to enter the premises to which a temporary event notice relates, at any reasonable time, to assess the likely effect of the notice on the promotion of the crime prevention objective (s.108).

8.10 TEMPORARY EVENTS AND PREMISES LICENCES

Provided the limits are adhered to, the temporary event procedure can also be used by personal licence holders in respect of premises where a premises licence is already in place. Accordingly, as long as no more than 12 temporary event notices are submitted for any one premises and the events do not last for more than 15 days in total, temporary event notices could be issued for the following uses:

- to provide regulated entertainment in premises currently licensed for the sale of alcohol;
- the provision of late night refreshment where the premises are not currently licensed for that purpose;
- the sale of alcohol where the premises are not currently licensed for that purpose;
- the sale of alcohol for a period beyond the normal hours permitted under the premises licence, or outside the terms of a condition which applies to that licence.

Alternatively, a publican could use a temporary event notice where he has been hired to run a temporary bar for example at a wedding or anniversary party, etc. at a venue which is not licensed for the sale of alcohol.

8.11 TEMPORARY EVENTS AND CLUB PREMISES CERTIFICATES

Temporary event notices may also be given by non-personal licence holders in respect of clubs covered by club premises certificates. Thus where a club wishes to admit members of the public and sell alcohol to them, it may do so for the period specified under a temporary event notice. However, the club will only be able to do this on a limited number of occasions, as only 12 such notices may be given in respect of the same club premises in any calendar year. The club secretary (assuming that he is not a personal licence holder) would be limited to a maximum of five notifications, but of course these notices could come from a number of different club members up to the annual limit.

8.12 APPEALS

Where a chief officer of police gives an objection notice, either:

- the premises user may appeal against the decision by a licensing authority to give a counter notice (Sched.5, para.16(2)); or
- the chief officer of police may appeal against the decision of the licensing authority not to give a counter notice (Sched.5, para.16(3)).

However, there is no right to appeal against the licensing authority's decision to issue a counter notice where the authority considers that the permitted limits have been exceeded. In these circumstances, the premises user would have to apply for a judicial review of the decision.

Appeals should be made to the magistrates' court covering the area in which the premises concerned are situated (Sched.5, para.16(4)). The appeal is commenced by giving notice to the chief executive for the magistrates' court within the period of 21 days beginning with the day on which the appellant was notified by the licensing authority of the decision to be appealed against (Sched.5, para.16(5)).

However, no appeal can be brought later than five working days before the temporary event is to occur (Sched.5, para.16(6)).

These provisions involve very little bureaucracy – they are described by the Secretary of State in the Guidance as 'light touch arrangements'. They enable licensees to extend their premises licences and to operate outside the conditions which apply to their premises, subject only to a potential police objection if the crime prevention objective is compromised. The scope for lengthy events involving the sale of alcohol and the provision of music is broad and potentially intrusive to others. However, most events will cause no problems and there is a welcome liberalising of the existing clumsy arrangements by which charitable and community groups have secured occasional permissions. In relation to those events which may disturb others, the

Guidance reminds its readers of the existing police powers to close down any licensed premises (including those for temporary events) which are disorderly, likely to become disorderly, or causing disturbance by way of excessive noise.

CHAPTER 9

Club premises certificates

9.1 WHAT IS A CLUB PREMISES CERTIFICATE?

Club premises certificates (2003 Act, Part 4) replace club registration certificates. Previously clubs would obtain their registration from the magistrates' court by establishing that they had met qualifying requirements. Generally, the registration would be granted for one year and thereafter would be renewed at five-yearly intervals.

Under the Licensing Act 1964, registered members clubs were classified as those where members had joined together for the promotion of a specific social, sporting or political purpose and jointly purchased alcohol in volume for supply to members. Examples of clubs of this type would be sports clubs, working men's clubs, the Royal British Legion, and clubs affiliated to political parties. These clubs, run by their own membership, were distinguished from proprietary clubs and remain so under the new licensing system.

Registered members clubs were treated differently from other licensed premises under the 1964 Act because club premises were private, generally not open to the public, and operated under strict rules. Additionally, alcohol and entertainment were not supplied for profit. There were technically no sales by retail of alcohol at these premises to members. They therefore generated licensing issues which were different from those found in premises which were commercially run and which provided alcohol and entertainment for the public.

This difference in treatment between commercially run premises providing licensable activities direct to the public and members clubs is maintained by the 2003 Act. Under this Act, clubs which meet certain specified criteria ('qualifying clubs') are able to supply alcohol and other 'qualifying club activities' under the authority of a club premises certificate.

9.2 QUALIFYING CLUB

A club is classified as a qualifying club in relation to a qualifying club activity if it meets the following conditions (s.62):

- there must be an interval of at least two days between nomination/application for membership and either admission to membership or admission, as candidates for membership, to any of the privileges of membership;
- for applicants becoming members without prior nomination or application, there must be an interval of at least two days before they can enjoy the privileges of membership;
- the club must be established and conducted in good faith as a club;
- the club must have at least 25 members;
- no alcohol is supplied, or intended to be supplied, to members on the club premises except by or on behalf of the club.

In addition, if the club intends to supply alcohol to members and guests, there are additional conditions that must be satisfied (s.61(2) and s.64):

- the purchase and supply of alcohol must be managed by a committee made up of elected members over the age of 18 years;
- nobody should receive any commission, percentage or similar payment deriving from the purchase of alcohol;
- nobody should receive any monetary benefit from the supply of alcohol to members or guests, apart from any benefit to the club as a whole, or any indirect benefit derived from a general gain to the club as a whole.

9.3 ASSOCIATE MEMBERS

Qualifying clubs are able to admit associate members and their guests (i.e. members and guests from another club) as well as their own members and guests. Associate members and their guests will therefore have the benefit of any qualifying club activities provided on the club premises (s.67).

9.4 ESTABLISHED CLUB CONDUCTED IN GOOD FAITH

In determining whether a club satisfies the condition of being established and conducted in good faith, the licensing authority must consider the following matters (s.63):

- any restrictions on the club's freedom to purchase alcohol;
- whether money or property belonging to the club may be used for purposes other than for the club's benefit or charitable, benevolent or political purposes;
- the provision of information to members regarding the club's finances;
- the club's accounts and the accuracy thereof;
- the nature of the premises occupied by the club.

Thus qualifying clubs under the 2003 Act are essentially the same as those classed as registered members clubs under the 1964 Act.

9.5 QUALIFYING CLUB ACTIVITIES

The activities which may be authorised by a club premises certificate, i.e. the 'qualifying club activities' are (s.1(2)):

- the supply of alcohol by, or on behalf of, a club to, or to the order of, a member of the club;
- the sale by retail of alcohol by, or on behalf of, the club to a guest of a member of the club for consumption on the premises where the sale takes place;
- the provision of regulated entertainment where that provision is by or on behalf of a club for members of the club or members of the club and their guests.

9.6 PROPRIETARY CLUBS

In defining the qualifying club activities the legislation makes it clear that the first of these qualifying club activities does not include any supply which is a sale by retail (s.1(3)).

Some organisations which claim to be clubs, but which in fact are not within the ownership or control of their members, are not eligible to be qualifying clubs. These are proprietary clubs and any supply of alcohol to members would be a sale by retail. These clubs will require a premises licence in order to provide any licensable activity.

9.7 PROVIDENT/FRIENDLY SOCIETIES

For the purposes of the 2003 Act, registered industrial and provident societies, registered and incorporated friendly societies, and miners' welfare institutes are treated as satisfying certain of the general conditions and additional conditions for being a qualifying club if specified requirements relating to their constitutions and management are met (ss.65–66). They are therefore eligible to apply for club premises certificates.

9.8 APPLICATION PROCESS

The procedure for applying for a club premises certificate is very similar to that for a premises licence.

Applications are made by qualifying clubs to the licensing authority in whose area the club premises is situated or mainly situated. If the club is situated across two or more licensing authority areas, the club can nominate one of the authorities to be the relevant licensing authority (ss.68 and 71(2)).

The application must be made using the form set out in Part B of Sched.9 to the PLCPC Regulations (PLCPC Regulations, reg.18) and must be accompanied by (s.71(4)):

- a club operating schedule;
- a plan of the premises (scale and details to be shown on the plan are the same as for premises licence applications: see **para.5.10**);
- a copy of the club rules;
- the appropriate fee.

On or before making an application for a club premises certificate, the club must make a declaration as to qualifying club status by completing and submitting to the licensing authority the form set out in Part A of Sched.9 to the PLCPC Regulations (PLCPC Regulations, reg.17). This will usually be submitted at the same time as the application for the club premises certificate.

9.9 CLUB OPERATING SCHEDULE

The club operating schedule, which is incorporated into the application form, is similar to the operating schedule that accompanies an application for a premises licence, and should include the following details (s.71(5)):

- the qualifying club activities to which the application relates;
- the proposed hours of operation for the relevant qualifying club activities;
- any other times during which the club premises will be open to members and their guests;
- whether alcohol is to be supplied, and if so whether the alcohol will be supplied for consumption on the premises or both on and off the premises;
- a statement of the steps the club proposes to take to promote the licensing objectives; and
- such other matters as may be prescribed.

As with the premises licence, the club operating schedule will be incorporated into the club premises certificate if the application is successful. The steps that the club intends to take to promote the licensing objectives will be translated into the conditions to be included in the certificate.

9.10 ADVERTISEMENT AND NOTIFICATION OF APPLICATIONS

All applications for club premises certificates must be advertised (s.71(6)(a)). The requirements for advertisement are the same as those for applications for premises licences as described in **para.5.12**.

Notice of the application must also be given to each responsible authority (see **para.5.12** for definition of responsible authority) and such other persons as may be prescribed. This is done by sending to them a copy of the application together with accompanying documents on the same day as the application is made to the licensing authority (s.71(6)(b) and PLCPC Regulations, reg.27).

9.11 DETERMINATION OF APPLICATION

The procedure for determination of a club premises certificate is also similar to that for a premises licence.

Following advertisement and notification of the application, responsible authorities and interested parties may object to the application by making relevant representations to the authorities. (For definitions of responsible authorities, interested parties and relevant representations, see **Chapter 5**.)

In the absence of any relevant representations, and provided the application has been lawfully made and properly advertised, the application must be granted. The conditions attached to the club premises certificate will be consistent with those detailed in the operating schedule together with mandatory conditions where relevant (s.72(2)).

If relevant representations are received by the authority, a hearing must be held within 20 working days of the end of the period for making representations (PLCPC Regulations, reg.5 and Sched.1) to consider these representations, unless all parties agree that a hearing may be dispensed with (s.72(3)).

Following the hearing, the licensing authority may (s.72(4)):

- grant the application as submitted;
- grant the certificate subject to modifications considered necessary for the promotion of the licensing objectives;
- grant the certificate subject to any mandatory conditions;
- exclude any of the qualifying club activities; or
- reject the application.

9.12 CONDITIONS

In the absence of relevant representations, the certificate may only be subject to those conditions that give effect to the operating schedule (s.72(2)), together with those described in **para.9.13** where supply of alcohol for consumption off the premises is permitted (s.73).

It should also be noted that if the rules of the club permit the sale by retail of alcohol or the provision of regulated entertainment to associate members of the club or their guests, conditions cannot be attached to a club premises certificate preventing these activities (s.75).

Where a club premises certificate authorises the exhibition of films, it is mandatory that the certificate include a condition requiring that admission of children must be restricted in accordance with the recommendations of either the relevant film classification body or the licensing authority (s.74).

Where a club premises certificate authorises the performance of a play, licensing authorities cannot attach conditions relating to the nature of the play performed or the manner of its performance, unless such conditions are justified as a matter of public safety (s.76).

Where relevant representations have been received, conditions may only be imposed where they are necessary for the promotion of the licensing objectives. In this respect, the Guidance reminds licensing authorities to bear in mind that qualifying clubs make an important contribution, and bring significant benefits, to local communities. In addition, as the general public do not normally have access to their premises and they operate under strict codes of conduct, licensing authorities are advised that conditions should not be attached to their certificates unless these conditions can be demonstrated to be strictly necessary.

Where conditions are required, licensing authorities are advised to draw upon the model conditions listed in the Guidance and reproduced here at **Appendices B2–B5** where necessary and appropriate.

9.13 SUPPLY OF ALCOHOL FOR CONSUMPTION OFF THE PREMISES

A club premises certificate may authorise the supply of alcohol by a club to its members for consumption off the premises only if it also authorises the supply of alcohol to a member of the club for consumption on the premises (s.73(1)).

If the above condition is met, a club premises certificate authorising such supply must include three conditions (s.73(2)):

- the supply must be made at a time when the premises are open for the purposes of supplying alcohol, in accordance with the club premises certificate, to members of the club for consumption on the premises (s.73(3));
- any alcohol supplied for consumption off the premises must be in a sealed container (s.73(4));
- any supply of alcohol for consumption off the premises must be made to a member of the club in person (s.73(5)).

It should be noted that the sale by retail of alcohol to a guest of a member for consumption *off* the premises is not a qualifying club activity.

9.14 VALIDITY OF CERTIFICATE

A club premises certificate will be valid indefinitely unless it is either withdrawn (see **para.9.17**) or surrendered (s.80).

9.15 DUTIES OF CLUB IN RELATION TO CERTIFICATE

The secretary of the club must notify the licensing authority of any change (ss.82 and 83) in:

- the name of the club;
- the club rules;
- the relevant registered address of the club.

If the change of name or club rules is not notified within 28 days then the club secretary commits an offence (s.82(6)).

The club must also ensure that:

- the certificate or a certified copy is kept at the premises (s.94(2));
- the certificate or certified copy is under the control of a nominated person (s.94(2));
- a summary of the certificate or a certified copy is prominently displayed at the premises (s.94(4)); and
- a notice specifying the position of the nominated person is prominently displayed at the premises (s.94(4)).

Failure to comply with these duties is an offence under the 2003 Act (s.94(5) and (6)).

9.16 BENEFITS OF CLUB PREMISES CERTIFICATE

There are a number of advantages of holding a club premises certificate when compared to a premises licence:

- there is no requirement for any member or employee to hold a personal licence;
- there is no requirement to specify a DPS;
- if there are door supervisors, there is no mandatory condition that they have to be licensed by the Security Industry Authority;
- these clubs are not subject to police powers of instant closure on grounds of disorder or public nuisance;
- these clubs are not subject to potential orders of the magistrates' court for the closure of all licensed premises in an area where disorder is happening or expected.

In addition, the rights of the police to enter premises holding a certificate are very limited. In summary, the power only arises where the police suspect that drugs offences are being committed or that there is likely to be a breach of the peace.

Under the Licensing Act 1964 registered members clubs were also allowed to sell alcohol to under 18 year olds and allow them to consume it on the club premises. This concession has now been abolished and it is an offence under the new legislation for clubs to sell or supply alcohol to minors (s.146). It is permissible for 16 or 17 year olds to consume beer, wine or cider in club premises but the purchase must have been made by an adult. In addition, the drinks can only be consumed with a table meal and in the presence of someone who is over 18 (s.149(5)).

It should be noted that a club may still need to apply for a premises licence instead of or as well as a club premises certificate if it wishes to hold regular public events or to sell alcohol to non-members. If a club does hold a premises licence, then a personal licence holder and a DPS will be required if the sale of alcohol is involved.

Alternatively, if a club wishes to offer its facilities commercially for the use of the general public on specific occasions only, an individual on behalf of a club may give temporary event notices for this purpose (see **Chapter 8**).

9.17 WITHDRAWAL OF CLUB PREMISES CERTIFICATE

If a club ceases to meet any of the criteria for a qualifying club as described in **paras.9.2** and **9.4** above, the licensing authority may withdraw the club premises certificate (s.90(1)).

If the reason for withdrawal is because the club's membership has fallen below the minimum required of 25 people, the withdrawal will not take effect until three months after the authority issued notice of withdrawal. If, at the end of the three-month period, the membership numbers have risen to the minimum required, the certificate will not be withdrawn (s.90(2)).

9.18 VARIATION OF CLUB PREMISES CERTIFICATE

A club may make an application to vary its club premises certificate in any way other than to vary *substantially* the premises to which it relates (s.84(1)). The procedure for an application to vary is essentially the same as for the original grant. Applications are made to the licensing authority which granted the original certificate.

The application must be made using the form set out in Sched.10 to the PLCPC Regulations (PLCPC Regulations, reg.19) and must be accompanied by the club premises certificate (or a statement of why this is not possible) together with the appropriate fee (s.84(2)).

The application to vary must be advertised in accordance with the relevant regulations (as described in **para.5.12**). Notice of the application must be given to each responsible authority, and such other persons as may be prescribed, by submitting a copy together with accompanying documents on the same day as the application is given to the licensing authority (s.84(4) and PLCPC Regulations, reg.27).

Responsible authorities and interested parties may make objections in the form of relevant representations about any of the variations applied for. If no relevant representations are made, the licensing authority must grant the variation as applied for (s.85(2)).

If objections are made, a hearing must be held within 20 days of the end of the period during which representations can be made to consider the representations (Hearings Regulations, reg.5 and Sched.1), unless all parties agree that a hearing is not required (s.85(3)). Following the hearing, and if it considers it necessary for the promotion of the licensing objectives, the licensing authority will either modify the conditions of the certificate or reject the application for the variation (s.85(4)). Otherwise, the licensing authority must grant the variation in the terms sought.

9.19 APPEALS

Appeals relating to club premises certificates may be made in the following circumstances.

1. Clubs may appeal against the rejection of an application for a club premises certificate or an application to vary a certificate (Sched.5, para.10).
2. If a certificate is granted, the club may appeal against the imposition of conditions or the exclusion of a qualifying club activity (Sched.5, para.11(2)).
3. Anyone who made relevant representations during the course of an application may appeal against the decision to grant the certificate, or that different conditions should have been imposed, or that qualifying club activities should have been excluded (Sched.5, para.11(3)).
4. Where a licensing authority modifies the conditions before granting a variation, the club may appeal against such modification (Sched.5, para.12(2)).
5. Where a person made relevant representations in relation to an application to vary, they can appeal against the decision to vary, or against the modification, or that a different modification should have been made (Sched.5, para.12(3)).

CHAPTER 10

Review of premises licences and club premises certificates

10.1 REVIEW OF PREMISES LICENCE

Under the 1964 Act licensing regime, the magistrates had an opportunity to examine any problems identified at licensed premises when the licence was due for renewal. However with renewals granted on a triennial basis, it was unlikely that any problems would coincide with the time when renewals were considered. The only other opportunities for reassessment came in the course of proceedings to revoke the licence, on breach of any undertakings given by licensees, or where transfers took place. As a counterbalance to the latitude which is provided to licensees to determine their own licensing arrangements under the 2003 Act, a procedure has been provided for the review of a premises licence at any time.

According to the Secretary of State's Guidance, the provision of such a review procedure enables the minimum of bureaucracy to be involved at the initial stage of the grant and variation of a premises licence. If any problems associated with crime and disorder, public safety, public nuisance or the protection of children from harm arise at a later stage, the licence can be reviewed at that time.

10.2 WHO CAN REQUEST A REVIEW OF A PREMISES LICENCE?

An interested party (see **para.5.14**) or a responsible authority (see **para.5.12**) may, at any time, apply to the licensing authority for a review of a premises licence (s.51(1)), if they consider that there is an issue relating to one of the licensing objectives occurring at that particular premises.

Thus, a local resident may consider that the steps taken to prevent noise nuisance specified in the original grant are not sufficient and request a review. Similarly, following an increase in crime in the area, the police may be of the opinion that the crime prevention measures that are in place in the licence are no longer effective and request a review.

Licensing authorities may not initiate their own reviews of premises licences. However, where a local authority is both the relevant licensing authority and a responsible authority, for example where it is also the local environmental health authority, it may apply for a review in its capacity as a responsible authority and then determine the application in its capacity as the licensing authority.

An application for a review must be made on the prescribed form (PLCPC Regulations, reg.16 and Sched.8) and in the prescribed manner (s.51(3)). However, the Guidance encourages authorities to use a warning system in the hope that shortcomings could be remedied without the need for formal proceedings.

A review of the licence will also normally follow any action by the police to close down the premises for up to 24 hours on the grounds of disorder or public nuisance (s.167) (see **para.11.16**).

10.3 GROUNDS FOR REVIEW

The application for review must relate to the promotion of the licensing objectives. It must also relate to the particular premises as opposed to general problems in a locality. The licensing authority may reject a ground for review, and thus reject the application, if it considers:

- the ground is not relevant to one or more of the licensing objectives (s.51(4)(a));
- where the application was made by an interested party, that the ground is (s.51(4)(b)):
  - frivolous or vexatious (see **para.5.15**); or
  - repetitious.

A ground is considered to be repetitious if it relates to the same premises and is identical or substantially similar to (s.51(5)):

- a ground for review specified in an earlier application for review; or
- representations considered when the premises licence was first granted; or
- representations made when the application for grant was first made that were excluded then as not relevant, vexatious or frivolous; and

in addition to the above grounds:

- a reasonable interval has not elapsed since that earlier review or the grant of the licence (normally at least 12 months).

Thus, where a request for a review is made by an interested party, the licensing authority must first consider whether the complaint made is relevant to the licensing objectives. If it is considered relevant, then the authority must decide whether it is vexations or frivolous and then whether or not it is repetitious. If the licensing authority rejects a ground for review as being frivolous, vexatious or repetitious, it must notify the applicant of the decision. If the ground was rejected for being frivolous or vexatious, the authority must also give reasons for the decision (s.51(6)).

10.4 PROCEDURE FOR REVIEW (LICENSING ACT 2003, S.51(3))

An applicant for review must submit the appropriate form (PLCPC Regulations, Sched.8) detailing the grounds for review together with supporting information to the relevant licensing authority (PLCPC Regulations, reg.16). On the same day, notice of the application to review must also be given to each responsible authority and the premises licence holder by sending them a copy of the application together with any relevant enclosures (PLCPC Regulations, reg.29).

The licensing authority must advertise the application (s.51(3)(b)) by displaying a notice at or near the premises to be reviewed, at the licensing authority's offices and, if possible, on the licensing authority's website for a period of 28 days after receiving the application (PLCPC Regulations, reg.38). The premises licence holder, interested parties and responsible authorities may make representations during this 28-day period.

10.5 DETERMINATION OF APPLICATION TO REVIEW

Once the above procedure has been completed, the licensing authority must hold a hearing within 20 working days of the end of the period during which representations can be made (Hearings Regulations, reg.5 and Sched.1) to consider the application and any relevant representations made in respect of it (s.51(2)).

Following the hearing, the licensing authority may decide that no action is necessary for the promotion of the licensing objectives, or it may decide that informal action, such as informal warnings or recommendations for improvements within a specified time, will be the most appropriate way forward.

However, where the licensing authority considers that formal steps are required, it may take any of the following actions (s.52(4)):

- modify (add, alter or omit) the conditions of the licence;
- exclude a licensable activity from the scope of the licence;
- remove the DPS;
- suspend the licence for a period not exceeding three months; or
- revoke the licence.

Where the decision is to take either of the first two actions outlined above, it should be noted that modifications of conditions and exclusion of licensable activities may be imposed either permanently or for a temporary period up to three months (s.52(6)).

Licensing authorities are directed to identify the cause of the problems which have prompted the review and to direct the remedial action accordingly. The response of the authority should be to implement measures which are both necessary and proportionate. For example, if a premises licence were to be reviewed because of disturbances on Saturday night, the authority could curtail the trading hours at weekends for a temporary period. Even in those circumstances, the authority would be expected to consider the financial impact on the business in order to determine whether this would be a proportionate step.

The Guidance advises that where reviews arise and the licensing authority determines that the crime prevention objective is being undermined because the premises are being used to further crimes, it is expected that revocation of the licence would be seriously considered – even in the first instance.

Having determined an application for review, the licensing authority must notify its decision and the reasons for making it to the premises licence holder, the applicant, any person who made relevant representations and the chief officer of police for the relevant area (s.52(10)).

10.6 APPEALS

An appeal against the decision in relation to a review of a premises licence may be made by the applicant for the review, the premises licence holder, or anyone who made relevant representations (Sched.5, para.8(2)).

10.7 CLUB PREMISES CERTIFICATES

The 2003 Act also contains provisions for reviewing club premises certificates. The procedures and powers of the licensing authority in this respect are broadly similar to those which apply in any review of a premises licence.

10.8 REVIEW OF CLUB PREMISES CERTIFICATE

In relation to club premises certificates, in addition to interested parties and responsible authorities, a member of the club in question may also apply to the relevant licensing authority for a review of the certificate (s.87(1)).

As with premises licences, the relevant licensing authority may not itself initiate a review of a club premises certificate. However, again the local authority in its capacity as a responsible authority may request such a review and then the same local authority in its capacity as licensing authority is able to determine the review.

An application for a review of a club premises certificate is made on the same form as the application to review a premises licence (s.87(3) and PLCPC Regulations, reg.20 and Sched.8).

The licensing authority can at any stage reject a ground for review if it is not relevant to any of the licensing objectives or, if made by an interested party or club member, it is frivolous, vexatious or repetitious (see **para.10.3**) (s.87(4)).

The procedure for the review of a certificate is the same as for review of premises licences described in **para.10.4** above (s.87(3)), except that a copy of the application must be given to the club rather than the licence holder.

The licensing authority must then hold a hearing to consider and determine the application for review and any relevant representations made in respect of it (s.88(2)). Following the hearing, the licensing authority may leave the certificate unaltered or it may take whichever of the following steps it considers appropriate for the promotion of the licensing objectives (s.88(4)):

- modify the conditions of the certificate;
- exclude a qualifying club activity from the scope of the certificate;
- suspend the certificate for a period not exceeding three months;
- withdraw the certificate.

Modification of conditions or exclusion of activities may be imposed either for a temporary period of up to three months or permanently (s.88(6)).

Following determination, the licensing authority must notify its decision and the reasons for making it to the club, the applicant, any person who made relevant representations and the chief officer of police for the area in which the club is situated (s.88(10)).

10.9 APPEALS

An appeal against the decision in relation to a review of a club premises certificate may be made by (Sched.5, para.13(2)):

- the applicant for the review;
- the club holding the certificate; or
- anyone who made relevant representations.

Appeals should be made to the magistrates' court for the area in which the club is situated, within 21 days of being notified of the decision being appealed against.

CHAPTER 11

What a licensee needs to know

The purpose of this chapter is to enable the practitioner to give some broad advice to prospective purchasers of licensed premises on their legal obligations and the sanctions that may be applied – either through the courts or through the licensing authority – if they break the law. The following areas are covered:

- offences involving children in licensed premises;
- offences in relation to unauthorised sales, activities, etc;
- procedural matters common to all offences under this legislation;
- the rights of persons to enter and/or inspect licensed premises;
- the power to close premises down.

11.1 CHILDREN

The protection of children from harm is one of the four main licensing objectives of the 2003 Act and is a significant priority in the new licensing regime. However, at the same time another aim of the new licensing system is to encourage family-friendly environments in licensed premises.

The 2003 Act is intended to address some of the deficiencies of the previous law and enables licensing authorities, where relevant representations have been made, to attach conditions relating to the access to licensed premises by children which reflect the individual character of the establishments concerned. In addition, the 2003 Act introduces and modifies a number of offences relating to the consumption of alcohol by children and the sale of alcohol to children.

11.2 CONDITIONS RELATING TO CHILDREN

The restrictions that may be placed on a premises licence or club premises certificate in relation to children's access will vary according to the individual circumstances of the premises or club and any representations made by responsible authorities and interested parties. It will also be subject to the test of being necessary for the promotion of any of the licensing objectives.

All applications for a licence or certificate must be accompanied by an operating schedule detailing the measures proposed to be taken in order to promote the objective of protecting children from harm. Where representations are made, the licensing authority may place conditions on the licence relating to times of access, ages of children and any other measures thought necessary to protect children.

The conditions need to be viewed in the context of the offence created by the 2003 Act which prohibits children under the age of 16 from being on premises which are exclusively or primarily used for the supply of alcohol (for consumption on those premises) unless they are accompanied by an adult. There is a similar prohibition on children under the age of 16 being on any premises which supply alcohol for consumption on the premises (irrespective of whether it is the primary use) between midnight and 5 a.m. These offences are discussed in more detail later in this chapter. Licensees should however, bear in mind that converted licences will still include any previous restrictions relating to children, unless an application to remove such a restriction has been made by an application to vary.

It follows that in premises which are not used exclusively or primarily for the supply of alcohol on the premises, e.g. a restaurant or hotel, there would be no statutory prohibition on the presence of children until midnight and in the period up to that time children under the age of 16 would have unrestricted access to licensed premises, in the absence of conditions included in the operating schedule of the relevant premises licence.

Government guidance requires licensing authorities to identify in their policy statements the types of premises which will attract robust conditions for the protection of children. The most obvious examples are premises providing entertainment of an adult nature, those that have a known association with drug taking, or premises which include a strong element of gambling. In relation to premises of this type, there is a presumption against the admission of children so that 16 and 17 year olds will also be excluded from the premises.

The times at which children will be permitted to enter licensed premises and the circumstances in which they can be there (with an adult for example) can be determined either by the statutory provisions of the 2003 Act or the conditions in a premises licence. It follows that there will be no children's certificates, as there were under the 1964 legislation.

Prospective purchasers or licensees will need to understand that it is the use to which they put their premises which will determine the risk of prosecution if children are found to be present. A pool of model conditions relating to the protection of children from harm is listed in the Guidance and is reproduced here at **Appendix B5**. These may be drawn upon by licensing authorities where necessary and appropriate.

Of course it may well be – as happens at present – that some licence holders will not wish to have children on their premises at all. Many publicans, for example, have chosen never to apply for children's certificates on the basis that the presence of children would not meet the approval of their existing customers. Where it is intended that children should be excluded entirely from the premises, then this will be indicated in the operating schedule. In those circumstances, it would not be necessary to specify steps (by way of conditions) to promote the protection of children from harm, since no children will be in a position where harm could occur.

No conditions, incidentally, could *require* admission of children to premises. In the absence of a restriction, whether children are admitted will be entirely at the discretion of the licensee.

11.3 OFFENCES RELATING TO CHILDREN

As indicated above it is an offence under the 2003 Act to allow unaccompanied children (those under the age of 16) access to relevant premises if those premises are used exclusively or primarily for the supply of alcohol for consumption on the premises (s.145(1)(a)). In this context 'relevant premises' means those operating under a premises licence, club premises certificate or a temporary event notice. The requirement that children are accompanied means that a child must be in the company of an individual aged 18 or over (s.145(2)).

Where premises sell or supply alcohol for consumption on the premises, but this is not their exclusive or primary use, then unaccompanied children under the age of 16 will be permitted access, subject to the discretion of the licensee and to any conditions on the licence. However between midnight and 5 a.m. on premises of that type (perhaps a nightclub where the primary activity is the provision of music and dancing) the licence holder will commit an offence if he permits unaccompanied children (under the age of 16) to be present if the premises are open for the supply of alcohol during that period (s.145(1)(b)).

The offences of permitting unaccompanied children in these circumstances can be committed by the following individuals (s.145(3)):

- anyone working at the premises in a capacity that gives that person authority to request the child to leave;
- a premises licence holder;
- the DPS;
- any member or officer of a club who is present in a capacity which enables that person to request the child to leave; and
- a premises user (where a temporary event notice is in effect).

There may be a defence if the person charged believed that the child was aged 16 or over or that the accompanying person was aged 18 or over, and either he took all reasonable steps to establish the individual's age or nobody could reasonably have suspected from the individual's appearance that the individual was aged under 16 or under 18 (s.145(6)).

The penalty for this offence is a fine at level 3 (s.145(8)), currently £1,000.

11.4 THE SALE OF ALCOHOL TO CHILDREN

The 2003 Act is more restrictive than the regime under the Licensing Act 1964 in relation to sales or supplies of alcohol to those under the age of 18. In fact, describing the new legislation as *more* restrictive does not really do justice to the way in which the 2003 Act treats 16 and 17 year olds, because it allows no circumstances in which those under 18 can be sold intoxicating liquor unless in chocolate!

It is an offence for any person to sell alcohol to any individual under the age of 18 (s.146(1)). Whilst under the 1964 legislation that offence related to sales on licensed premises, the new offence covers sales by any person in any location.

There are similar offences in relation to a club so that supplies of alcohol to club members who are under the age of 18 are also now prohibited (s.146(2) and (3)). Previously clubs were exempt from the provisions which made it illegal to supply alcohol to minors, although their club rules often either restricted or prohibited those supplies.

Some schools, for example, created Sixth Form social clubs which permitted the supply of limited quantities of alcohol to 16 and 17 year olds at weekends. There are no circumstances in which those supplies could now be lawful.

As with the offence of permitting unaccompanied children on to relevant premises, a defence is provided for persons charged with this offence in similar terms. Namely, that they believed that the individual was aged 18 or over and they had either taken steps to establish the individual's age or no one would have suspected from the individual's appearance that he was under the permitted age (s.146(4)).

There is a more significant penalty however in relation to this offence, namely that the maximum fine is up to level 5 (s.146(7)), currently £5,000.

11.5 ALLOWING THE SALE OF ALCOHOL TO CHILDREN

Apart from the sale or supply itself, there is an offence of knowingly allowing another person to make that sale or supply. This offence relates to relevant premises, i.e. those operating under a premises licence, club premises certificate or temporary event notice (s.147(1)).

This offence can be committed by anyone who works at the premises in a capacity that gives that person authority to prevent the sale or supply of alcohol (s.147(2)). For club premises, it would apply to any member or officer who was present at the time of the supply in a capacity which enabled him to prevent it (s.147(4)).

This offence also carries a level 5 fine (s.147(5)).

11.6 CONSUMPTION OF ALCOHOL BY CHILDREN

It is an offence for an individual under the age of 18 knowingly to consume alcohol on premises where a premises licence, club premises certificate or temporary event notice is in place (s.150(1)).

More importantly, from the point of view of risk to the licensee, it is also an offence knowingly to allow a child to consume alcohol on relevant premises (s.150(2)). This offence can be committed by anyone who works at the premises in a capacity that gives that person authority to prevent the consumption taking place (s.150(3)(a)) and there are similar provisions in relation to the supply of alcohol by a club (s.150(3)(b)).

No offence, however, is committed where a 16 or 17 year old accompanied by an adult drinks beer, wine or cider, with a table meal (s.150(4)). Licensees will need to understand that this exception is in more restrictive terms than the comparable provisions under the 1964 legislation.

Up to the second appointed day (24 November 2005), 16 and 17 year olds will be able to buy and to consume beer or cider (but not wine) for consumption with a meal in a part of the premises which is not a bar and which is usually set apart for the service of meals.

From the second appointed day onwards, the 16 and 17 year olds concerned can still drink alcohol with their meal, but the alcohol will have to be bought by an adult. The consumption can only take place in the presence of an adult, although there is no requirement that the accompanying adult should be the one who made the purchase.

For the offence of consuming alcohol, a child can be fined up to £1,000. For allowing consumption, the fine is set at level 5 (s.150(5)).

In all circumstances other than those set out above relating to consumption of alcohol by 16 and 17 year olds with a table meal, any individual who buys or attempts to buy alcohol for consumption on relevant premises by a child commits an offence punishable at level 5 (s.149(7)(b)).

11.7 MISCELLANEOUS OFFENCES RELATING TO CHILDREN

It is appropriate to make a brief mention of three further offences relating to those under 18.

First, the sale of liqueur confectionery is lawful provided that the purchaser is 16 or over (s.148(1)(a)), but other foodstuffs containing alcohol can only be bought by over 18s. The relevant proportion in determining whether a product is 'alcoholic' is 0.5% of alcohol by volume.

Prospective licensees should also be aware that it is an offence knowingly to deliver alcohol to children (s.151(1)). There is a significant risk for businesses which take orders by mail order or over the internet and then despatch alcohol to a requested address. The first risk is that the sale itself may be taking place to a minor. The second risk is that the delivery may not be to one of the locations which are specifically mentioned in s.151 of the 2003 Act. In simple terms, if the alcohol is delivered to the buyer's home address or his place of work, then the fact that it is then received by a child will not result in the commission of an offence.

Lastly, as in the Licensing Act 1964, it is an offence to allow a person under the age of 18 to sell or supply alcohol unless each of those sales or supplies has been specifically approved (s.153).

11.8 UNAUTHORISED LICENSABLE ACTIVITIES

Central to the enforcement of the new licensing regime is the provision that it is an offence to carry on, or attempt to carry on, a licensable activity without or not in accordance with a premises licence, a club premises certificate or a temporary event notice, as appropriate (s.136(1)(a)). It is also an offence knowingly to allow a licensable activity to be undertaken without the proper authorisation (s.136(1)(b)).

These offences cover the operation of premises that are entirely unlicensed as well as activities that are in breach of the relevant authorisation. Thus if a premises were licensed for only one activity and a second licensable activity were carried out, one or other of these offences would be committed. In addition, these offences also relate to breaches of the terms and conditions included in licences.

Where the licensable activity is the provision of regulated entertainment, a person who is involved in the performance of that entertainment but has no other involvement, will not commit an offence under this section. However, if in addition to the performance the individual is also involved in the organisation of the event, then that individual may be committing the above offences (s.136(2)).

The maximum sentence on conviction of these offences is up to six months' imprisonment, or a fine not exceeding £20,000, or both (s.136(4)). However, these offences cover a wide range of acts of varying severity and it will be up to the courts to decide the relevant sentence.

11.9 EXPOSING ALCOHOL FOR UNAUTHORISED SALE

Exposing alcohol for sale by retail in circumstances where the sale would not be under or in accordance with a premises licence, club premises certificate or temporary event notice is an offence under the 2003 Act (s.137(1)). For example, if alcohol were displayed in a shop as being for sale at a time when the premises licence did not authorise such sale, then an offence would be committed even without a sale taking place.

The sentence on conviction of this offence is up to six months' imprisonment, or a fine up to £20,000, or both (s.137(3)). Additionally, the court may order that the alcohol in question be confiscated and either destroyed or dealt with in whatever manner the court may consider appropriate (s.137(4)).

11.10 KEEPING ALCOHOL ON PREMISES FOR UNAUTHORISED SALE

It is an offence to have in your possession or under your control alcohol with the intention of selling it by retail or supplying it where such sale or supply would be an unauthorised licensable activity (s.138(1)).

On conviction for this offence the sentence is a fine not exceeding level 2. In addition, the court may order the forfeit of the alcohol in question which may then be destroyed or dealt with as the court orders (s.138(4) and (5)).

11.11 DUE DILIGENCE

In relation to offences of carrying on unauthorised licensable activities, exposing alcohol for unauthorised sale or keeping alcohol on premises for unauthorised sale, defences of due diligence are available (s.139(2)). The person charged would need to demonstrate that his act was due to a mistake or to reliance on information given to him or to an act or omission by another person or some other cause beyond his control. In addition, he would need to demonstrate that all reasonable precautions had been taken and all due diligence exercised to avoid the commission of the offence (s.139)(1)).

11.12 ALLOWING DISORDERLY CONDUCT ON LICENSED PREMISES

The 2003 Act creates the offence of knowingly allowing disorderly conduct on relevant premises (i.e. premises for which a premises licence, club premises certificate or temporary event notice is in force) (s.140(1)). This offence is of vital importance in ensuring the safety of customers in licensed premises. It should be noted that it is not necessarily the outbreak of disorder itself, but the failure to address the issue either through controlling the problem or requesting police assistance, that may result in the commission of the offence.

This offence differs from a similar offence under the 1964 Act which only refers to permitting 'violent, quarrelsome or riotous' conduct.

The offence may be committed by (s.140(2)):

- any person who works at the premises in a capacity (whether paid or unpaid) that gives him the authority to prevent such conduct;
- a premises licence holder or DPS;

- an officer or member of a club operating under a club premises certificate who is present at the time of the disorder and who has the authority to prevent it;
- a premises user who has given a temporary event notice in respect of those premises.

The sentence on conviction of this offence is a fine of up to level 3 (£1,000) (s.140(3)).

11.13 SALE OF ALCOHOL TO A PERSON WHO IS DRUNK

Under the 2003 Act it is an offence knowingly to sell or attempt to sell alcohol to a person who is drunk, or to allow alcohol to be sold to such a person (s.141(1)). This is similar to s.172(3) of the Licensing Act 1964 save that the 1964 legislation rendered only the holder of the justices' licence liable to prosecution and there was no requirement for the prosecutor to demonstrate that the sale by the licensee was made knowingly.

The 2003 legislation extends these provisions to club premises (s.141(3)) and extends the categories of those that can be prosecuted to the individuals set out in **para.11.12** (s.141(2)).

The sentence on conviction of this offence is a fine up to level 3 (currently £1,000).

The Guidance advises that this offence will be rigorously prosecuted in order to control excessive consumption and drunkenness and thus reduce the risk of anti-social behaviour occurring elsewhere after customers have left the relevant premises.

It is worth noting that a person who is drunk or disorderly will himself commit an offence if he fails to leave relevant premises at the request of the premises licence holder or (amongst others) a person employed on the premises with authority to make the request (s.143(1)). In any proceedings brought on charges of allowing disorderly conduct, it will obviously assist a licensee (or other defendant) to show that such a request was made and ignored.

The offence of failing to leave licensed premises when requested to do so is not restricted to premises licensed to sell alcohol, but applies to premises licensed for any licensable activity.

11.14 MISCELLANEOUS PROVISIONS IN RELATION TO OFFENCES

Whilst prospective purchasers of licensed premises are unlikely to seek advice before acquisition on procedural matters relating to offences, the following general points are worth noting.

1. There are now three potential prosecutors for licensing offences. They are the licensing authority, the Director of Public Prosecutions and (in relation to underage sales) trading standards officers (s.186(2)).
2. Most licensing authorities have drawn up enforcement protocols which will demonstrate where enforcement responsibilities lie and also the circumstances in which prosecution is likely to follow.
3. The list of potential defendants has been widely expanded. Where offences are committed with the consent or connivance of the director of a corporate body (or a similar officer or manager) or through attributable neglect, then that individual, as well as the corporate body, commits the offence (s.187(1)).
4. Similar provision is made in relation to partnerships or unincorporated associations (s.187(4) and (6)).
5. Whilst all of the offences set out above are summary offences, i.e. only prosecuted in the magistrates' court, the normal time limit for issuing proceedings has been extended. The limitation period is one of 12 months rather than six months (s.186(3)).
6. None of the offences set out above are subject to powers of arrest.

11.15 RIGHTS OF ENTRY

The rights and powers of the police and other authorised persons to enter a licensed premises have been greatly extended under the Licensing Act 2003. The 'authorised persons' include an officer of the licensing authority, an inspector under the Fire Precautions Act 1971 or an inspector under the Health and Safety at Work Etc. Act 1974. A local authority officer authorised for environmental health purposes also has a right of entry (s.13(2)).

When application is made for a premises licence (including a provisional statement or a variation) then a constable or an authorised person has the right to enter the premises in order to assess the likely effect of any grant on the promotion of licensing objectives. Similar powers arise when a premises licence is reviewed (s.59).

There are comparable powers in relation to club premises (s.96). Under the 1964 legislation, the police had no right to enter club premises (save in relation to a breach of the peace). There is still a difference for club premises in that the right of entry can only be exercised provided that either the police have or an authorised person has given 48 hours' notice. However, rights of entry are immediate (and can be enforced by the use of reasonable force if necessary) where there is reasonable cause to believe that a drugs offence has been or may be committed or that there is likely to be a breach of the peace (s.97).

Finally, the police or any other authorised persons have the right to enter premises to ensure that licensable activities are being carried out under the appropriate authorisations, although this right does not apply to premises for which the only authorisation is a club premises certificate (s.179).

In relation to all of these rights of entry and inspection, anyone obstructing either the police or an authorised person in the exercise of their powers commits an offence.

11.16 CLOSURE ORDERS

In the course of making preliminary enquiries the practitioner will have identified whether powers have been used to close relevant premises or whether enforcement of that type has been threatened.

The Government has been keen during the transitional period to emphasise that the perceived liberalising of the licensing laws has been balanced by wide and robust powers of enforcement.

The most obvious of those is the power to close down premises which are either causing or likely to experience disorder (s.160). There are significant extensions of the police powers to close premises and the premises at risk are not limited to those which sell alcohol. As a result, premises which provide either regulated entertainment or late night refreshment or which are simply covered by a temporary event notice may be subject to closure.

The police have the power to close all premises which are operating under a premises licence or a temporary event notice within a specified geographical area. The immediate period of closure cannot exceed 24 hours and the use of the power would clearly follow an expectation of particular disorder in that area. This provision replaces and extends the previous powers under s.188 of the Licensing Act 1964 which gave the justices power to close licensed premises because of the risk of a riot or tumult.

Of more concern to a prospective licensee is the risk of a closure order for identified premises (s.161). A senior police officer is empowered under the 2003 Act to close specific premises for up to 24 hours on the grounds that such closure is necessary in the interests of public safety because of actual or likely disorder, or that public nuisance is being caused by the noise emanating from those premises and that closure is necessary to prevent that nuisance.

The requirement is that the disorder should be in the vicinity of and related to the premises which are to be closed, and before making the order a senior police officer must consider the conduct of the premises user. Where, for example, the police are satisfied that the person managing the premises appreciates the problem and is taking steps to deal with it, a formal order may be avoided.

Once the closure order comes into force, application must be made by the police to the magistrates' court to consider that order.

The court's powers are (s.165(2)):

- to revoke the closure order and any extension of it;
- to order the premises to remain closed until the licensing authority has conducted a review of the premises licence;
- to order the premises to remain closed until that time subject to specified exceptions or conditions.

There is a right of appeal to the Crown Court against any decision by the magistrates' court (s.166).

It is an offence to permit the premises to remain open in contravention of a court order of closure. Anyone convicted of this offence is liable to imprisonment up to three months, a fine not exceeding £20,000, or both (s.165(7) and (8)).

Where a licensing authority has received notice from a magistrates' court confirming that the court has exercised its powers in relation to a closure order, then the authority must review the premises licence for those premises and determine the review within 28 days of receiving the notice (s.167). This appears to be the case even if the only action taken by the justices is to revoke the order.

The review must be notified to the licence holder and to responsible authorities (PLCPC Regulations, reg.37) and must also be advertised (PLCPC Regulations, reg.38). Relevant representations may be made by responsible authorities and interested parties (PLCPC Regulations, reg.39) (s.167(4)).

The powers of the licensing authority on a review of this type are as follows (s.167(6)) (provided of course that the steps taken are to further the licensing objectives):

- to modify the conditions of the premises licence;
- to exclude a licensable activity;
- to remove the DPS from the licence;
- to suspend the licence for up to three months;
- to revoke the licence.

Where the decision is to modify conditions or exclude a licensable activity, this may be for a specified period, not exceeding three months (s.167(8)).

The above decisions available to the licensing authority do not come into effect until either the end of the time allowed for appeal or, if the decision is appealed, until the appeal is determined (s.168(2)).

It is an offence for a person, without reasonable excuse, to allow premises to remain open following the licensing authority's decision to revoke the licence (subject to appeal). On conviction, the offence is punishable by up to three months' imprisonment or a fine not exceeding £20,000, or both (s.168(8) and (9)).

CHAPTER 12

Transitional arrangements

12.1 MOVING FROM THE OLD SYSTEM TO THE NEW

In implementing the new legislation, provision has been made for a changeover period. This 'transitional period', as it is termed in the 2003 Act, runs from the first appointed day, 7 February 2005, to the second appointed day, 24 November 2005.

During this period all holders of existing justices' licences are entitled to apply for a personal licence and all licences in existence on 7 February 2005 under the old licensing regimes may be converted to premises licences. Similarly, transitional arrangements are provided to enable registered members clubs to convert their existing club registration certificates to club premises certificates.

Although this period extends for nine and a half months, applications for conversion to personal and premises licences and club premises certificates may only take place during the first six months. The remaining three and a half months are to allow time for the licensing authorities to process all the applications.

It should be noted that in considering applications for conversion to both personal licences and premises licences the licensing authority may only take into account police objections relating to the prevention of crime and disorder objective. The other licensing objectives are not relevant to these transitional arrangements.

All new licences will take effect from the second appointed day (Sched.8, para.6(4) and para.18(2)).

12.2 PERSONAL LICENCES

As explained in **Chapter 4**, personal licences are only required by those wishing to sell, supply or authorise the supply of alcohol. During the conversion period (first six months of transitional period) those holding a justices' licence (either on- or off-licence) granted under the Licensing Act 1964 are able to apply for a personal licence without having to provide a criminal record/conviction certificate and without having to possess the new licensing qualification as set out in **para.4.4**.

Where licences have been issued in joint names, all those individuals named on the licence may apply for a personal licence under the transitional provisions.

The procedure for this 'conversion' to a personal licence is as follows.

1. Application is made to the licensing authority where the licensee is 'ordinarily resident' (the location of the licensed premises is irrelevant) (Sched.8, para.23(1)(a)).
2. Within 48 hours of the application, a copy of the application must be sent by the applicant to the chief officer of police for that same area (Sched.8, para.23(1)(c)).
3. The documents required to accompany the application are (Sched.8, para.23(3)):
   (a) completed statutory form (PL Regulations, reg.8 and Sched.4);
   (b) justices' licence or certified copy of licence;
   (c) two photographs, one of which has been endorsed verifying likeness;
   (d) disclosure of convictions and declaration form (PL Regulations, Sched.3);
   (e) the appropriate fee, currently £37.

Although the 2003 Act states that a copy of the licence may be sent, it is not advisable to send the original as this will also be required for conversion to the premises licence. It is sensible to have a number of certified copies made and use these in the relevant applications.

The police may object to the application for conversion where a statement of relevant convictions is made in the application. However, this will only be in exceptional circumstances, where granting the personal licence to the applicant would undermine the crime prevention objective (Sched.8, para.25).

The police have 28 days in which to object, and if they do object they must issue an objection notice as described in **Chapter 4** (Sched.8, paras.25(2) and (3)). If an objection is made, a hearing must be held within 10 working days following the end of the police objection period (Hearings Regulations, reg.5 and Sched.1) to consider the grounds for objection (Sched.8, para.26(3)(a)). The licensing authority may then reject the application if it considers this to be necessary for the promotion of the crime prevention objective (Sched.8, para.26(3)(b)(i)).

However, if no objection is made by the police, and the licensing authority is satisfied that the applicant holds a justices' licence, the licensing authority must grant the personal licence (Sched.8, para.26(1)). The authority has no discretion in this matter.

If the licensing authority fails to determine the application within three months of receiving the application, it is deemed to be granted (Sched.8, para.26(4)).

During the transitional period, the responsibility for any variation, extension of hours, or transfer of any existing licences remains with the current licensing authority until the second appointed day (24 November 2005). Consequently, anyone wishing to be transferred on to a justices' licence should apply through the old regime to the licensing justices.

If a person is transferred on to a justices' licence during the transitional period, they can still apply for a personal licence under the transitional provisions (Sched.8, para.23(1)(a)). This differs from the provisions relating to premises which are the subject of a new justices' licence. If such a licence is granted after 7 February 2005 the transitional provisions do not apply (subject to one important provision concerning opening hours) and any application would have to be for a new premises licence under Part 3 of the 2003 Act.

Additionally, any individual who is not a current holder of a justices' licence may apply for a personal licence during the period of transition following the procedure laid out in **Chapter 4** and making the application to the local authority rather than the magistrates' court. This, of course, is a new application rather than a conversion. It follows that the applicant must have an accredited licensing qualification.

As personal licences only authorise the sale/supply of alcohol from establishments operating under a premises licence, they do not have effect until the second appointed day when premises licences come into force.

12.3 PREMISES LICENCES

Within the six-month period following the first appointed day, existing licences which are in force on the first appointed day (alcohol, public entertainment, theatre, cinema, late night refreshment house, night café licences) may be converted into premises licences (Sched.8, para.2(2)).

The new premises licence will authorise the licensable activities specified in the original licence or licences and will be subject to any conditions or restrictions attached to the original licences (Sched.8, para.6(5), (6) and (8)).

An application for conversion of an existing licence into a premises licence may be made either by the holder of the current licence or with the consent of the current holder (Sched.8, para.2(3)). Thus where an existing licence is in joint names, an applicant who is also one of the licence holders will need the consent of the other licence holders before an application for conversion can be made. Similarly, if a pub holding company wishes to apply for conversion of the existing justices' licences to premises licences for each of the pubs it owns, the company will need the consent of the individual licensees concerned.

If more than one licence currently exists in respect of any premises, an application may be made to convert one or more of those licences into a single premises licence. This will be a frequent requirement where premises licensed for the sale of alcohol are also licensed for public entertainment.

The procedure for conversion to a premises licence is as follows.

1. The application is made on the form set out in Part A of Sched.1 to the Licensing Act 2003 (Transitional Provisions) Order 2005, SI 2005/40 (the TP Order) and details the current licensable activities (TP Order, art.2).
2. Application is made to the licensing authority in whose area the premises are situated (Sched.8, para.2(2)).
3. Within 48 hours of the application, a copy of the application must also be sent to the chief officer of police for the police area in which the premises are situated (Sched.8, para.3(1)).
4. The documents required to accompany the application are (Sched.8, para.2(6):
   (a) the existing licence(s) or a certified copy;
   (b) any relevant certificates or certified copies thereof (e.g. children's certificates, extensions to permitted hours, etc.);
   (c) a plan of the premises;
   (d) form of consent by existing licensee(s) (TP Order, art.2(5) and Sched.3);
   (e) if the sale of alcohol is involved:
      – details of the DPS;
      – consent form from proposed DPS (TP Order, art.2(4) and Sched.2);
   (f) the appropriate fee.

Plans must normally be on a scale of 1mm:100mm (TP Order, art.1(2)). However, it may be possible to agree a different scale with the licensing authority (TP Order, art.3(2)).

The following information is required to be shown on the plan (TP Order, art.3(3)):

- the extent of the boundary of the building, if relevant, and any external and internal walls of the building and, if different, the perimeter of the premises;
- the location of points of access to and egress from the premises;
- if different from above, the location of escape routes from the premises;
- in a case where the premises is used for more than one existing licensable activity, the area within the premises used for each activity;

- in a case where an existing licensable activity relates to the supply of alcohol, the location or locations on the premises which is or are used for consumption of alcohol;
- fixed structures (including furniture) or similar objects temporarily in a fixed location (but not furniture) which may impact on the ability of individuals on the premises to use exits or escape routes without impediment;
- in a case where the premises includes a stage or raised area, the location and height of each stage or area relative to the floor;
- in a case where the premises includes any steps, stairs, elevators or lifts, the location of the steps, stairs, elevators or lifts;
- in a case where the premises includes any room or rooms containing public conveniences, the location of the room or rooms;
- the location and type of any fire safety and any other safety equipment;
- the location of a kitchen, if any, on the premises.

The police may object to the application for conversion, but only on the following grounds (Sched.8, para.3(2)):

- if an appeal is pending against a decision to revoke or reject an application for renewal of an existing licence; *or*
- there has been a material change in circumstances since the grant or last renewal of the original licence;

and the police are satisfied that the conversion in either of these circumstances would undermine the crime prevention objective.

If the police do object, they must issue an objection notice within 28 days of receipt of the application (Sched.8, para.3(5)). When a police objection is received, the licensing authority must hold a hearing within 10 days of the end of the police objection period (Hearings Regulations, reg.5 and Sched.1) to consider the objection and, if it is thought necessary for the promotion of the crime prevention objective, reject the application (Sched.8, para.4(3)).

Where no police objection is made, the licensing authority must grant the application for conversion, provided the application is duly made.

If the licensing authority has not made a determination within two months of receipt of the application, it is deemed to have been granted (Sched.8, para.4(4)).

The new premises licence takes effect from the second appointed day (24 November 2005) (Sched.8, para.6(4)). However, if an existing licence is revoked after the conversion to a premises licence but before the second appointed day, the new premises licence will lapse. If the revocation is only in relation to certain of the existing licensable activities, the new premises licence will be amended to remove the relevant activities (Sched.8, para.8).

12.4 CONDITIONS ATTACHED TO CONVERTED LICENCES

The new premises licence reflects the authorisations, conditions and restrictions that existed on the original licence (Sched.8, para.6(5) and (6)). Thus, if an existing justices' licence allowed sales of alcohol during permitted hours only, i.e. there was no provision for extended hours, the converted licence would also only authorise sales during those hours. If the original licence was subject to any extensions, these would also be reflected in the converted licence. Furthermore, where, for example, a special hours certificate to sell alcohol until 2 a.m. was granted subject to the requirement that the establishment provides music, dancing and substantial refreshment, then the converted licence would only authorise the sale of alcohol until this time subject to the same requirement. When making the application for conversion the applicant must specify all existing licensable activities. These include the activities authorised by the licence and other licensable activities which may be carried on by virtue of the existence of the licence. Such activities are referred to as 'embedded benefits' and for a converted Justices Licence include provision of hot food until 30 minutes after permitted hours, drinking up time, sale of hot food to residents 24 hours a day and provision of recorded music throughout the day, amongst others.

It should be noted that where the new statutory provisions impose prohibitions or restrictions then the conversion process will not enable licensees to proceed as if the 1964 Act still applied to the premises. For example, the admission of children under the age of 14 to bar areas in on-licensed premises is permitted where a children's certificate is in force. However, it is an offence under the 2003 Act to allow unaccompanied children under the age of 16 years access to licensed premises if those premises are used exclusively or primarily for the supply of alcohol for consumption on those premises. It will, accordingly, be an offence for a licensee to permit 14-year-old children into the premises (if it is primarily a drinking establishment) irrespective of the fact that they could lawfully be accommodated under the previous licence.

Similarly, exemptions have been lost in the area of regulated entertainment. Under s.182 of the Licensing Act 1964 many establishments have benefited from the 'two in the bar' rule, whereby premises operating under a justices' licence were exempt from the requirement for a public entertainment licence if that entertainment was provided by up to two performers. This exemption is not included in the new legislation and therefore cannot be included in any converted licence (Sched.8, para.1(2)). If licensees wish to provide entertainment of this nature, it will be necessary to apply for a variation of the premises licence.

The new converted premises licence will also be subject to any statutory provisions relating to conditions – for example there were statutory provisions as to conditions to be attached to seasonal licences, six-day licences, early closing licences and Part IV restaurant licences.

However, the rules relating to drinking-up time will not be transferred to the converted licences. The pre-2003 rules regarding permitted hours and drinking-up time relate to both the sale and consumption of alcohol, whereas under the new legislation, only the sale of alcohol, not consumption, is classed as a licensable activity. Consequently, the controls on consumption specified in the old regime will not apply after the second appointed day and will not be carried forward automatically to converted licences.

As undertakings and assurances which are currently attached to a number of off-licences have no statutory force, they will not be transferred to new premises licences as conditions on conversion. This may cause problems in view of the fact that undertakings have often been used to ensure that the conduct of licensed premises does not cause disturbance, particularly to local residents. The Guidance states that where there are problems arising from the removal of these undertakings, the answer will be for those adversely affected to seek a review of the premises licence.

The premises licence will be subject on conversion to any relevant mandatory conditions as outlined in **para.5.18** despite the fact that those conditions would clearly not have existed at the time of the application (Sched.8, para.6(3)).

Despite the clear intention in these transitional provisions that – subject to the legislative changes set out above – the applicant should obtain a licence which reflects his previous licensing arrangements, there will still be scope for argument. The applicant's interpretation of the conditions required to maintain the existing position may well differ from the view taken by the licensing authority. The authority may take the view, for example, that the applicant is seeking to better his position and that the conversion application should be accompanied by one for variation. Licensees will need to check that their applications are carefully drafted and that the premises licence obtained does not reduce their previous entitlements.

12.5 VARIATION OF NEW PREMISES LICENCE

It is possible to make an application to vary any of the existing terms, conditions and restrictions of an existing licence at the same time as the application for conversion to a premises licence (Sched.8, para.7). The procedure for an application to vary at the same time as conversion is the same as for a straightforward variation as described in **Chapter 7**.

An application to vary in this manner is made in Part B of the statutory form at Sched.1 to the TP Order for the conversion of existing licences to premises licences and is made to the relevant licensing authority. This part of the form requires brief details of the proposed variation together with an additional operating schedule outlining the proposed new licensable activities and/or the varied times during which these activities will be conducted.

The application should be copied to the responsible authorities and advertised for the benefit of interested parties so that they can make any relevant representations as appropriate. (Advertisement and notification requirements are the same as for a variation as described at **para.7.2.**) However, it should be noted that any representations made can only relate to the proposed variations and not to any of the hours, terms or conditions to which the new converted licence is subject and which were transferred from the original authorisation.

If no representation is made by either a responsible authority or an interested party, the application to vary must be granted. If a relevant representation is made, there must be a hearing at which all parties may present their argument to the licensing authority. Following a hearing, the licensing authority will determine the application and will refuse the variation only if it is necessary for the promotion of the licensing objectives.

Refusal of the application to vary will not affect the application to convert. The latter may be granted while the variation is rejected. Any rejection of the application to vary will not result in the licensing authority having any rights to make changes to the converted licence. If the conversion is granted, all hours, terms or conditions, etc. relating to the original licence are automatically transferred.

If an application for variation under the transitional provisions has not been determined within two months from the date the application was made, it is deemed to have been refused (Sched.8, para.7(3)).

12.6 PROVISIONAL LICENCES

There is no specific transitional process for the conversion of an existing provisional grant of a justices' licences to a premises licence prior to completion of the works. However, under the transitional arrangements, where the grant of a provisional licence has been made and the premises have been completed in a manner which substantially complies with the plans deposited under the 1964 Act, the licensing authority 'must have regard to the provisional grant of a justices' licence when determining the application for the grant of a premises licence' (Sched.8, para.12(1)).

The proposed time period for when a licensing authority 'must have regard to the provisional grant' is the period from 7 February 2005 until 24 November 2006 (i.e. a year after the second appointed day) (TP Order, art.6).

12.7 OPENING HOURS

Where an existing holder of a justices' licence applies during the transitional period for a premises licence under the provisions of Part 3 of the 2003 Act (i.e. not a conversion), the licensing authority cannot normally restrict the hours during which alcohol may be sold to hours which are less than the current 'permitted hours' for that licence (Sched.8, para.11(1)(a)). This procedure will cover 'new' justices licences granted between 7 February 2005 and the 24 November 2005 (TP Order, art.5).

However, such a restriction may be permitted where there has been a material change in circumstance since the original licence was granted or renewed, or where relevant representations are made by the police advocating that such restricted hours are necessary for the promotion of the crime prevention objective (Sched.8, para.11(3)). This is a prohibition on the licensing authority and it does not appear that the authority would be able to reduce these hours even if the application was submitted on the basis that the applicant did not want all of the hours which were previously available to him.

12.8 CLUB PREMISES CERTIFICATE

Similar transitional arrangements also apply to clubs. Within the six-month period following the first appointed day, where a registered club holds an existing club certificate, the club may apply to the licensing authority in whose area the club is situated to convert the club certificate to a club premises certificate (Sched.8, para.14(1) and (2)).

The application must:

- be made on the statutory form (TP Order, Part A of Sched.4);
- specify the existing qualifying club activities (Sched.8, para.14(3));
- be copied to the chief officer of police for the police area in which the club is situated within 48 hours of making the application (Sched.8, para.15(1));
- be accompanied by (Sched.8, para.14(5) and TP Order, art.7 and Sched.4):
  - the existing club certificate or a certified copy;
  - a plan of the premises;
  - the club rules; and
  - the appropriate fee.

The information required to be included on the plan is as detailed for a conversion to a premises licence above.

As with the application to convert to a premises licence, the police can only object to the application to convert to a club premises certificate on limited grounds (Sched.8, para.15(2)), thus:

- if an appeal is pending against a decision to revoke or reject an application for renewal of an existing club certificate; *or*
- there has been a material change in circumstances since the grant or last renewal of the original club certificate;

and the police are satisfied that the conversion in either of these circumstances would undermine the crime prevention objective.

If the police do object to the application to convert they must issue a notice of objection within 28 days of receipt of the application.

When a police objection is received, the licensing authority must hold a hearing within 10 days of the end of the police objection period (Hearings Regulations, reg.5 and Sched.1) to consider the objection and, if it is thought necessary for the promotion of the crime prevention objective, reject the application.

Where no police objection is made, the licensing authority must grant the application for conversion (Sched.8, para.16(2)).

If the licensing authority has not made a determination within two months of receipt of the application, it is deemed to have been granted (Sched.8, para.16(4)).

The new club premises certificate, if granted, is granted on the same terms as the original certificate and subject to the same conditions and restrictions. It will come into effect on the second appointed day (24 November 2005) (Sched.8, para.18).

12.9 VARIATION OF NEW CLUB PREMISES CERTIFICATE

As with the new premises licence, a variation to a new club premises certificate can be made at the same time as the application for conversion (Sched.8, para.19). The procedure for variation is the same as for variation of a club premises certificate as outlined at **para.9.18**. Application for variation of a newly converted club premises certificate is made on Part B of the application form at Sched.4 to the TP Order.

If the licensing authority fails to determine the application to vary within two months from receipt of the application, it is deemed to have been rejected (Sched.8, para.19(3)).

12.10 APPEALS

There are provisions under the transitional arrangements for appeals in the following circumstances.

1. With regard to personal licences, appeals may be made (Sched.8, para.27):
   (a) by the applicant, where the licensing authority refuses the grant of a personal licence;
   (b) by the police, where the licensing authority grants an application for a personal licence following issue of an objection notice.

2. With regard to premises licences, appeals may be made (Sched.8, para.9):
   (a) by the applicant, where the licensing authority refuses the grant of an application for conversion of an existing licence;
   (b) by the police, where the licensing authority grants an application for conversion of an existing licence following issue of an objection notice.
3. With regard to the variation of a new premises licence, an appeal may be made:
   (a) by the applicant, against a decision by the licensing authority to refuse the application to vary;
   (b) by the applicant, where the application is deemed to have been refused by non-determination.
4. With regard to club premises certificates, an appeal may be made (Sched.8, para.21):
   (a) by the applicant, where the licensing authority refuses the grant of an application for conversion of an existing club certificate;
   (b) by the police, where the licensing authority grants an application for conversion of an existing club certificate following issue of an objection notice.

12.11 JURISDICTION DURING TRANSITIONAL PERIOD

During the transitional period, the pre-2003 Act licensing regimes will continue to administer their respective systems and all existing licences and permissions will remain in force throughout this period. Any applications for new licences, or renewals, variations, transfers, etc. to existing licences that are to take effect before the end of the transitional period, will continue to be the responsibility of the pre-2003 Act licensing authorities. Additionally, any enforcement or appeals relating to existing licences will continue to be dealt with in accordance with the law prior to the 2003 Act.

However, at the same time, applications for conversion of existing licences to the new system as described above will be administered by the local authorities under the new licensing regime. Furthermore, applications for new personal licences, or new premises licences, or new club premises certificates may be made to the local authorities under the 2003 Act where those licences are not required to have effect until after the second appointed day (24 November 2005). It follows that grants or refusals in relation to these applications can be appealed to the magistrates' court notwithstanding that the licences applied for will not have immediate effect.

From 24 November 2005 all new licences will have effect and all existing licences will cease to have effect.

CHAPTER 13

Preliminary enquiries

In this chapter the conveyancer is directed to the issues which need to be considered at the outset of any transaction involving licensed premises. Obviously, the majority of the work and the risk in such a transaction falls upon the buyer, but in order to speed up the process there is a great deal of information which can be gathered by those acting for the seller or the buyer as soon as instructions are received.

13.1 PRELIMINARY INFORMATION GATHERING

As soon as instructions are received from a prospective seller of licensed premises the solicitor should request from the seller all the official documents that a prudent solicitor for the other side will be requesting as soon as an agreement has been negotiated. Typically, for a large public house or a hotel which provides entertainment, this will include (prior to the second appointed day, 24 November 2005) the following:

- justices' licence;
- public entertainments licence;
- supper hour certificate;
- children's certificate (pursuant to s.168(a) of the Licensing Act 1964);
- special hours certificate;
- gaming permits;
- approved plans;
- fire certificate;
- registration from the local authority for the provision of food;
- certificates confirming the safety of the electrical installations and emergency lighting system;
- licence from the Performing Rights Society or the other organisations dealing with copyright in relation to the playing of music or videos;
- any agreements with the local authority in relation to the use of tables or seating on pavements outside the premises.

After the second appointed day (24 November 2005), the premises licence itself will include the authority for the sale or supply of alcohol and the provision of entertainment, but many of the remaining items set out above will be material, as will evidence of the annual payment made to the licensing authority which has granted the premises licence.

Whether under the 1964 or the 2003 legislation, there is a licensing register available for inspection. In the former case, that register is with the magistrates' court. In the latter, it is with the local authority. In either event the seller's solicitor should obtain information from the register if the seller himself is unable to provide a comprehensive set of documents.

For the buyer's solicitor the licensing register will also be a useful starting point. Inspection of any register maintained by licensing justices is limited by statute to council tax payers, owners of licensed premises or licence holders within the district of the court. Generally speaking, however, court staff will make the register available to members of the public on request.

The registration should include the name of the owner of the premises, because every person applying for a new justices' licence or for a renewal was required to provide that information. In addition, the register can include the name of any person who has an estate or interest in the premises prior or paramount to that of the occupier. That person's name will also be entered on the register as an owner of the premises, but only if that individual has applied to the chief executive to the licensing justices for the entry to be made. As a result of these provisions, the licence itself may only reveal the owner as declared either on grant or on renewal. It will be necessary to inspect the register to discover the name of any individual who has made a subsequent application to be included.

Once jurisdiction has moved from the licensing justices to the licensing authority, there will be no such restrictions on access to the licensing register. The register kept by the licensing authority must contain a record of each premises licence, club premises certificate and personal licence issued by that authority. In addition, it must keep a record of each temporary event notice received. The authority must provide facilities for making information available for inspection by any person free of charge during office hours. In addition, on request, the licensing authority must supply any person with a copy of the information contained in any entry in its register, although the provision of information in this way may be subject to a reasonable fee.

The other matter worthy of note is that any freeholder has the right under the 2003 Act to be notified of licensing matters relating to his property. Any person with a property interest in the premises should give notice of that interest to the licensing authority if he wishes to be informed of changes to the register. The notice is effective for a period of 12 months and accordingly will have to be renewed annually.

In addition to the licensing registers, the buyer's representative can also arm himself with the relevant statement of licensing policy. Again, whether the jurisdiction arises from the licensing justices or from the licensing authority, there will be a policy document which indicates the approach of that body to issues of principle and which also provides assistance on matters of procedure.

At this stage in the transaction, the buyer should certainly acquaint himself with this document. If he is considering a radical overhaul of the premises – perhaps the provision of live music or adult entertainment – then it will be essential before contracts are exchanged for the buyer to review that future investment in the light of the policy document for the area where he proposes to run his business.

13.2 AN APPROPRIATE APPLICANT?

Before looking at the matters which will be the subject of enquiry from a buyer, there is one matter which requires immediate consideration between the prospective buyer and his representative. That issue is whether the buyer will be able to secure a grant or the transfer of the relevant licence. Again, this will depend upon whether the jurisdiction lies with the justices or the local authority.

The question of whether the buyer is a fit and proper person has been covered in **Chapter 2**. It is such an important issue that it will need to be addressed before the property work gets underway. In the jurisdiction of the licensing justices, this issue will turn largely on whether there are previous convictions, but also – if the buyer is a new entrant to the trade – on a willingness to undertake a training course. There will of course be a substantial number of transactions where the potential buyer is not intending to run the premises himself in any event. If he is intending to put in tenants or a manager to run the premises, any questions on suitability will obviously apply to those individuals.

Under the 2003 Act the initial questions are very different. In order to secure a premises licence (or to obtain its transfer if it already exists) the applicant must be a person who carries on or proposes to carry on a business which involves the use of the premises for licensable activities. There are other categories which will less frequently be encountered, including a charity or the proprietor of an educational institution. Once those purely legal aspects have been considered, there is still the question of character to be reviewed in order to ascertain whether there is likely to be an objection from the police on the basis that the grant would undermine the crime prevention objective. The same issue will arise if the prospective buyer proposes to be the DPS (for premises which will include in the licensable activities the sale or supply of alcohol) or if the buyer proposes to apply for a personal licence. It is important to remember that the DPS must be the holder of a personal licence. If a prospective buyer does not have a licence of his own, then the practitioner will need to consider the timescale of the proposed purchase. If it is not practical for the client to obtain his personal licence prior to completion then another DPS will need to be found. Bear in mind also that all supplies of alcohol under the premises licence must be made or authorised by the person who holds a personal licence.

Some licensing authority policy documents have suggested that there must always be a personal licence holder on the premises at times when supplies of alcohol are made in order to comply with the mandatory condition set out in s.19. Policies in those terms have been challenged and there is no legal requirement for a personal licensee to be present at all times. Nonetheless, the licence holder may be required to demonstrate (perhaps on a review) that all supplies were authorised as a matter of fact. Some large retailers have taken the view that the safest course is to have a personal licensee on the premises at all times. This will vary from business to business. The starting point for any licensing authority is likely to be consideration of the size of the premises and the hours during which they operate. If this is likely to cause difficulties the most prudent course would be to consult with the licensing authority and of course in the course of preliminary enquires the prospective buyer will discover both the number of personal licensees currently employed at the premises and whether this issue has been one of dispute with the licensing authority.

13.3 PRELIMINARY ENQUIRIES

With no apologies for stating the obvious, the preliminary enquires raised on the purchase of the licensed premises broadly fall into three categories, namely:

- property enquiries;
- business enquiries; and
- licensing enquiries.

The commercial conveyancer, as the name suggests, is assumed to need no assistance on the first two categories. What follows here is a list of enquiries which will arise frequently, or which should be considered by the practitioner before being narrowed down by the nature of the property to the needs of the client concerned.

As in any transaction, no list of potential enquiries is necessarily exhaustive. The information supplied either by the selling agents or by the buyer himself may prompt further investigation. As with pure property issues of title, etc., no reference is made here to such matters as planning consent or structural issues, since they will be within the general experience of any conveyancer. Similarly on the commercial side no reference is made here to such things as trading figures or accounts since those enquiries will again be of general application on the acquisition of a commercial undertaking.

13.4 ENQUIRIES RELEVANT TO JUSTICES' LICENCES

13.4.1 General enquiries

Please supply a copy of the current justices' licence permitting the sale of intoxicating liquor and advise whether or not there are any conditions attached to the licence or any undertakings or assurances which have been given to the licensing justices.

It may be that the buyer will have this information from the enquiries referred to above in relation to the licensing register. If not, then the practitioner should bear in mind that conditions on justices' on-licences or undertakings on justices' off-licences are often endorsed on the back of the paper licence. As a result, the practitioner should ensure that a copy of the entire licence, i.e. front and back, has been provided. A review of the conditions is essential in considering the viability of the business which the buyer intends to operate.

Please confirm that the licensees are currently as quoted on the licence and advise their present and future addresses for service of the licensing notices.

By the nature of the purchase, the licensees are likely to be moving away, and this will be the time to obtain confirmation of the addresses for service. If the buyer serves the application to transfer the licence at the same time as the application for the protection order, then all of the statutory requirements will have been dealt with on the basis of the information provided by the sellers and there will be no need to spend further time – or perhaps encounter further difficulty – in trying to trace outgoing licensees after the protection order has been granted.

Please advise the Petty Sessional Division in which the premises are situated and advise the name, address and telephone number of the clerk to the licensing justices.

Again the buyer may already have obtained this information in order to secure the licensing policy or as part of the initial information gathering set out above. If, however, the information gathering process is effectively starting with preliminary enquiries then this is the obvious first step. The enquiry could perhaps be supplemented by asking whether there is any particular individual in the clerk's office to whom licensing enquiries should be made.

Please supply the names and addresses for the chief officer of police, proper local authority, and the clerk of the parish town or community council.

Again, these are matters which can be ascertained but will be readily available to the seller and therefore most easily obtained from that source.

Please advise the days on which the local magistrates' court sits and any specific day on which the court would normally deal with protection orders.

There are still many courts which only sit once or twice a week. In view of the fact that seven clear days' notice of intention is normally required for a protection order application, it is essential to know from the outset those days on which such an application would be heard, particularly if there is a need to exchange contracts as quickly as possible.

Please advise the dates of the next three transfer sessions.

This information is required to ensure that the practitioner knows the last date available to his client for the transfer of the licence. The protection order ceases to have effect on the date of the second transfer sessions after its grant. The reason for asking for three dates is to cover the possibility that the first one will arise before the buyer is in a position to obtain his protection order.

Please supply a copy of the licensing policy published by the local licensing justices.

Once again the buyer may well have already obtained this policy, but if not then time may be saved if the seller can supply a policy straightaway, rather than waiting for a copy to be obtained from the clerk to the licensing justices.

Have the licensing justices granted a certificate under s.68 of the Licensing Act 1964? If so, please supply a copy.

If the answer to this enquiry is in the affirmative, then the buyer has confirmation that he can sell or supply intoxicating liquor as an ancillary to a table meal for one hour after the close of normal permitted hours (see **Chapter 2**). The certificate will indicate whether it also applies to the afternoon period on Christmas Day.

Have the licensing justices granted a special hours certificate under s.77 of the Licensing Act 1964, and if so have any limitations been imposed on the certificate? Please supply a copy.

The production of this certificate will confirm the days and the hours for which it has been granted and any limitations imposed under s.78(a) or s.80 of the Licensing Act 1964 on the original application. The additional enquiry is required because under s.81(a) of the 1964 Act it is possible on an application to revoke a certificate for the court either to attach a limitation or to vary the limitation, rather than taking the revocation route. Production of the original certificate may not reveal that alteration.

Have the licensing justices granted a certificate under s.168(a) of the Licensing Act 1964? If so, please supply a copy.

There is a general prohibition under the 1964 legislation on persons under the age of 14 being in the bar of licensed premises during permitted hours. Where a certificate has been granted, no offence is committed by the licensee if a child under the age of 14 is in a bar area provided that the child is in the company of someone over the age of 18 and the certificate is operational. Bar areas would not include areas which were set apart for the service of table meals. The buyer will need to know the areas covered by the certificate and also the conditions placed on the certificate, the most important of which will be the time at which the certificate ceases to be operational.

If there are certificates or orders granted under s.69 or s.77 or s.168(a), please confirm that a notice has been exhibited in the premises stating the effect of the order and supply a copy.

This is a requirement, although one that is often overlooked and one which is rarely enforced. The transaction is unlikely to turn on whether the seller has complied, but the enquiry is a useful reminder of the obligation for the incoming party and could be useful in checking that the information supplied about these certificates is correct.

13.4.2 Plans

Please supply copy layout plans of the premises which clearly define the licensed areas open to the public and any areas to which certificates or orders under s.68, s.77 and s.168(a) apply. If no plans are available, please describe the areas referred to. In the case of a Part IV licence which permits the sale of intoxicating liquor to residents, please identify the 'dry' room.

It is imperative that the buyer knows the extent of the licensed premises and the areas where the extensions to permitted hours will apply. Often plans are unavailable and in the absence of plans supplied by the seller, the buyer may be able to inspect plans held by the police or by the clerk to the licensing justices if there is any doubt as to the areas defined. Reference to s.168(a) is to identify areas covered by a children's certificate. Reference to the 'dry' room refers to the requirement that there should be a room other than a bedroom available to residents where intoxicating liquor may not be sold unless the licensing justices have certified that no such provision needs to be made.

Have all structural alterations made to the premises received prior approval of the licensing justices, the local authority and the fire authority?

This enquiry covers a great deal of ground and can therefore be divided if it is appropriate to do so. The gist of the enquiry is to ensure that structural alterations covered by s.20 of the Licensing Act 1964 have received the prior approval of the licensing committee in view of the fact that retrospective consent cannot be given. Where a s.20 approval has been given, most committees will provide a signed copy of the plan showing the alterations, and a copy of that plan should also be requested.

The reference to the local authority and the fire authority goes beyond the fact that both of those authorities are likely to have been served with any application for structural alterations made to the licensing justices. Clearly, structural alterations are likely to require a consent of one form or another from the local authority (planning consent or building regulation consent). In addition, for premises which have a fire certificate – or have been exempted under the Fire Precautions Act 1971 – there is still a requirement to notify the fire authority of structural alterations.

Has approval been given for any structural alterations which have yet to be carried out? If so, then please supply full details, together with copy plans.

The buyer will obviously want to see what modifications have received approval if they have not yet been implemented. The only other point to note is that some committees will set a time for the completion of structural alterations and the buyer should obviously be aware of that, although there is no statutory compulsion to carry out alterations once they have been approved.

Justices do have the power to order alterations and so this enquiry can be supplemented by checking that no direction to make structural alterations has been received.

Have any notices been received seeking revocation of the justices' licence pursuant to s.20(a) of the Licensing Act 1964?

The section enables an application to be made by any person for the revocation of a justices' licence. If there is an application pending, then very few buyers would wish to proceed without awaiting the outcome. Practitioners should note that the revocation of an existing licence before the second appointed day (24 November 2005) will result in either the new licence not being granted by the licensing authority or a part only of that licence being granted. The issue of revocation for that reason remains significant in the circumstances where a premises licence has been approved under the transitional arrangements.

13.4.3 Where premises are subject to a provisional justices' licence

Finally, enquiries which will be appropriate where the premises are subject to a provisional justices' licence.

Please confirm that there are no restrictive covenants affecting the premises that restrict the sale of intoxicating liquor.

The general enquiries concerning covenants should have something of this nature, but where premises have never traded, it is obviously sensible to make these specific enquiries before any provisional grant is made final.

Please supply a copy of the provisional grant and confirm (if the grant is time limited) the date on which the grant will expire. Please supply copies of the approved plans, together with any approved modifications.

Where a provisional grant has been made, it has been the practice of many licensing committees to limit those grants to a period of 12 months. The purpose of this enquiry is therefore to find out the nature of the grant and whether there is any limitation on the time that a buyer would have to apply for a final grant. Apart from the plans approved at the time of the grant, the licence holder also has the facility to modify those plans before the final stage is reached. The buyer should ensure for that reason that all of the plans (original and modifications) are available.

Schedule 8 to the 2003 Act does include a provision that the licensing authority on an application for the grant of a new premises licence will be required to 'have regard' to the provisional grant made under the 1964 legislation where that grant has not been declared final and where the premises have been completed in accordance with the approved plans. There is accordingly some benefit from the 'old' provisional grant under the new system.

Please confirm that the holder of the provisional grant will provide his consent to the transfer of the licence.

Provisional grants are often held by individuals involved in the planning stage of a new project who have little or no intention of trading from the premises. Where a practitioner is dealing with premises which have the benefit of a provisional grant, it is imperative to have both the contact details and the consent from the holder of the provisional grant to ensure that that licence is transferred to the buyer, who will then be able to apply for the final grant when the premises are complete.

13.5 PUBLIC ENTERTAINMENTS

Please confirm if any public entertainment is provided on the premises and please specify the nature of that entertainment and both the days and the times at which it is provided.

Please confirm whether there is a public entertainment licence for the premises and if so supply a copy together with a plan showing the area covered by the licence.

Some entertainment which is undoubtedly public is exempted by s.182 of the Licensing Act 1964 – the 'two in a bar rule' for example. Buyers need to ascertain exactly what entertainment is provided to check whether a licence is required and, if one is held, that it covers the actual provision.

Please supply copies of all conditions which are applied to this licence.

Public entertainment licences often have both specific and general conditions. Both types must be viewed with the licence. They will be of particular importance where the licence is to be 'converted' into a premises licence.

Please confirm that all of the licence conditions have been complied with.

Are there any current proceedings to revoke the licence or for breach of any licence conditions?

The existence of a special hours certificate depends upon there being in force a current public entertainment licence for the premises. The buyer needs for that reason to ensure that there has been no lapse of the public entertainment licence and no threats to its continuation. The next enquiry covers the first point.

Please confirm that the public entertainment licence has remained in force continuously over the course of the whole period during which a special hours certificate has been held for the premises.

Once satisfied as to the duration of the public entertainment licence the only remaining check will be that the licence and the certificate cover the same physical area.

Have the licensees ever received any warning from any party that proceedings may be taken to revoke the licence or to prosecute any breach of its terms? If so, please supply copies.

In order to elicit any indications that proceedings are being contemplated.

13.6 ENQUIRIES RELATING TO CONVERSION

Please confirm that an application for conversion of existing licences for the premises has been submitted during the transitional period and supply a copy of the application.

The transitional period runs from 7 February 2005 and subject to the very limited objections which can be raised by the police and to the correct procedures being followed, the existing licences will be converted to a premises licence on the second appointed day (24 November 2005). Applications to convert must have been submitted within six months from 7 February 2005.

Please confirm the date on which the application was submitted and whether any objection has been received from the police.

The importance of the date is that if the licensing authority fails to determine the application within a period of two months following receipt, then the application will be treated as granted. The only police objection that can be raised in these circumstances is where an appeal is pending against the revocation or refusal of a renewal for an existing licence. Even then the police can only give a notice of objection if they are also satisfied that the conversion of the existing licence would undermine the crime prevention objective.

Where existing licences are not held by the applicant for the premises licence, then please provide the consents of the existing licence holders.

Applications can only be made for conversion where existing licences are held by the applicant for a premises licence, or the holder of the licence consents to the application being made. This will often mean that an application for conversion must include consents from tenants or employed managers who have been the holders of liquor or public entertainment licences.

Please confirm whether the application for conversion was accompanied by an application for variation and, if so, supply a copy. Please also confirm the date of the submission of the variation application.

Often an application for a conversion will be accompanied by a variation to cover extended hours or extended activities. The presumption in favour of a grant does not apply to the variation and at the end of the two-month period from submission the application will be deemed to have been refused if the licensing authority has not given it approval.

Please supply copies of all representations received as a result of an application to vary.

Whether in the context of variation or new applications or review, it will be very important for the buyer to secure as much information as possible as to potential problems in the running of the relevant premises. An enquiry of this nature will flag up sensitivity perhaps from the police or from local residents on issues of nuisance or disorder.

As a result of any representations made, please confirm whether the licensing authority has held a hearing and, if so, confirm the outcome.

The steps to be taken by the licensing authority where representations have been made are either to modify the conditions of the licence or to reject the whole or part of the application. If the response to this enquiry is not specific on these issues, then it should be followed up to ensure the buyer is aware of exactly what areas were causing concern and how they have been resolved.

13.7 FURTHER ENQUIRIES

13.7.1 General enquiries relating to premises licenses

Please confirm that the premises have a current premises licence and supply a copy. Please also supply a copy of the operating schedule and the plans submitted to the licensing authority.

This is the fundamental enquiry in that it will identify the relevant licensable activities, the areas in which they can be carried on, and the conditions to which the licence is subject.

Was the seller the applicant when the premises licence was first granted by the licensing authority? If so, please supply a copy of the application which was submitted.

At the start of the new licensing system and for some time to come, a large proportion of transactions will involve the original applicant. Disclosure of the original application will reveal to a potential buyer whether more ambitious plans for the premises have been curtailed and who the potential objectors might be if the buyer has plans for future expansion. Replies to the following enquiry could provide more information of this nature if there have been representations in relation to the relevant licence and a hearing regarding issues raised.

Have representations been raised by any interested parties or responsible authorities on the application for the grant of the premises licence? If so, please provide copies and confirm the outcome of any hearing held by the licensing authority to deal with those representations.

Please confirm that the charge for the premises licence has been paid to the licensing authority and supply the authority's receipt for the fees covering the current period.

Please confirm that the seller and all those persons working on the premises have complied with the conditions set out in the licence.

The buyer will be looking for some assurance that the premises have been run in accordance with the licence. As far as possible the buyer will be looking to assure himself that there is no prospect of a review of the licence, which could of course occur shortly after he takes over responsibility for the premises. There is a further enquiry later on that specific point.

Please confirm that the mandatory conditions under s.19 of the Licensing Act 2003 have been complied with.

These conditions require that (1) no supply of alcohol may take place from the premises unless there is a DPS, who must be the holder of a personal licence; and (2) that the supply should be made or authorised by a personal licence holder. The enquiries following ensure that the detail is provided to back up any assurance that the mandatory conditions have been observed.

Please confirm the full name and address of the designated premises supervisor and confirm that he will remain as designated premises supervisor until completion.

There are many transactions where the buyer will be looking to ensure the replacement of the DPS, and others where the buyer will be equally concerned to ensure his retention. The important factor however is that since no sales can take place unless there is a DPS in place, the buyer should discover at the earliest opportunity what the situation is in respect of the DPS.

Please confirm that the designated premises supervisor will provide his consent to a variation of the premises licence to change the designated premises supervisor.

In order to change the DPS, an application will need to be submitted to the licensing authority served on both the police and the current DPS.

Please confirm that the designated premises supervisor has not given notice to the licensing authority to be removed as the designated premises supervisor for these premises.

Such a notice has effect as soon as it is received by the licensing authority (unless a later time is specified on the notice) and needs to be served on the holder of the premises licence within 48 hours.

Please specify the names, addresses and the number of hours worked each week by all personal licence holders working on the premises.

The mandatory condition is of course that the supply of alcohol should be made by or authorised by a person who holds a personal licence. The buyer needs to find out so far as he can whether the current number of personal licensees on the premises is regarded as adequate and also, if the buyer proposes to reduce the numbers, whether that is likely to cause problems by way of review. Cross-reference will be required here to the conditions on a premises licence which may refer to the number of personal licensees on the premises – particularly at particular times on particular days.

Please confirm that the mandatory condition under s.21 of the Licensing Act 2003 has been complied with.

This applies where there is a condition on the premises licence which requires door supervision. The mandatory condition is that any individual working in such a capacity must be licensed by the Security Industry Authority.

Since the premises licence was granted, have there been any applications to vary the licence? If so, specify the outcome of any applications made.

Please supply details of any representations made by interested parties or responsible authorities in response to these applications.

These two enquiries may well assist a buyer who is considering a variation of his own. Once again they may unearth useful information as to potential objectors.

Apart from any alterations to the premises covered by applications to vary, please specify whether any other alterations – however minor – have been made to the premises since the premises licence was originally granted.

The purpose of this enquiry is to ascertain whether alterations have been carried out at the premises which should have been the subject of a variation. The only guidance at present in the 2003 Act is that major variations cannot be dealt with under the variation procedure, but would have to be dealt with by way of a new licence application. For guidance at the other end of the scale, i.e. minor variations, practitioners are advised to look at the policy document published by the relevant licensing authority.

Have any notices been served on the licence holder by way of application for review? If so, please supply copies.

Applications for review can come from interested parties or responsible authorities. Any applicant must give notice to the holder of the premises licence.

If a review has been held, then please indicate the outcome of the review and supply a copy of the licensing authority's notice of determination.

The steps that can be taken by a licensing authority on review are specified in the 2003 Act and a review is likely to cause major concern for a prospective buyer. It is essential that he discovers whether a review has resulted in a major impairment to the business, perhaps a suspension of the licence, or is directed at an individual, perhaps the DPS. Where there is a review and an adverse finding, then the buyer should also ascertain whether any appeal has been lodged. Bear in mind that appeals against determinations on review can be made by not only the licence holder, but also the applicant for the review or any other party that made relevant representations.

Has the licence holder received any correspondence or other intimation from responsible authorities or interested parties either threatening the possibility of an application for a review or serving as a warning that such action will be taken? If so, please supply copies or details.

It is assumed that any individuals or authorities who wish to object to the conduct of premises are likely to do so in the first instance by way of letter but clearly the buyer will wish to know if there has been any other threat of action. Again, this is a possible route for a buyer to find out whether there is a major difficulty on the horizon.

Please provide details of any convictions of either the licence holder or any persons working on the premises for any offences under the Licensing Act 2003.

There are many offences under the legislation but the most significant in terms of potential trouble will be those relating to the permitting of disorderly conduct, sales made to drunken individuals, sales made to children, or the permitting of unauthorised children to be on licensed premises.

Please confirm that no orders have been served for the closure of the licensed premises at any time. If such orders have been served, then please supply copies.

There are two types of closure order, namely, a closure order for a whole licensing area or a closure order relating to a specific premises. The latter will be the one that will give a buyer the greatest concern, although both would be matters requiring investigation.

Where a closure order has been made for these premises, please provide the following documents:

- *copy of any cancellation notice from the police, or*
- *notification of the outcome of the hearing by the magistrates' court to consider the order, and*
- *any appeal pursued as a result of that hearing, and*
- *the outcome of the review conducted by the licensing authority following the closure order.*

13.7.2 Transfer of premises licence

Please confirm that the seller will consent to the transfer of the premises licence and that he will agree to the transfer having immediate effect from the date agreed for completion.

This enquiry envisages the most likely situation, namely, that the licence holder is available to give his consent (there is an alternative procedure under s.43 where the consent cannot be obtained) and where the transfer will be applied for in a manner which will enable the transfer to take place on the date of completion. Often the buyer will wish this to be a condition of the contract.

13.7.3 Interim authorities

In the event of death, mental incapacity or insolvency of the licence holder, the premises licence will lapse. In any of these circumstances, the following enquiries should be raised.

Please confirm that an interim authority has been obtained to permit the continuation of the premises licence following the death/mental incapacity/insolvency of the licence holder and supply a copy.

If there is no interim authority, then please specify how the licensable activities are permitted to continue.

The time limits for any application in these circumstances are very narrow and it is anticipated that there will be many occasions when the appropriate notice is not given. There is an alternative procedure under s.50 for reinstatement of the licence on transfer, but again that is subject to short time limits. The only course in the absence of reinstatement or an interim authority will be an application for a new premises licence. In the meantime, the only way in which licensable activities could be continued at the premises is on the basis of a temporary event notice.

Please confirm that an application has been made for the transfer of the licence and supply a copy.

The interim authority period begins with the day on which the interim authority notice is received by the relevant licensing authority and ends two months after that date. An application for a transfer to a new licence holder is therefore required within this period. Practitioners should note in addition that the premises licence lapses unless the person giving the interim authority notice has also served a copy on the police. It may accordingly be worth a supplemental enquiry to check that the interim authority notice has been properly served.

13.7.4 Provisional statements

Where the premises are subject to a provisional statement, please supply a copy. Please also supply copies of any representations made by interested parties or responsible authorities at the time when the provisional statement was approved.

Practitioners will be aware from earlier chapters that a provisional statement under the 2003 Act is not as definite as a provisional grant under the 1964 legislation. As a result, enquiries need to be made as to any objectors at the original hearing as those objectors may have the opportunity to raise objections at the later application for a full premises licence.

Please confirm that there has been no material change in circumstances relating either to the relevant premises or to the area in the vicinity of those premises since the provisional statement was made.

The wording here is taken from s.32(3)(b) of the 2003 Act. The answer may be of some comfort to the buyer but the fact remains that 'material change' is open to interpretation. Bear in mind however that in order to have a second opportunity to object, any person wishing to make representations will have to demonstrate that they could not reasonably have made those representations at the original hearing.

13.7.5 Temporary activities

Many licensed premises make a significant proportion of their income from special events on site or events conducted on other premises. Under the 1964 legislation those events are covered by special orders of exemption (if they go beyond permitted hours) or by occasional licences for events off site. The buyer may wish to take over that client base and in view of the transition to the new licensing system may need to apply for temporary event notices to cover events for which arrangements have already been made.

Please supply copies of all special orders of exemption granted for events on the licensed premises, together with letters in support.

Please supply copies of all occasional licences granted to enable the licensee to run events away from the licensed premises and provide letters in support.

The author takes the view that there is a significant difference between special orders and occasional licences in terms of future licensees. Special orders extend the hours relating to a particular premises for a particular event. Occasional licences however authorise the applicant to make sales at alternative premises. Accordingly, if the buyer is taking over these commitments prior to the second appointed day (24 November 2005), then he should reapply for the occasional licences to be granted in his own name once he becomes the licence holder.

Please supply copies of all temporary event notices submitted by the premises user in the previous 12 months.

The purpose of this enquiry is to calculate whether the limit for the premises has been exhausted. Applications by any associate of the premises user or any individual in business with the premises user will be treated as applications by the premises user himself. If it is a matter of concern, then the enquiry should be broadened to cover those categories as well.

Please supply any notices of objection to temporary event notices, or any counter notices from the licensing authority.

Whilst the personal allocation to a personal licensee will not be of great significance to an incoming buyer, the service of counter notices by the licensing authority will indicate whether these allocations (personally or for the premises) have been used. Objection notices from the police will indicate any potential areas of concern.

13.7.6 Club premises

If the property being bought is a club, then the following enquiries should be raised.

Please confirm that the club still meets the qualifying club criteria set out in s.62 of the 2003 Act.

In summary, those criteria are as follows.

- No admission to membership without an interval of two days.
- No admission to the privileges of membership for two days after a person has become a member.
- That the club is conducted in good faith.
- That the club has at least 25 members.
- That alcohol is not supplied or intended to be supplied to members on the premises otherwise than by or on behalf of the club.

Please confirm if the club is supplying alcohol and if so please provide confirmation that the club complies with the conditions in s.64 of the 2003 Act.

These are conditions that the supply of alcohol is managed by an elected committee and that no person receives any benefit (financially) from the purchase of alcohol by the club.

Please supply a copy of the club premises certificate.

Please confirm whether on the grant of the certificate any representations were made by interested parties, or responsible authorities and, if so, supply copies.

If there was a hearing to consider representations, please confirm the outcome of that hearing.

Please supply a copy of the club's operating schedule, a plan of the premises and a set of the club rules which accompanied the application for the certificate.

Replies to the enquiries above should give the prospective buyer the basic information concerning the club's licensing arrangements and confirmation that the club qualifies to hold the certificate. Practitioners should consider however whether additional enquiries should be raised comparable to those which would relate to a premises licence. For example, enquiries could be made to see whether variations have been sought to the certificate or whether the club has altered its rules since the certificate was granted. Clubs are required to notify the licensing authority of any rule changes. In addition, although reviews are less likely for club premises, there are provisions in ss.87 and 88 for a review which can in the worst cases result in withdrawal of the certificate. Further enquiries may be necessary and should mirror those set out above in relation to reviews and revocation.

Please confirm whether the club has the benefit of registration under Part III of the Gaming Act 1968 in relation to gaming machines. If so, then please supply a copy of the registration and copies of any club rules relating to the operation of machines.

Many members clubs have secured registration under this part of the Gaming Act to operate machines with a higher pay-out than those permitted in public houses. Registration will have been secured on the basis that the profits from such machines will be for the benefit of the membership and will be separately accounted for. Prospective buyers will need to obtain details of those arrangements.

13.7.7 Health and safety

In common with all commercial premises, licensed premises will be subject to inspection by the local authority. Buyers will need to be aware of any notice serviced under the health and safety legislation since those notices may inhibit these sort of premises or require works to be completed.

Please confirm that no improvement notices or prohibition notices have been served by the local authority under the health and safety legislation. If any such notices have been served, then please supply copies.

13.7.8 Late night refreshment

Where premises provide hot food or hot drink enquiries will need to be made to ensure either that no premises licence is required or that the premises licence is in force and covers the activities on site.

Please confirm the hours during which hot food or hot drink is supplied to members of the public from the premises.

If supplies are made in these circumstances between 11 p.m. and 5 a.m., please confirm that there is a premises licence in force and supply a copy.

If supplies of hot food are made between 11 p.m. and 5 a.m. and no licence is held, please specify whether the supply is exempt and confirm to whom those supplies are being made.

There is a long list of exempt supplies set out in Sched.2 to the 2003 Act. They can most easily be summarised by reference to the heading which states 'Exempt supplies: clubs, hotels etc. and employees'. Please note also that supplies of hot food by vending machine will require a premises licence, although supplies of hot drinks from a machine will not.

Where a premises licence is in force, the buyer may need to raise further enquiries concerning objections to the licence, variations and reviews, as set out earlier in this chapter.

13.8 MISCELLANEOUS ENQUIRIES RELATING TO LICENSED PREMISES

Despite the wholesale reform of licensing law, and the absorption of various licences – particularly late night refreshment, public entertainment and liquor licences – into the same document, there are a still a number of ancillary areas where enquiries will be required.

13.8.1 Fire certificates

Premises providing accommodation may require a certificate from the fire authority. The requirement arises where sleeping accommodation is provided for more than six persons (whether guests or staff) or there is some sleeping accommodation above the first floor or below the ground floor.

If an enquiry has not been raised in general enquiries, then it should be in the following terms:

Is there a fire certificate for the premises and, if so, please supply a copy. Further, please confirm that the conditions of the fire certificate have been complied with and that no alterations have been made to the premises without the approval of the fire authority.

13.8.2 Gaming permits

Has a permit been issued for the premises pursuant to s.34 of the Gaming Act 1968? If so, please confirm the number of machines permitted and supply copies of the permits.

There is no provision for the transfer of permits or machines and so buyers will have to make arrangements for new permits to be secured.

Ancillary enquiries will be required as to the machines themselves. Whilst strictly not a licensing issue, gaming machines in licensed premises will generally be the property of a third party and if so a copy should be obtained of the leasing agreement so that a decision can be taken as to whether attempts should be made with the owner to secure the retention of the machines.

Very often it is the owner of the machines that will make the application for the permits and so contact should be made with the owners to clarify those arrangements.

13.8.3 Environmental health

Please supply copies of any notices served by environmental health officers in connection with food safety or statutory nuisance.

Although all notices affecting the property should be revealed by replies to general enquiries practitioners will want to raise specific enquiries and will need to consider which areas to cover and whether there are any particular areas at risk with the premises which are being sold. The most obvious powers are under the Food Safety Act 1990 and Regulations under that Act where there are provisions which require works to be carried out. Alternatively, in the area of noise, there may be abatement notices issued under the Environmental Protection Act 1990.

13.8.4 Copyright

Please supply copies of all licences granted for the reproduction of copyright music or for any visual displays.

13.8.5 Neighbours

Please provide details of any complaints from local residents or businesses regarding noise or any other issues arising from the conduct of the premises.

Local residents have considerable power under the 2003 Act, where complaints can lead to a review and to potential revocation of the licence. Buyers should take any steps that they can to ascertain before a transaction proceeds whether there are likely to be disputes with those living or working nearby.

13.9 FUTURE BUSINESS

Steps should be taken as soon as possible to secure either bookings or contacts which may assist the buyer when he takes over the premises. The following two enquiries may assist.

Please supply details of any advance bookings and confirm that any deposits will be transferred to the buyer on the completion.

In so far as those advance bookings post-date completion, whilst the parties may well sort out these matters between themselves, it is the sort of issue which could easily be overlooked and which could cause unnecessary problems with customers who have little or no interest in the change of ownership, but every interest in the success of the intended event. Where significant contributions to trade are made by sports teams (perhaps darts or pool) then a buyer might wish to supplement this enquiry with a request for details of the organisers of these teams to ensure continuity.

Is the seller a member of any local marketing association or does he receive referrals from any tourist board or commercial agency? Please supply full details.

Again, this is a sensible enquiry to ensure continuity of business. The seller is likely to apportion any subscriptions or membership fees which have been paid to these organisations.

13.10 CONDITIONAL CONTRACTS

Different conditions will be placed in contracts for the sale of licensed premises according to whether the transaction takes place under the terms of the Licensing Act 1964 or the Licensing Act 2003.

For existing premises where the sale takes place before the second appointed day (24 November 2005), the contract will be conditional upon the grant of a protection order and the provision of a consent from existing licensees who transfer the licence at a future date. For existing premises under the 2003 Act there will be a contractual obligation on the holder to transfer the premises licence, such transfer to be effective on completion.

For premises to be built or in the course of conversion, a contract for a sale prior to 24 November 2005 will be conditional upon a provisional grant coming into force. The clause should ensure that the condition provides for the possibility of an appeal. If a provisional grant was opposed (but still granted), then the objector would have a right to appeal and the coming into force of the grant could not be said to be before the end of the 21-day period available for that appeal to be lodged. If the appeal is lodged then the grant would not come into force until conclusion or withdrawal of the appeal.

For new premises under the 2003 Act the contract might be conditional on the coming into force of the premises licence, or on the coming into force of the provisional statement, depending on the circumstances of the particular case.

Sample clauses are set out at **Appendix C**.

PART 2

Other licensing issues

CHAPTER 14

Food premises licensing

New EU food hygiene legislation will apply from 1 January 2006. **Paragraphs 14.1–14.4** will discuss the regime in place until this date. **Paragraph 14.5** will discuss the new regulations in more detail.

14.1 FOOD PREMISES REGISTRATION

All food premises are legally required to be registered with their local authority under the Food Premises (Registration) Regulations 1991, SI 1991/2825 (Food Premises Regulations) (as amended), made under the Food Safety Act 1990. This includes market stalls, delivery vehicles and other moveable structures (see **para.14.1.2** for further details of definition of a food premises).

The main purpose of this registration is to provide information on the number, location and types of food premises in the area, so that the Environmental Health Department is aware of their existence and can arrange for all food premises to be inspected to ensure public safety. Food premises may be inspected routinely or as a result of a complaint. The number of routine inspections depends on the type of food hazards involved in the business and history of compliance with food safety legislation.

A local authority cannot refuse to register a premises. However, it is an offence to carry on a food business from premises that are not registered and there is a maximum fine of £1,000 for failing to register.

14.1.1 What is a food business?

A food business is defined as any business in the course of which commercial operations with respect to food or food sources are carried out.

14.1.2 Which food premises require registration?

Food premises are defined as any premises used for the purposes of a food business. Registration is required for:

- premises where a food business is carried on for five or more days (whether or not consecutive) in any consecutive five-week period;
- premises where two or more food businesses are carried on by the same or by different people/organisations for five or more days (whether consecutive or not) within any consecutive five-week period.

Where the premises are used by more than one person, it is the aggregate of use by all of them which counts towards the five-day period.

A large building containing smaller permanent premises where several different food businesses are carried on (e.g. the food court of an airport terminal) will not need to be registered, but each of the smaller individual food businesses must be registered. Where all of the smaller premises are used by the same food business, only one registration is required.

In markets where vehicles, moveable stalls and barrows (not provided by or used by the market controller) are used, the individual stalls, etc. will have to be registered and, in most cases, registration will also be required for the market itself. However, in markets where moveable stalls, barrows, etc. are provided by the market controller for the use of others, individual registration of the stalls, etc. is not required, although the market itself must be registered.

Vehicles used for food businesses, such as ice cream vans or mobile food stalls, are exempt from registration unless used within a market (as explained above). However, the premises where the vehicles are stored must be registered.

Staff canteens, directors' dining rooms and their kitchens attract registration under the regulations.

14.1.3 Exemptions from registration

Premises which are used for less than five days, whether or not consecutive, in any period of five consecutive weeks are exempt from registration.

In addition, premises where commercial food operations are carried out which pose little or no risk to human health and those where the use is by charities or voluntary organisations are also exempt.

Those premises where food operations are subject to control or registration by other legislation are excepted from registration under this legislation. Thus the following are exempt:

1. Premises which are used only for the activities detailed in (a) to (f) below and which are registered or licensed for that purpose:
   (a) slaughterhouses;
   (b) poultry meat slaughterhouses and cutting premises;
   (c) meat export cutting premises, cold stores and transhipment centres;

(d) meat product plants approved for export to another country in the EU
(e) dairies or dairy farms;
(f) milk distribution centres.

2. Premises where the activities listed in (a) to (g) below take place, unless the retail sale of food also takes place there:
(a) places where game is killed for sport, e.g. grouse moors;
(b) places where fish is taken for food, but not processed, e.g. river banks;
(c) places where crops are harvested, cleaned, stored and/or packed, except where the crops are wrapped in the way in which they will be sold to the consumer;
(d) places where honey is harvested;
(e) egg production or packing premises;
(f) livestock farms and markets and shellfish harvesting areas;
(g) places where no food is kept, such as kitchens used only for washing up.

The following premises are also exempt from registration:

- private cars, aircraft, and ships (except where the latter are permanently moored or used for pleasure excursions in inland or coastal waters);
- tents, marquees, awnings and similar structures (not including stalls);
- places supplying food or drink in the course of religious ceremonies;
- premises where the only food sold is through vending machines;
- places where the supply of biscuits, cakes, drinks is ancillary to the main business which is not the sale of food (e.g. hairdressers);
- places run and used by voluntary/charitable organisations where no food (except tea, coffee, sugar, biscuits, etc.) is stored (e.g. some village and church halls);
- some domestic premises where food is prepared for another food business;
- houses where bed and breakfast accommodation is provided in not more than three bedrooms.

14.1.4 Application procedure

Application for registration must be made on the prescribed form to the appropriate local authority at least 28 days before the commencement of the business. The application should be made by either the proprietor of the food business or the person who permits the premises to be used as a food business.

The application form is set out at Sched.4 to the Food Premises Regulations and requires the following information:

- address of premises;
- name of food business;
- type of premises;
- type of food handled;
- whether vehicles are kept at the premises;
- proprietor's name;
- whether seasonal;
- number of employees.

There is no fee for registration, and no requirement for renewal of registration once registered, but any changes in the information supplied must be notified to the registering authority.

14.1.5 Register

The local authority is required to keep a register containing the name and address of each registered food premises and the type of business operated there. This is open to inspection by the public and copies can also be requested, although the local authority may charge a fee for the latter.

The local authority is also required to maintain a supplementary record which contains the other details supplied by food businesses on the registration forms. This is confidential and therefore not open to the public, but is open to inspection by the police and authorised officers. The proprietor of a food business should be allowed access to any information supplied on the registration form relating to their business.

14.2 BUTCHERS' SHOPS LICENSING

The Food Safety (General Food Hygiene) (Butchers' Shops) (Amendment) Regulations 2000, SI 2000/930 (Butchers' Shops Regulations) require the annual licensing of most butchers' shops by the local authority. It is an offence to operate an unlicensed butcher's shop or to operate in breach of the licence. Upon conviction, the court may impose a fine of up to £5,000.

14.2.1 What is a 'butcher's shop'?

'Butcher's shop' is defined by the Butchers' Shops Regulations as any food premises, other than catering premises, in or from which commercial operations are carried out in relation to unwrapped raw meat, and raw meat and ready-to-eat food are both placed on the market for sale or supply. This includes most retail butchers' shops, mobile shops, market stalls, some on-farm shops as well as mixed business premises such as supermarkets which operate butchery services.

Premises that are not covered by these Regulations include:

- retail outlets handling and selling raw meat only;
- retail food outlets which do not sell any raw meat;
- shops such as delicatessens and grocers that sell only uncooked meat products/preparations and ready-to-eat foods;
- shops handling and selling pre-wrapped bought in raw meat together with ready-to-eat foods;
- catering premises;
- food premises that are licensed or approved by other product-specific food hygiene legislation;
- market stalls handling and selling only raw meat, raw meat products and meat preparations.

14.2.2 Application procedure

Application forms must be submitted to the local authority at least 28 days prior to commencement of operation or expiry of the previous licence.

The local authority must determine the application and notify applicants of the decision in writing within 28 days of receiving the application. The licence remains in force for one year from the date of issue.

Any material change to the layout of the shop or change of ownership or management which may reduce the safety of food sold or supplied from the shop must be notified to the local authority.

14.2.3 Licence conditions

Before the local authority can grant a licence, the premises themselves and the systems and practices utilised must meet hygiene and safety standards which are greater than those required by the general hygiene regulations.

The three main licence conditions are as follows.

1. Compliance with the Food Safety (General Food Hygiene) Regulations 1995, SI 1995/1763, and the Food Safety (Temperature Control) Regulations 1995, SI 1995/2200.
2. Formal training in food hygiene for all staff:
   (a) for food handlers – basic or Level 1 food hygiene training from an accredited body;
   (b) for at least one supervisor – intermediate or Level 2 training in food hygiene and in the principles of hazard analysis critical control point procedures (HACCP).
3. HACCP procedures must be in place.

The Butchers' Shops Regulations require that records of staff hygiene training and HACCP procedures are maintained.

14.3 FOOD PREMISES APPROVAL

Certain types of food premises, generally manufacturers and wholesalers of products of animal origin, such as dairies, meat products manufacturers or wholesale fish markets are subject to product-specific regulations (Meat Products (Hygiene) Regulations 1994 (as amended), SI 1994/3082, Minced Meat and Meat Preparations (Hygiene) Regulations 1995 (as amended), SI 1995/3205, Egg Products Regulations 1993 (as amended), SI 1993/1520, Dairy Products (Hygiene) Regulations 1995 (as amended), SI 1995/1086, Food Safety (Fishery Products and Live Shellfish) (Hygiene) Regulations 1998 (as amended), SI 1998/994).

These types of premises are required to be approved by the local authority and generally their products must display a health mark or be accompanied by a health certificate.

14.4 MEAT PREMISES LICENSING

The following operating meat plants are required to be licensed:

- red or white meat slaughterhouses;
- farmed game processing facilities;
- farmed game handling facilities;
- wild game processing facilities;
- cutting plants;
- cold stores;
- re-packaging centres;
- re-wrapping centres.

14.5 EU FOOD HYGIENE REGULATIONS

New EU food hygiene legislation will apply in the UK from 1 January 2006. This legislation will replace and amend the hygiene legislation referred to in the above paragraphs and therefore the registration/licensing requirements outlined in **paras.14.1–14.4** will no longer apply after 1 January 2006.

There are three main EU Hygiene Regulations:

- Regulation (EC) 852/2004 on the hygiene of foodstuffs;
- Regulation (EC) 853/2004 laying down specific hygiene rules for food of animal origin; and
- Regulation (EC) 854/2004 laying down specific rules for the organisation of official controls of products of animal origin intended for human consumption.

The new legislation is less prescriptive. It introduces risk-based procedures based on the application of HACCP principles and requires food premises to be either registered or approved. As it is contained in EU Regulations, it is directly applicable in the UK and there is no requirement for it to be implemented by national legislation.

New UK legislation will, however, be necessary in order to identify the offences under the new rules, provide for the enforcement of the EU Regulations, and revoke the existing food hygiene legislation. The new legislation (the Food Hygiene Regulations (England)) is currently still only in draft form.

As noted above, the EU food hygiene rules are broadly drawn and therefore do not contain the same level of detail as the previous legislation. The Food Standards Agency is, however, required to produce guidance (currently in draft form) which will contain a more detailed explanation of the legal requirements with which food businesses will have to comply from 1 January 2006.

Regulation 852/2004 applies to all food businesses. Regulation 853/2004 applies, in addition to Regulation 852/2004, to food businesses handling products of animal origin.

A 'food business' is defined as any undertaking, whether for profit or not and whether public or private, carrying out any stage of production, processing and distribution of food. This includes businesses involved in primary production – in many cases for the first time.

A 'food business operator' is the natural or legal person(s) responsible for ensuring that the requirements of food law are met within the food business under their control.

Certain activities are not included in the scope of the Regulations:

- primary production for domestic use;
- domestic preparation, handling or storage of food for private domestic consumption;
- the direct supply, by the producer, of small quantities of primary products to the final consumer or to local retail establishments directly supplying the final consumer;
- collection centres and tanneries which fall within the definition of food business only because they handle raw material for the production of gelatine or collagen.

The draft Guidance also considers the following to be excluded from the scope of the Regulations:

- the occasional preparation of food by individuals or groups for gatherings or for sale at charitable events;
- in circumstances where the provision of food and drink is ancillary to the main business, such as where hairdressers provide their customers with refreshment.

The rules that will apply to a food business from 1 January 2006 will depend on the type of food handled or sold. The requirements are therefore different depending on which of the following a food business is categorised as:

- restaurants, caterers and businesses selling food to the final consumer;
- businesses (other than restaurants, caterers and businesses selling food to the final consumer) manufacturing food not of animal origin;
- businesses (other than restaurants, caterers and businesses selling food to the final consumer) making or handling foods of animal origin.

14.5.1 Registration

Restaurants, caterers and other businesses selling food to the final consumer will have to register their food businesses with their local district council. (Where food is sold to the final consumer there is no distinction made between food of animal origin and that which is not of animal origin.)

Other food businesses processing or handling foods of non-animal origin will also require registration. The registration requirements are the same as for restaurants, caterers, etc. selling to the final consumer but they are classified separately as other requirements under the EU food hygiene legislation are slightly different.

Registrations are to be made on a standard form and need to provide full details of all the activities undertaken.

For new businesses, registration forms need to be submitted at least 28 days before food operations commence. Once establishments are registered, the food business operator must ensure that the council has up-to-date information on its establishments by notifying the council of any subsequent changes such as change of food business operator or change to the food operations undertaken. Such notifications should be made as soon as possible and in any event no later than 28 days after the change occurred.

If a food business is already registered under the current legislation and no changes have been made since registration or the last inspection visit, then no further action is required to be made in order to comply with the new legislation. If there have been any changes, then it will be necessary to notify the relevant district council.

As well as the registration requirements, food business operators must also comply with general hygiene requirements set out in Regulation 852/2004 and establish, implement and maintain food safety management procedures based on HACCP principles.

14.5.2 Approval

Foods of animal origin include fresh meat (including game meat), minced meat, meat products, meat preparations, shellfish, fish and fishery products, milk and dairy products, eggs and egg products, rendered animal products and miscellaneous products including frogs legs and snails.

Food businesses that handle food of animal origin must from 1 January 2006 (with some exceptions for wild game meat), be approved by the competent authority. If a food business requires approval, it does not require registration as well. Approval will replace both current approvals and licences.

Under the new food hygiene Regulations a food business handling food of animal origin will need to be reassessed for approval even if it is already approved or licensed. However, the current approval/licence will continue until the reassessment is carried out and the food business operator need not take any action until contacted by the competent authority. New businesses will be required to apply for approval to the relevant enforcement authority.

Food businesses which are currently licensed by the local authority to supply game for the domestic market or to produce minced meat and meat preparations for the domestic market, will need to be approved under the new food hygiene Regulations.

As well as approval of establishments, food business operators must also comply with general hygiene requirements set out in the new Regulations and establish, implement and maintain food safety management procedures based on HACCP principles. In addition, products of animal origin will have to bear an identification mark.

In contrast to some of the current licensing regulations, the above requirements apply to these food businesses irrespective of the throughput of the premises.

14.5.3 Butchers' shops

The requirements introduced by the new EU hygiene legislation are essentially the same as the current butchers' licensing requirements. Consequently, the national butchers' licensing scheme is being withdrawn from 1 January 2006 and butchers' shops will be required to register with their local council in the same way as other local businesses selling food to the final consumer.

CHAPTER 15

Premises licensed for betting and gaming

15.1 INTRODUCTION

For the conveyancer involved in property transactions relating to premises which are or are to be used for any betting or gaming facilities, it is essential to understand the basic principles of betting and gaming law so that the necessary licences or permits may be obtained to ensure that the buyer will be able to provide, or continue to provide, these facilities.

The Gambling Act 2005 received Royal Assent on 7 April 2005, although at the time of writing no date has been given for its coming into force. As such, this chapter concentrates mainly on current legislation whilst an outline of the main provisions in the 2005 Act is provided at **para.15.17**.

The current legislation has established a separate regime for each of the three different types of gambling.

1. Betting (including pool betting) is governed by the Betting, Gaming and Lotteries Act 1963 (BGLA 1963).
2. Gaming is regulated by the Gaming Act 1968 (1968 Act).
3. Lotteries are governed by the Lotteries and Amusements Act 1976 (1976 Act).

15.2 BETTING REGULATION

Betting is not legally defined but relates to the wager of money on the outcome of an uncertain future event.

Under the Betting, Gaming and Lotteries Act 1963, all betting in streets and other public places (except racecourses) is prohibited. Premises used for betting are subject to the following licensing requirements.

1. Premises used for betting must be authorised by a betting office licence.
2. As a prerequisite to the grant of a betting office licence, an individual must hold either a bookmaker's permit or a betting agency permit.

The licensing authority responsible for dealing with applications for the grant of these permits and licences is the betting licensing committee of the local justices.

15.3 GAMING REGULATION

Gaming is the playing of a game of chance or mixed chance and skill (otherwise than in an athletic game or sport) for winnings in money or money's worth.

Gaming in the street or public places, or in any place to which the public has access is prohibited by the Gaming Act 1968. Accordingly, gaming is not allowed in pubs, etc. except for the playing of prescribed games such as dominoes and cribbage and certain local games approved by the local licensing justices.

Gaming on premises to which the public does not have access is strictly regulated by the Gaming Act 1968. Under this Act, gaming is classified as either Part I, Part II or Part III gaming, with different requirements being prescribed for each type.

Of relevance to the conveyancing practitioner will be the requirement for bingo clubs and casinos to hold licences under Part II of the 1968 Act; the registration of clubs under Parts II and III; and the licensing of gaming machines under Part III of the Act, particularly the use of amusement with prizes machines.

There are exemptions from the requirements of the 1968 Act for non-commercial forms of gaming. Accordingly, gaming at charitable, etc. entertainments which are not held for private gain (1968 Act, s.41), the provision of amusement with prizes at exempt entertainments such as bazaars, fetes, etc. (1976 Act, s.15), and the provision of amusements with prizes at certain commercial entertainments provided under a permit from a local authority (1976 Act, ss.16 and 17) are not regulated by the 1968 Act.

Prior to any licence being granted under the Gaming Act 1968, a certificate of consent is required from the Gaming Board for Great Britain. The majority of applications are then made to the gaming committees of the local justices.

15.4 REGULATION OF LOTTERIES

There is no legal definition of a lottery, but it is generally held to be a distribution of prizes by lot or chance where entry is secured by the payment of a stake.

The Lotteries and Amusements Act 1976 provides that lotteries run for private or commercial gain are illegal. However, the 1976 Act provides exceptions in the case of small lotteries, private lotteries, societies' lotteries and local authority lotteries.

15.5 BOOKMAKER'S PERMIT OR BETTING AGENCY PERMIT

Betting transactions are prohibited on any premises by s.1 of the Betting, Gaming and Lotteries Act 1963 except for those authorised by a betting office licence (BGLA 1963, s.9).

As noted above, to be eligible for a betting office licence an individual must hold either a bookmaker's permit or a betting agency permit. Accordingly, the first essential consideration when acting for the buyer of such premises is that he is either in possession of such a permit or eligible to apply for one.

A bookmaker is defined (BGLA 1963, s.55) as a person (other than the Totalisator Board) who 'on his own account or as a servant or agent to any person, carries on, whether occasionally or regularly, the business of receiving or negotiating bets or conducting pool betting operations; or by way of business in any manner holds himself out, or permits himself to be held out, as a person who receives or negotiates bets or conducts such operations'.

If a bookmaker is acting on his own account he requires a bookmaker's permit; if he is acting on behalf of another bookmaker he requires a betting agency permit.

15.5.1 Eligibility

An *individual* is eligible to obtain the grant of a bookmaker's permit or betting agency permit if he fulfils the following criteria:

- he is age 21 or over (BGLA 1963, Sched.1, para.15(a));
- he has not been disqualified from holding such a permit;
- he is resident in Great Britain on the date of the hearing of the application;
- he has been so resident in Great Britain for six months prior to the application (BGLA 1963, Sched.1, para.15(c));
- he has not been refused the grant or renewal of such a permit in the previous 12 months (BGLA 1963, Sched.1, para.15(e));
- a permit that he did hold has not been cancelled within the previous 12 months (BGLA 1963, Sched.1, para.15(f));
- he has not been refused the renewal of a bookmaker's permit under s.4 of the Horseracing Betting Levy Act 1969 within the preceding 12 months;
- he has obtained the approval of the Horseracing Betting Levy Board for his application (BGLA 1963, Sched.1, para.15(ee)).

A body corporate may also apply for the grant of a bookmaker's permit provided the company has been incorporated in Great Britain (BGLA 1963, Sched.1, para.15(d)). The permit must however be held by an individual on behalf of the company. A body corporate will not be eligible for grant of a permit if such a grant has been refused or cancelled within the preceding 12 months.

If the holder of a bookmaker's permit or betting agency permit has been convicted of certain offences under the BGLA 1963 or of offences involving fraud or dishonesty the court may order that the permit be forfeited and cancelled (BGLA 1963, s.11(1)). If this happens, the holder is disqualified from holding either permit for a period of five years unless the court directs otherwise (BGLA 1963, s.11(4)).

15.5.2 Application procedure

The procedure and timetable for applications is set out in Sched.1, paras.5–7 to the BGLA 1963, and the Betting (Licensing) Regulations 1960, SI 1960/1701. Application is made to the chief executive of the betting licensing committee for the area where the premises is situated giving at least 28 clear days' notice. If the individual making the application is acting on behalf of a body corporate, the application must be sent to the licensing committee for the area where the registered office of the company is situated. The application must be accompanied by two references as to the character of the applicant. Copies of the application must also be sent within seven days to the police and the collector of customs and excise.

Finally, the application has to be advertised in a local paper within 14 days of the application being made. This notice should give details of the application and must indicate that anyone wishing to object to the grant must send to the chief executive of the committee two copies of a brief statement in writing of the grounds of the objection. The notice must also indicate the final date for receipt of objections which must not be a date earlier than 14 days after the publication of the advertisement.

The legislation states that the notice must appear in a newspaper circulating in the area where the premises are situated. However, this does not mean that the publication is limited to a local newspaper. A national newspaper may be used provided it can be shown that it circulates in the area of the licensing authority. Indeed, it is common for such notices to be placed in *The Sporting Life*.

Within seven days of the advertisement appearing in the newspaper a copy of the whole newspaper containing the advertisement must be sent to the chief executive of the licensing committee.

If there have been no objections to the application or if all objections have been withdrawn, the permit may be granted without a hearing. However, if objections have been made and not withdrawn or if the committee considers that there are grounds for refusing the application, a hearing must be held to consider the application and any objections.

15.5.3 Grounds for refusal

Provided an applicant meets the eligibility requirements set out above, an application for a bookmaker's permit may only be refused on the following discretionary grounds (BGLA 1963, Sched.1, para.16):

- the committee is not satisfied that the applicant is, or satisfactory evidence is supplied that the applicant is not, a fit and proper person; or
- the committee is satisfied that if the permit were to be granted the business would be managed or carried on for the benefit of a person who is not eligible to hold a permit.

For a betting agency permit, grant must be refused if the agent cannot show that he is the holder of an accreditation from the holder of a bookmaker's permit or the Totalisator Board. Grant may be refused if the committee is not satisfied that the applicant is, or satisfactory evidence is supplied that the applicant is not, a fit and proper person (BGLA 1963, para.17).

15.5.4 Change of directors of company

Where the holder of a bookmaker's permit is a body corporate, conveyancers should be aware that, under the provisions of para.25 of Sched.1 to the BGLA 1963, it is a requirement to notify the chief executive to the licensing justices and the police of any change in directors as soon as is reasonably practical. Failure to do so is an offence, conviction of which will result in a fine of up to £200.

15.6 BETTING OFFICE LICENCE

From a practical point of view it is important to note that betting committees are only required to meet on four occasions a year – in January, April, July and October. At their discretion, they may hold extra sessions at other times if required (BGLA 1963, Sched.1, paras.3 and 4). It is therefore essential that the conveyancer gives early attention to applications for a betting office licence and the requisite bookmaker's permit or betting agency permit.

As there is no provision to transfer a betting office licence to the buyer of a property which is a betting office, any purchase of such premises will involve an application for a new licence with the attendant risk that the application may be refused.

15.6.1 Eligibility

Having applied for or obtained a bookmaker's permit or, being accredited by a bookmaker or the Totalisator Board as an agent for the purpose of receiving or negotiating bets, having obtained or applied for a betting agency permit, the applicant is then eligible to apply for a betting office licence.

As an application for a betting office licence is contingent on the applicant either holding or having applied for a bookmaker's or a betting agency permit, anyone who has been disqualified from holding such a permit will also be disqualified from holding a betting office licence.

There is no requirement that an applicant for a betting office licence has to show a legal interest in the premises for which he is seeking a licence.

A betting office licence can be held by an individual on behalf of a limited company.

15.6.2 Application procedure

An application for the grant of a betting office licence is made using the form prescribed in Sched.1 to the Betting (Licensing) Regulations 1960. The procedure and timetable to be followed is essentially the same as set out above for applications for bookmaker's and betting agency permits (BGLA 1963, Sched.1) with some additional requirements.

Accordingly:

1. Notice of application in the prescribed form is submitted to the chief executive of the betting licensing committee for the area where the premises are situated.
2. Within seven days of the application being made, copies of the notice must be sent to:
   (a) the chief officer of police for the police area in which the premises are situated;
   (b) the appropriate local authority, i.e. the district council or the London Borough Council in whose district the premises are situated; and
   (c) the collector of customs and excise for the licensing authority's district.
3. A notice must be placed in a newspaper circulating in the area within 14 days of the application being made.
4. A copy of the notice published in the newspaper must also be displayed at the entrance or proposed entrance to the premises not less than 14 days before the date given in the notice as the date by which objections must be made. The notice may be placed inside the premises provided that it is capable of being read from outside the premises. The applicant must also take reasonable steps to ensure that the notice remains displayed until and including the day by which objections are to be lodged.

All notices must include a plan of the premises which must be sufficient to show the layout and location of the premises and the means of access to them.

It should be noted that if the applicant knowingly makes a false statement in the application he is guilty of an offence which carries a penalty on conviction of a fine up to £5,000.

As with applications for bookmaker's and betting agency permits, a copy of the whole newspaper containing the notice of application must be sent to the chief executive of the betting licensing committee within seven days of the advertisement appearing in the newspaper.

The application may not be heard by the licensing committee earlier than 14 days after the date given in the advertisement as the date by which objections must be submitted.

As a final step the chief executive to the committee must send notice of the time, date and place of the hearing not earlier than the date given for objections to be submitted and not less than seven days before the date set for the hearing of the application to:

- the applicant;
- the police;
- the collector of customs and excise; and
- any objector whose objection has not been withdrawn.

If objections have been made, the chief executive must also send the applicant a copy of the objections at the same time the notice of the hearing is sent.

In addition the chief executive must post a notice detailing that the meeting is to take place at the appropriate courthouse. This must be displayed where it can conveniently be read by the public (BGLA 1963, Sched.1, para.7).

It should be noted that many licensing committees require the grant of planning consent prior to consideration of an application for a betting office licence. If planning consent has not been obtained, this may be regarded as a ground for adjournment. The committee may also be entitled to adjourn consideration of the application if there is no immediate prospect of the premises becoming operational.

Most betting licensing committees have policies which set out their requirements for matters such as plans, any requirement for planning permission, notification to fire authorities, proof of service of notices, polices on demand, etc. and the practitioner would be advised to consider these prior to making any application.

15.6.3 Grounds for refusal

Grounds for refusal of grant of a betting office licence are either mandatory or discretionary. A betting licensing committee *must* refuse an application for grant if it is *not* satisfied:

- that the applicant will be the holder of a bookmaker's or betting agency permit at the date on which the licence would come into force;
- that the premises are or will be enclosed; and
- that there is or will be direct access to the street (BGLA 1963, Sched.1, para.19(a)).

Applications *may* be refused on the grounds that:

- the premises are not suitable for use as a betting office, having regard to their character, condition, layout or location;
- it would be inexpedient to make a grant having regard to the demand in the locality for the time being and to the number of licensed betting offices to meet the demand; or
- the premises have not been properly conducted under their licence (BGLA 1963, Sched.1, para.19(b)).

When refusing an application for grant the committee must give details of its reasons for refusal. It should be noted that the committee cannot refuse an application for reasons other than the statutory grounds.

In exercising its discretionary power in relation to demand the committee should have regard to the following conclusions outlined in (*R (ex p. Hestview Limited)* v. *Snaresbrook Crown Court 2001* [2001] LLR 214).

1. In considering an application for grant or renewal, the committee should normally consider the issue of demand first, but does not always have to do so.
2. Assessing actual demand 'for the time being' may be done in a variety of ways and is not limited to a list of 'key indicators'.
3. Demand includes latent demand; if latent demand is unmet, then the demand test is satisfied; in determining whether latent demand is being met, the quantity, quality and type of the existing facilities may be relevant.
4. The requirement for witness evidence and market research regarding demand is a matter for each licensing committee depending on the facts of the case.
5. A finding of latent demand may be made on the basis that the applicant is prepared to invest money in the premises concerned.
6. In the absence of demand, applications should be refused if made merely to entice customers away from the current licensed offices or to stimulate demand; however in deciding whether there is an unmet demand, the licensing authority should not be overly concerned with whether the consequence of granting a licence may be that customers are enticed away from other offices or whether a new licence would stimulate demand.

7. How an authority assesses demand may change with time;
8. In determining expediency a licensing authority may take into account the future as well as the position 'for the time being'.
9. If an application is, in effect, an application for the transfer of a licence from one premises to another close by, with some increase in size, little or no analysis or re-analysis of demand may be required.
10. The absence of demand 'for the time being' is an important factor but not decisive; the licensing authority has a discretion to grant or renew.
11. Where there is only a small imbalance between supply and demand, a licensing authority may have regard to public policy considerations.

If an application is refused, the applicant has a right of appeal to the Crown Court.

The discretionary power to refuse an application on the basis of inexpediency as a result of lack of demand is equally applicable to both the grant of a new licence and the renewal of a licence and is therefore of great relevance to the purchaser of a licensed betting office. It is therefore important to ensure continuing operation of the betting office while a sale is taking place as other bookmakers seeking to obtain a betting office licence in the area may take advantage of a temporary closure or change of ownership to try to convince the betting licensing committee that their application should be preferred to that of the buyer of an existing business.

If the purchaser is to make an application for the grant of a betting office licence at the April meeting of the committee, which is when applications for renewal are also made, it may be expedient for the seller to make an application for renewal to keep the premises operating until the buyer has obtained his grant.

Conveyancers should make appropriate preliminary enquiries having regard to the grounds on which an application may be refused and should also give careful consideration to local policies, the existence of other licences in the area, and any information that may indicate that others may be considering making a similar application.

15.6.4 Rules for licensed betting offices

Schedule 4 to the BGLA 1963 specifies the rules for the conduct of betting offices which include the following:

- the premises must be closed on Christmas Day and Good Friday;
- admission of anyone apparently under the age of 18 years is not permitted;
- the betting office permit must be displayed on the premises but other forms of notice or advertisement on the premises are restricted (see below);

- the rules relating to the exhibition of television or video pictures and vocal commentary are set out;
- the provision of music, dancing or other entertainment is not permitted;
- the consumption of alcohol is prohibited but other refreshment is permitted.

As noted above advertisements in betting offices are restricted. The detailed provisions relating to this are contained in the Licensed Betting Offices Regulations 1986, SI 1986/103. These Regulations also prescribe closing hours, and set out the requirement for the external display of a notice banning under 18s and the internal display of a notice of the terms under which betting is conducted.

15.7 RENEWAL OF BOOKMAKER'S PERMIT, BETTING AGENCY PERMIT OR BETTING OFFICE LICENCE

Bookmaker's permits and betting agency permits and betting office licences are valid for a three-year 'licensing period' and may then be renewed. The latest such period runs from 1 June 2003 to 31 May 2006. If an application is granted within the last five months of a licensing period it is valid until the end of the next licensing period (BGLA 1963, Sched.1, para.29).

In February of the year when permits and licences are due for renewal the chief executive to the betting licensing committee must give notice of the day in April when the committee will meet to consider applications for renewal as follows:

- written renewal notices must be sent to all permit and licence holders specifying the date, time and location of the meeting and the date by which applications for renewal must be received;
- an advertisement must be placed in a newspaper circulating in the area stating the date, time and location of the meeting and advising that any person wishing to object to renewal should, by a specified date, send two copies of a statement of their grounds for objection to the chief executive of the committee.

If an objection is received, the objector must be notified of the date of the hearing and a copy of the objection must be sent to the applicant. Unopposed applications for renewal may be dealt with by the chief executive to the betting licensing committee without a hearing.

If a hearing for an application for renewal is adjourned beyond the expiry date for the permit or licence, then the permit or licence will continue in force until the application is determined or any appeal to such determination is heard.

15.8 GAMING LICENSING

As noted above, the control of gaming can be said to depend on the extent to which a commercial profit is likely to be made from it. There are therefore a number of exceptions for activities which are considered to be sufficiently non-commercial. Those that are likely to be of relevance to the conveyancer are discussed in **paras.15.13** and **15.16**.

Under Part I of the Gaming Act 1968, gaming may also take place in a club without the necessity for licensing or registration if certain criteria are fulfilled. See **para.15.16** for further details.

Under the Gaming Act 1968, three kinds of commercial gaming are permitted: casinos, bingo and gaming machines. Part II of the Gaming Act 1968 governs the grant of licences to premises for gaming of all types. Schedule 2 to the 1968 Act regulates the procedures for the grant, renewal, cancellation and transfer of gaming licences. The regulation of gaming machines is governed by Part III of the 1968 Act.

The Gaming Act 1968 established the Gaming Board for Great Britain, the functions of which include:

- overseeing gaming facilities throughout the country;
- advising the Secretary of State on regulations to be made under the Gaming Act 1968;
- investigating the suitability of applicants;
- advising justices on relevant matters;
- opposing applications before the gaming committee;
- appealing to the Crown Court against justices' decisions.

15.9 BINGO CLUBS AND CASINO GAMING LICENCES

A gaming licence will be required for bingo clubs and casinos. The appropriate licensing authority is the gaming licensing committee of the local petty sessions area and the committee is required to meet four times a year in January, April, July and October. Other dates may be set for meeting by the committee.

15.9.1 Preliminary considerations

The following should be brought to the attention of prospective buyers before an application for the grant of a licence is made:

1. Casinos can only be located in certain areas of the country – the permitted areas are set out in the Gaming Clubs (Permitted Areas) Regulations 1971, SI 1971/1538.

2. Only permitted games are allowed in casinos (1968 Act, Sched.2, para.3) – the most common games are American Roulette, Blackjack, Punto Banco and Casino Stud Poker.
3. The applicant should familiarise himself with:
   (a) the Gaming Board's current Memorandum of Advice;
   (b) the Gaming Board's current policies (set out in its annual reports);
   (c) the Gaming Board Guidelines to the casino industry.
4. A certificate of consent from the Gaming Board is a prerequisite to the grant of any gaming licence;
5. All casino staff and bingo club staff must hold a certificate of approval issued by the Gaming Board.

15.9.2 Board consent

To be eligible for the grant of a licence, the applicant must have obtained a certificate of consent from the Gaming Board in respect of the particular premises (1968 Act, Sched.2, para.3). The certificate is in force for a limited period of time and application for a licence must be made within this specified time. If the certificate obtained is limited to a bingo club licence, then the applicant is only eligible to apply for a bingo licence.

The criteria that must be satisfied before such a consent is issued are as follows.

1. If the applicant is an individual, he must be over 21 years of age, resident in Great Britain and have been resident throughout the preceding six-month period.
2. If the applicant is a body corporate it must have been incorporated in Great Britain.
3. The Board must be satisfied that the applicant is likely to be capable of and diligent in securing that:
   (a) the provisions of the Gaming Act 1968 and any relevant regulations made under it will be properly conducted;
   (b) gaming on those premises will be fairly and properly conducted;
   (c) the premises will be conducted without disorder or disturbance.

In reaching its decision, the Board may take into account the character, reputation and financial standing of the applicant and anyone else by whom the club would be managed or for whose benefit the club would be carried on. The Board may also consider 'any other circumstances appearing to them to be relevant in determining whether the applicant is likely to be capable of and diligent in securing compliance with the Act and regulations'.

15.9.3 Application for grant of a gaming licence

Detailed provisions for the application for a new gaming or bingo-only licence are set out in Sched.2, paras.5–7 to the Gaming Act 1968.

An application for the grant of a licence can be made at any time by:

- an existing club, in relation to premises currently being used by that club or premises that are intended to be used if the licence is granted;
- a club that is intended to be formed, for whose purpose the relevant premises will be used if the licence is granted.

Application is made using the prescribed form to the chief executive of the gaming licensing committee for the area in which the premises are situated and must be accompanied by the certificate of consent issued by the Gaming Board and a plan of the premises.

Copies of the application must be sent within seven days of making the application to the following:

- the Gaming Board;
- the chief officer of police for the area;
- the local authority for the area;
- the fire authority for the area;
- the collector of customs and excise for the area.

Within 14 days of making the application, the applicant must ensure that a notice is published in a newspaper circulating in the area containing the following information:

- the name of the applicant;
- the name of the club;
- the location of the club premises;
- whether the application is for a bingo licence or another licence under the Act;
- a statement inviting anyone wishing to object to send two copies of a brief statement in writing of the grounds of the objection to the licensing authority before the date specified in the notice.

A copy of the newspaper containing the notice must be sent to the chief executive of the committee as proof of publication. A notice similar to the one placed in the newspaper must also be displayed outside the entrance to the premises to be licensed (or inside provided it can be easily seen by people outside) not later than 14 days before the date specified in the advert.

The chief executive of the licensing committee will send notice in writing of the date, time and place of the meeting to consider the application to the following:

- the applicant;
- all those served with a copy of the application;
- anyone who has objected and not withdrawn their objection;

and will also display a notice of the meeting at the courthouse. If any objections have been made, a copy must be enclosed with the notice of hearing sent to the applicant.

Although power exists for the licensing committee to grant a licence without a hearing if there are no objections, in practice a hearing normally takes place. If objections are made and not withdrawn, the applicant, the objector, all recipients of the notice and the Gaming Board are entitled to be heard.

15.9.4 Renewal of a gaming licence

Gaming licences are valid for only 12 months and must therefore be renewed each year. The application to renew may not be made earlier than five months nor later than two months before the date on which the licence is due to expire. However, there is a power to consider applications outside this period if the committee is satisfied that the failure to apply was due to inadvertence and application is made before the end of such extended period as the committee allows.

The procedure and timetable for renewal is basically similar to that for an application for grant and is set out in Sched.2, para.12 to the Gaming Act 1968 and the particulars in the Gaming Clubs (Licensing) Regulations 1969, SI 1969/1110.

Within seven days of submitting the application to the gaming licensing committee, the applicant must send a copy to:

- the Gaming Board;
- the chief officer of police for the area in which the premises are situated;
- the local authority for that area;
- the fire authority for that area; and
- the collector of customs and excise for that area.

The responsibility for advertising the renewal application is that of the chief executive of the committee. Such notice must be published in a newspaper circulating in the area within 14 days of the application being made. The notice must state that anyone wishing to object to the renewal should submit two copies of a brief statement of the grounds of their objection by the date specified in the notice (Gaming Act 1968, Sched.2, para.13).

Copies of any objections received must be sent to the applicant and all other recipients of the application not less than seven days before the hearing of the renewal application.

If no objections have been submitted, the renewal application may be heard in the absence of the applicant. If objections are made and not withdrawn, the applicant, the objector, all recipients of the notice and the Gaming Board are entitled to be heard.

As with the grant of a licence, on renewal, the gaming licensing committee possesses the same powers to impose conditions. These may be conditions that restrict the hours of gaming to prevent disturbance or annoyance to other occupiers of premises in the vicinity. Conditions may also restrict the type of games to be played or they may restrict the gaming to certain parts of the premises.

It is important to note that an application for renewal may be deemed to be an application for a new licence if it seeks materially different facilities from those included in the current licence.

15.9.5 Grounds for refusal of grant or renewal

The grounds on which the justices may or must refuse to grant a licence are set out in paras.18–20 and 22 of Sched.2 to the Gaming Act 1968 and should be addressed by the applicant prior to making an application.

The gaming committee may refuse to grant a licence if it is not shown to its satisfaction that a substantial demand already exists for gaming facilities of the kind to be provided if the licence were granted. In considering whether existing facilities are or are not sufficient, the committee should have regard to both the quantity and quality of those facilities. It can therefore take into account the fact that the proposed premises will provide more suitable facilities than already exist.

If it is shown to the satisfaction of the committee that such a demand already exists in its area, the committee still has the discretion to refuse the application if it is not satisfied that there are no gaming facilities of that type available in the area, or in another area that is reasonably accessible to prospective players, or that the existing facilities are insufficient to meet the demand.

However, even if the committee considers that the demand has not been demonstrated to its satisfaction, it still has a discretion to grant the application.

The committee may also refuse an application for grant or renewal if it is satisfied that (Gaming Act 1968, Sched.2, para.20):

- the relevant premises are unsuitable by reason of their layout, character or location;
- the applicant is not a fit and proper person to be the holder of a licence under the 1968 Act;
- if the licence were granted or renewed, the club would be managed by, or carried on for the benefit of, a person other than the applicant who would himself be refused renewal of the licence on the grounds that he is not a fit and proper person;
- the licensing authority, the Board, the police, the local authority or the fire authority have been refused reasonable facilities to inspect the premises;
- any duty payable under various statutes remains unpaid;
- any bingo duty remains unpaid.

If any bingo duty that is payable has not been made, then the gaming committee *must* refuse an application to grant or renew, it has no discretion in this matter.

There are also a number of other discretionary grounds on which renewal may be refused (Gaming Act 1968, Sched.2, para.21):

- a lack of demand for the gaming facilities offered;
- a conviction of any person of offences under the Act or Regulations in connection with the relevant premises;
- the premises have been conducted in a manner that has failed to prevent disturbance or disorder;
- while a licence has been in force for the premises, gaming has been conducted on the premises dishonestly;
- the premises have become the resort for criminals or prostitutes or used for other unlawful purposes;
- fire precautions have not been observed.

As noted above all casino and bingo club staff must hold certificates of approval and, if such a certificate has been revoked in respect of a staff member for the relevant premises, there is a further discretionary ground for refusal of renewal.

15.10 TRANSFERS OF GAMING LICENCES

There are provisions for the transfer of gaming licences (Gaming Act 1968, Sched.2, paras.58–61). The proposed transferee requires a certificate of consent from the Gaming Board before an application for the transfer of the existing licence can be made. The same rules apply to the application for consent as applied for the original applicant, and the application for transfer must be made during the period of validity of the consent.

An application for transfer may be made at any time in the prescribed form to the chief executive to the gaming licensing committee. Copies of the application must be sent within seven days to:

- the Gaming Board;
- the police;
- the local authority; and
- the collector of customs and excise.

The applicant must publish a notice of the application in a newspaper circulating in the area within 14 days and this must include specified information and require objectors to give written notice of objection within the period specified in the notice. A similar notice must be displayed outside the premises.

The committee must grant the transfer unless one of the following grounds applies:

- the applicant is not a fit and proper person;
- the club is carried on for the benefit of a person to whom a transfer would not be granted;
- duty payable by the applicant under various statutes has not been paid.

15.11 RESTRICTIONS ON PARTICIPATING IN GAMING

In order to participate in gaming in licensed gaming establishments it is necessary to be a member of the gaming club or to be a *bona fide* guest of a member of the club (Gaming Act 1968, s.12). Eligibility requirements provide that at least 24 hours must have elapsed between becoming a member and participating in gaming.

Under 18s are excluded from entry to premises licensed for casino gaming and, whilst permitted to be present in bingo clubs, are excluded from participation in the games.

Gaming is not permitted on a Sunday between the hours of 4 a.m. and 2 p.m.

Detailed rules relating to the games that may be played, charges, levies, credit and prizes are set out in Part II of the Gaming Act 1968 and in the myriad of Regulations made under that Act. In this respect, the practitioner is advised to refer to a solicitor specialising in gaming law to advise the clients on the many rules and regulations that apply and offences that may be committed.

15.12 CHANGE OF DIRECTORS

If the gaming licence is held by a body corporate, any change of directors or change in the persons in accordance with whose directions or instructions the directors are accustomed to act, must be notified to the chief executive of the licensing committee, the police and the Gaming Board as soon as is reasonably practical.

15.13 GAMING ON PREMISES LICENSED FOR SALE OF ALCOHOL

No gaming licence is required in order to play dominoes and cribbage and other specially authorised games on premises licensed for the sale of alcohol (Gaming Act 1968, s.6).

Application for authorisation to play specified games is made by the premises licence holder (holder of justices' on-licence, other than a Part IV licence, prior to the coming into force of the 2003 Act) to the relevant licensing authority (licensing justices prior to the coming into force of the 2003 Act) for the area where the premises are situated. There are no provisions prescribing the form of such an application, but it may be sensible to send notice of the application to the police as well.

Such games as permitted by this section may be played for either prizes or stakes, but the licensing authority (licensing justices) may impose restrictions to prevent play for high stakes from taking place or in circumstances which constitute an inducement to resort to the premises primarily for the purpose of taking part in any such gaming.

15.14 GAMING MACHINES

The rules for providing facilities for gaming by way of machines are contained in Part III of the Gaming Act 1968. It should be noted that a licence for gaming machines is only required where an element of chance is involved. If the machine provides a game which is one of pure skill and there is no element of chance, a licence is not required.

Gaming by way of machines may take place on premises licensed or registered for other forms of gaming without any further permission (Gaming Act 1968, s.31).

15.14.1 Section 34 permits in premises licensed to sell alcohol

The holder of a premises licence granted under the 2003 Act (or a justices' on-licence, other than a Part IV licence, in force prior to the second appointed day (24 November 2005)) may apply for a permit to operate amusement with prizes (AWP) gaming machines under the provisions of s.34 of the Gaming Act 1968 (Gaming Act 1968, Sched.9, para.5(1)(a)). The application is currently made to the liquor licensing justices, but when the 2003 Act is in force the responsibility for the grant of these permits will transfer from the licensing justices to the local authority.

Under Sched.9, para.10A of the Gaming Act 1968, all AWP machines must be located in a bar of the premises. The 2003 Act amends this paragraph in respect of the meaning of 'bar' so that in this context it means any place which, by virtue of the premises licence, may be used for the supply of alcohol, and which is exclusively or mainly used for the supply and consumption of alcohol.

Under the transitional provisions of the 2003 Act conversion of the existing licence into a premises licence does not provide authorisation for activities that take place on the premises that are not existing licensable activities, such as AWP machines operated under a section 34 permit. Accordingly, as the law currently stands, a converted premises licence will not provide authorisation for AWP machines. However, it is expected that secondary legislation currently in draft form will be introduced before the second appointed day (24 November 2005) which will provide that s.34 permits will be deemed to have effect as if they had been granted to the holder of the premises licence.

Detailed compliance rules for the operation and use of AWP machines are set out in s.34 of the Gaming Act 1968. At the current time, the maximum charge for playing once on a machine is 30 pence, and the maximum pay-out per game is £5 or tokens exchangeable for non-monetary prizes not exceeding £8. Alternatively, the prize may be the opportunity to play one or more further games.

The permit is valid for three years and is renewable.

15.14.2 Section 34 permits in arcades and other public places

Section 34 permits may also be granted for premises other than those licensed to sell alcohol in order to operate gaming machines, but in this case the application is made to the appropriate local authority (Gaming Act 1968, Sched.9).

It should be noted that local authorities have the power to pass 'blanket' resolutions in relation to the grant and renewal of s.34 permits. These resolutions can refuse the grant of permits in respect of premises of a class defined in the resolution, or they can refuse renewal of licences already granted in that class. In addition, they can impose conditions limiting the number of machines for which a permit will be used (1968 Act, Sched.9, paras.3 and 4).

The restrictions on the class of premises which may be refused permits specifically exclude the arcade type of premises which are used, wholly or mainly, for the provision of amusements by means of machines to which Part III of the Gaming Act 1968 applies. However, the applicant must bear in mind that the power to grant a permit is discretionary and may therefore still be refused.

The power to impose conditions is limited to those authorised by the council resolution or, except in the case of arcades, limiting the number of machines that may be made available for gaming.

Permits are valid for three years and may then be renewed for a further three years. Local authorities do not have fixed dates for renewal, but it is important to ensure that renewal notices are submitted at least one month in advance of the expiry date.

Once a permit has been granted, the local authority may only refuse a renewal of a permit in relation to arcades on the following grounds:

- the local authority or its authorised representatives have been refused reasonable facilities to view the premises;

- by reasons of the conditions or manner in which machines, to which Part III of the Gaming Act 1968 applies, have been used on the premises or any other amusements have been provided or conducted on the premises, while the permit has been in force.

The latter has been interpreted by local authorities as including the conduct of staff on the premises which has encouraged the excessive use of gaming machines.

An application for a permit may be made either by the occupier or by any person who proposes, if the application for a permit is granted, to become the occupier of the premises. Accordingly, provided the seller agrees, it is possible to have a conditional contract to purchase the premises dependent on the grant of the s.34 permit. Application can be made in the name of a limited company.

Permits are not transferable and are no longer valid if the holder ceases to be the occupier of the premises. It is therefore essential that the purchaser obtain the grant of the permit prior to completion of the sale.

15.15 MEMBERS CLUBS AND MINERS' WELFARE INSTITUTES

15.15.1 Registration for gaming under Part II

Members clubs and miners' welfare institutes wanting to use their premises for gaming are eligible to apply for registration under Part II of the Gaming Act 1968.

To be eligible for registration, a club must be a *bona fide* members club, have at least 25 members and be of a more than temporary character (1968 Act, Sched.3, para.7(1)).

The procedures for application are set out in Sched.3 to the Gaming Act 1968. Application is made to the chief executive of the gaming committee on the prescribed form and containing the prescribed information. A copy of the application must also be sent to the police within seven days of making the application and to the collector of customs and excise for the area. A notice of the application must also be published in a newspaper circulating in the area with 14 days of making the application. There is, however, no requirement that the club post a notice of the application outside the entrance to its premises or to serve a copy of the application on either the local authority or the fire authority.

If the committee is not satisfied as to the eligibility of the club as set out above, it must refuse to register the club. In addition, the committee must refuse the application if it appears that the principal purpose of the club is gaming, unless satisfied that the gaming consists exclusively of bridge and/or whist (1968 Act, Sched.3, para.7(2)).

15.15.2 Part III registration

Part II registration relates to the use of premises of members clubs and miners' welfare institutes for gaming other than by machines. Registration under Part III of the Gaming Act 1968 permits gaming by machines in such premises (1968 Act, Sched.7).

Application for registration is made to the chief executive to the licensing authority and may be made at any time. Application is made on the prescribed form and should contain the prescribed information. A copy of the application must be sent within seven days of making the application to the police, but there is no requirement for copies to be sent to any other authorities. There is also no requirement for advertising the application either in the press or on the premises and so there is no procedure for receiving or hearing objections.

The licensing committee may refuse to register a club if it appears that the premises are frequented mainly by under 18 year olds, or if they are not satisfied that it is a *bona fide* members club or has fewer than 25 members or is of a temporary character.

15.16 EXEMPTION FOR GAMING IN CLUBS

As noted earlier, gaming may take place in a club without the requirement for either licensing or registration provided the following criteria are satisfied:

- games must be limited to those where there is no banker (s.2(1));
- games must be limited to those where the chances are equal as between players;
- there must not be a levy on stakes or winnings (s.4);
- there must not be any charge for taking part in gaming apart from prescribed permitted charges (Gaming Act 1968, s.3(1), s.40).

The membership subscription of a club is not to be taken as such a charge, even if gaming is the main object of the club, provided that payment is made quarterly or less frequently (s.3(3)).

15.17 GAMBLING ACT 2005

The Gambling Act 2005 received Royal Assent on 7 April 2005, no date has yet been given for its coming into force, although at the time of writing it is expected to be fully implemented by Autumn 2007.

This new legislation consolidates all gambling legislation, including betting, gaming and lotteries (other than the National Lottery and spread betting) into a single Act. Remote gambling will also be covered. All existing statutes relating to betting, gaming and lotteries will be repealed and a single, comprehensive regime established.

The main provisions of the Gambling Act 2005 can be summarised as follows.

1. The introduction of licensing objectives:
   (a) preventing gambling from being a source of crime, being associated with crime or being used to support crime;
   (b) ensuring that gambling is conducted in a fair and open way;
   (c) protecting children and other vulnerable people from being harmed or exploited by gambling.
2. The introduction of operating licences for facilities for gambling, personal licences for individuals, and premises licences for the use of premises.
3. The creation of a Gambling Commission which will replace the existing Gaming Board for Great Britain and which will, in addition, assume regulatory responsibilities for all gambling in the UK. The Commission will have power to:
   (a) issue operating licences for commercial gambling and personal licences for individuals;
   (b) license betting, gaming (to include bingo, casinos, gaming machine operators, and internet gaming) and certain lottery operators;
   (c) impose conditions on any licence granted;
   (d) review, amend or revoke licences;
   (e) enforce the law on gambling with powers of entry, seizure and search, and the power to initiate public prosecutions.
4. Local authorities will have the responsibility for licensing gambling premises and for issuing permits to authorise other gambling facilities. The Commission will be required to issue guidance to local authorities on the exercise of their power.
5. The current restriction on the geographical location of gaming premises will be removed (although local authorities will be given powers to prevent new casinos opening in their areas).
6. The requirement for an applicant to establish an unmet demand for gambling in the area is removed.
7. Membership requirements and the 24 hour rule for casinos and bingo clubs are abolished.
8. Casinos will be divided into four categories – small, large, regional and existing.
9. There will be one regional casino, eight large casinos, and eight small casinos in each local authority area.
10. Each of the regional, large and small casinos will have specified minimum table gaming and non-gambling areas and maximum number of gaming machines.

11. Existing casinos will continue to operate under transitional provisions with an increase to a 20 machines entitlement and an increased stake to £2.
12. All but small and existing casinos will be allowed to provide bingo and betting on the premises.
13. A separate remote gambling licence is required for gambling by internet, mobile phone, interactive television or similar method.

APPENDIX A

Extracts from legislation

A1	Licensing Act 2003, Part 3 – Premises licences
A2	Licensing Act 2003, Schedule 1, Part 1 – Provision of regulated entertainment: general definitions
A3	Licensing Act 2003, Schedule 4 – Personal licence: relevant offences
A4	Summary of spent convictions under the Rehabilitation of Offenders Act 1974

APPENDIX A1

Licensing Act 2003, Part 3 – Premises licences

Introductory

11 Premises licence

In this Act 'premises licence' means a licence granted under this Part, in respect of any premises, which authorises the premises to be used for one or more licensable activities.

12 The relevant licensing authority

(1) For the purposes of this Part the 'relevant licensing authority' in relation to any premises is determined in accordance with this section.
(2) Subject to subsection (3), the relevant licensing authority is the authority in whose area the premises are situated.
(3) Where the premises are situated in the areas of two or more licensing authorities, the relevant licensing authority is –
  (a) the licensing authority in whose area the greater or greatest part of the premises is situated, or
  (b) if there is no authority to which paragraph (a) applies, such one of those authorities as is nominated in accordance with subsection (4).
(4) In a case within subsection (3)(b) –
  (a) an applicant for a premises licence must nominate one of the licensing authorities as the relevant licensing authority in relation to the application and any licence granted as a result of it, and
  (b) an applicant for a statement under section 29 (provisional statement) in respect of the premises must nominate one of the licensing authorities as the relevant licensing authority in relation to the statement.

13 Authorised persons, interested parties and responsible authorities

(1) In this Part in relation to any premises each of the following expressions has the meaning given to it by this section –
'authorised person',
'interested party',
'responsible authority'.

(2) 'Authorised person' means any of the following –
- (a) an officer of a licensing authority in whose area the premises are situated who is authorised by that authority for the purposes of this Act,
- (b) an inspector appointed under section 18 of the Fire Precautions Act 1971 (c.40),
- (c) an inspector appointed under section 19 of the Health and Safety at Work etc. Act 1974 (c.37),
- (d) an officer of a local authority, in whose area the premises are situated, who is authorised by that authority for the purposes of exercising one or more of its statutory functions in relation to minimising or preventing the risk of pollution of the environment or of harm to human health,
- (e) in relation to a vessel, an inspector, or a surveyor of ships, appointed under section 256 of the Merchant Shipping Act 1995 (c.21),
- (f) a person prescribed for the purposes of this subsection.

(3) 'Interested party' means any of the following –
- (a) a person living in the vicinity of the premises,
- (b) a body representing persons who live in that vicinity,
- (c) a person involved in a business in that vicinity,
- (d) a body representing persons involved in such businesses.

(4) 'Responsible authority' means any of the following –
- (a) the chief officer of police for any police area in which the premises are situated,
- (b) the fire authority for any area in which the premises are situated,
- (c) the enforcing authority within the meaning given by section 18 of the Health and Safety at Work etc. Act 1974 for any area in which the premises are situated,
- (d) the local planning authority within the meaning given by the Town and Country Planning Act 1990 (c.8) for any area in which the premises are situated,
- (e) the local authority by which statutory functions are exercisable in any area in which the premises are situated in relation to minimising or preventing the risk of pollution of the environment or of harm to human health,
- (f) a body which –

(i) represents those who, in relation to any such area, are responsible for, or interested in, matters relating to the protection of children from harm, and
(ii) is recognised by the licensing authority for that area for the purposes of this section as being competent to advise it on such matters,

(g) any licensing authority (other than the relevant licensing authority) in whose area part of the premises is situated,
(h) in relation to a vessel –
(i) a navigation authority (within the meaning of section 221(1) of the Water Resources Act 1991 (c.57) having functions in relation to the waters where the vessel is usually moored or berthed or any waters where it is, or is proposed to be, navigated at a time when it is used for licensable activities,
(ii) the Environment Agency,
(iii) the British Waterways Board, or
(iv) the Secretary of State,

(i) a person prescribed for the purposes of this subsection.

(5) For the purposes of this section, 'statutory function' means a function conferred by or under any enactment.

14 Meaning of 'supply of alcohol'

For the purposes of this Part the 'supply of alcohol' means –
(a) the sale by retail of alcohol, or
(b) the supply of alcohol by or on behalf of a club to, or to the order of, a member of the club.

15 Meaning of 'designated premises supervisor'

(1) In this Act references to the 'designated premises supervisor', in relation to a premises licence, are to the individual for the time being specified in that licence as the premises supervisor.
(2) Nothing in this Act prevents an individual who holds a premises licence from also being specified in the licence as the premises supervisor.

Grant of premises licence

16 Applicant for premises licence

(1) The following persons may apply for a premises licence –
(a) a person who carries on, or proposes to carry on, a business which involves the use of the premises for the licensable activities to which the application relates,

(b) a person who makes the application pursuant to –
  (i) any statutory function discharged by that person which relates to those licensable activities, or
  (ii) any function discharged by that person by virtue of Her Majesty's prerogative,
(c) a recognised club,
(d) a charity,
(e) the proprietor of an educational institution,
(f) a health service body,
(g) a person who is registered under Part 2 of the Care Standards Act 2000 (c.14) in respect of an independent hospital,
(h) the chief officer of police of a police force in England and Wales,
(i) a person of such other description as may be prescribed.

(2) But an individual may not apply for a premises licence unless he is aged 18 or over.

(3) In this section –
'charity' has the same meaning as in section 96(1) of the Charities Act 1993 (c.10);
'educational institution' means –
(a) a school, or an institution within the further or higher education sector, within the meaning of section 4 of the Education Act 1996 (c.56), or
(b) a college (including any institution in the nature of a college), school, hall or other institution of a university, in circumstances where the university receives financial support under section 65 of the Further and Higher Education Act 1992 (c.13);
'health service body' means –
(a) an NHS trust established by virtue of section 5 of the National Health Service and Community Care Act 1990 (c.19),
(b) a Primary Care Trust established by virtue of section 16A of the National Health Service Act 1977 (c.49), or
(c) a Local Health Board established by virtue of section 16BA of that Act;
'independent hospital' has the same meaning as in section 2(2) of the Care Standards Act 2000 (c.14);
'proprietor' –
(a) in relation to a school within the meaning of section 4 of the Education Act 1996, has the same meaning as in section 579(1) of that Act, and
(b) in relation to an educational institution other than such a school, means the governing body of that institution within the meaning of section 90(1) of the Further and Higher Education Act 1992; and
'statutory function' means a function conferred by or under any enactment.

17 Application for premises licence

(1) An application for a premises licence must be made to the relevant licensing authority.

(2) Subsection (1) is subject to regulations under –
 (a) section 54 (form etc. of applications etc.);
 (b) section 55 (fees to accompany applications etc.).

(3) An application under this section must also be accompanied –
 (a) by an operating schedule,
 (b) by a plan of the premises to which the application relates, in the prescribed form, and
 (c) if the licensable activities to which the application relates ('the relevant licensable activities') include the supply of alcohol, by a form of consent in the prescribed form given by the individual whom the applicant wishes to have specified in the premises licence as the premises supervisor.

(4) An 'operating schedule' is a document which is in the prescribed form and includes a statement of the following matters –
 (a) the relevant licensable activities,
 (b) the times during which it is proposed that the relevant licensable activities are to take place,
 (c) any other times during which it is proposed that the premises are to be open to the public,
 (d) where the applicant wishes the licence to have effect for a limited period, that period,
 (e) where the relevant licensable activities include the supply of alcohol, prescribed information in respect of the individual whom the applicant wishes to have specified in the premises licence as the premises supervisor,
 (f) where the relevant licensable activities include the supply of alcohol, whether the supplies are proposed to be for consumption on the premises or off the premises, or both,
 (g) the steps which it is proposed to take to promote the licensing objectives,
 (h) such other matters as may be prescribed.

(5) The Secretary of State must by regulations –
 (a) require an applicant to advertise his application within the prescribed period –
  (i) in the prescribed form, and
  (ii) in a manner which is prescribed and is likely to bring the application to the attention of the interested parties likely to be affected by it;

(b) require an applicant to give notice of his application to each responsible authority, and such other persons as may be prescribed, within the prescribed period;

(c) prescribe the period during which interested parties and responsible authorities may make representations to the relevant licensing authority about the application.

18 Determination of application for premises licence

(1) This section applies where the relevant licensing authority –

(a) receives an application for a premises licence made in accordance with section 17, and

(b) is satisfied that the applicant has complied with any requirement imposed on him under subsection (5) of that section.

(2) Subject to subsection (3), the authority must grant the licence in accordance with the application subject only to –

(a) such conditions as are consistent with the operating schedule accompanying the application, and

(b) any conditions which must under section 19, 20 or 21 be included in the licence.

(3) Where relevant representations are made, the authority must –

(a) hold a hearing to consider them, unless the authority, the applicant and each person who has made such representations agree that a hearing is unnecessary, and

(b) having regard to the representations, take such of the steps mentioned in subsection (4) (if any) as it considers necessary for the promotion of the licensing objectives.

(4) The steps are –

(a) to grant the licence subject to –

(i) the conditions mentioned in subsection (2)(a) modified to such extent as the authority considers necessary for the promotion of the licensing objectives, and

(ii) any condition which must under section 19, 20 or 21 be included in the licence;

(b) to exclude from the scope of the licence any of the licensable activities to which the application relates;

(c) to refuse to specify a person in the licence as the premises supervisor;

(d) to reject the application.

(5) For the purposes of subsection (4)(a)(i) the conditions mentioned in subsection (2)(a) are modified if any of them is altered or omitted or any new condition is added.

(6) For the purposes of this section, 'relevant representations' means representations which –

(a) are about the likely effect of the grant of the premises licence on the promotion of the licensing objectives,
(b) meet the requirements of subsection (7),
(c) if they relate to the identity of the person named in the application as the proposed premises supervisor, meet the requirements of subsection (9), and
(d) are not excluded representations by virtue of section 32 (restriction on making representations following issue of provisional statement).

(7) The requirements of this subsection are –
(a) that the representations were made by an interested party or responsible authority within the period prescribed under section 17(5)(c),
(b) that they have not been withdrawn, and
(c) in the case of representations made by an interested party (who is not also a responsible authority), that they are not, in the opinion of the relevant licensing authority, frivolous or vexatious.

(8) Where the authority determines for the purposes of subsection (7)(c) that any representations are frivolous or vexatious, it must notify the person who made them of the reasons for its determination.

(9) The requirements of this subsection are that the representations –
(a) were made by a chief officer of police for a police area in which the premises are situated, and
(b) include a statement that, due to the exceptional circumstances of the case, he is satisfied that the designation of the person concerned as the premises supervisor under the premises licence would undermine the crime prevention objective.

(10) In discharging its duty under subsection (2) or (3)(b), a licensing authority may grant a licence under this section subject to different conditions in respect of –
(a) different parts of the premises concerned;
(b) different licensable activities.

19 Mandatory conditions where licence authorises supply of alcohol

(1) Where a premises licence authorises the supply of alcohol, the licence must include the following conditions.

(2) The first condition is that no supply of alcohol may be made under the premises licence –
(a) at a time when there is no designated premises supervisor in respect of the premises licence, or
(b) at a time when the designated premises supervisor does not hold a personal licence or his personal licence is suspended.

(3) The second condition is that every supply of alcohol under the premises licence must be made or authorised by a person who holds a personal licence.

20 Mandatory condition: exhibition of films

(1) Where a premises licence authorises the exhibition of films, the licence must include a condition requiring the admission of children to the exhibition of any film to be restricted in accordance with this section.
(2) Where the film classification body is specified in the licence, unless subsection (3)(b) applies, admission of children must be restricted in accordance with any recommendation made by that body.
(3) Where –
(a) the film classification body is not specified in the licence, or
(b) the relevant licensing authority has notified the holder of the licence that this subsection applies to the film in question,
admission of children must be restricted in accordance with any recommendation made by that licensing authority.
(4) In this section –
'children' means persons aged under 18; and
'film classification body' means the person or persons designated as the authority under section 4 of the Video Recordings Act 1984 (c.39) (authority to determine suitability of video works for classification).

21 Mandatory condition: door supervision

(1) Where a premises licence includes a condition that at specified times one or more individuals must be at the premises to carry out a security activity, the licence must include a condition that each such individual must be licensed by the Security Industry Authority.
(2) But nothing in subsection (1) requires such a condition to be imposed –
(a) in respect of premises within paragraph 8(3)(a) of Schedule 2 to the Private Security Industry Act 2001 (c.12) (premises with premises licences authorising plays or films), or
(b) in respect of premises in relation to –
(i) any occasion mentioned in paragraph 8(3)(b) or (c) of that Schedule (premises being used exclusively by club with club premises certificate, under a temporary event notice authorising plays or films or under a gaming licence), or
(ii) any occasion within paragraph 8(3)(d) of that Schedule (occasions prescribed by regulations under that Act).
(3) For the purposes of this section –
(a) 'security activity' means an activity to which paragraph 2(1)(a) of that Schedule applies, and

(b) paragraph 8(5) of that Schedule (interpretation of references to an occasion) applies as it applies in relation to paragraph 8 of that Schedule.

22 Prohibited conditions: plays

(1) In relation to a premises licence which authorises the performance of plays, no condition may be attached to the licence as to the nature of the plays which may be performed, or the manner of performing plays, under the licence.
(2) But subsection (1) does not prevent a licensing authority imposing, in accordance with section 18(2)(a) or (3)(b), 35(3)(b) or 52(3), any condition which it considers necessary on the grounds of public safety.

23 Grant or rejection of application

(1) Where an application is granted under section 18, the relevant licensing authority must forthwith –
   (a) give a notice to that effect to –
      (i) the applicant,
      (ii) any person who made relevant representations in respect of the application, and
      (iii) the chief officer of police for the police area (or each police area) in which the premises are situated, and
   (b) issue the applicant with the licence and a summary of it.
(2) Where relevant representations were made in respect of the application, the notice under subsection (1)(a) must state the authority's reasons for its decision as to the steps (if any) to take under section 18(3)(b).
(3) Where an application is rejected under section 18, the relevant licensing authority must forthwith give a notice to that effect, stating its reasons for the decision, to –
   (a) the applicant,
   (b) any person who made relevant representations in respect of the application, and
   (c) the chief officer of police for the police area (or each police area) in which the premises are situated.
(4) In this section 'relevant representations' has the meaning given in section 18(6).

24 Form of licence and summary

(1) A premises licence and the summary of a premises licence must be in the prescribed form.

(2) Regulations under subsection (1) must, in particular, provide for the licence to –
   (a) specify the name and address of the holder;
   (b) include a plan of the premises to which the licence relates;
   (c) if the licence has effect for a limited period, specify that period;
   (d) specify the licensable activities for which the premises may be used;
   (e) if the licensable activities include the supply of alcohol, specify the name and address of the individual (if any) who is the premises supervisor in respect of the licence;
   (f) specify the conditions subject to which the licence has effect.

25 Theft, loss, etc. of premises licence or summary

(1) Where a premises licence or summary is lost, stolen, damaged or destroyed, the holder of the licence may apply to the relevant licensing authority for a copy of the licence or summary.
(2) Subsection (1) is subject to regulations under section 55(1) (fee to accompany applications).
(3) Where an application is made in accordance with this section, the relevant licensing authority must issue the holder of the licence with a copy of the licence or summary (certified by the authority to be a true copy) if it is satisfied that –
   (a) the licence or summary has been lost, stolen, damaged or destroyed, and
   (b) where it has been lost or stolen, the holder has reported that loss or theft to the police.
(4) The copy issued under this section must be a copy of the premises licence or summary in the form in which it existed immediately before it was lost, stolen, damaged or destroyed.
(5) This Act applies in relation to a copy issued under this section as it applies in relation to an original licence or summary.

Duration of licence

26 Period of validity of premises licence

(1) Subject to sections 27 and 28, a premises licence has effect until such time as –
   (a) it is revoked under section 52, or
   (b) if it specifies that it has effect for a limited period, that period expires.
(2) But a premises licence does not have effect during any period when it is suspended under section 52.

27 Death, incapacity, insolvency etc. of licence holder

(1) A premises licence lapses if the holder of the licence –
  (a) dies,
  (b) becomes mentally incapable (within the meaning of section 13(1) of the Enduring Powers of Attorney Act 1985 (c.29)),
  (c) becomes insolvent,
  (d) is dissolved, or
  (e) if it is a club, ceases to be a recognised club.

(2) This section is subject to sections 47 and 50 (which make provision for the reinstatement of the licence in certain circumstances).

(3) For the purposes of this section, an individual becomes insolvent on –
  (a) the approval of a voluntary arrangement proposed by him,
  (b) being adjudged bankrupt or having his estate sequestrated, or
  (c) entering into a deed of arrangement made for the benefit of his creditors or a trust deed for his creditors.

(4) For the purposes of this section, a company becomes insolvent on –
  (a) the approval of a voluntary arrangement proposed by its directors,
  (b) the appointment of an administrator in respect of the company,
  (c) the appointment of an administrative receiver in respect of the company, or
  (d) going into liquidation.

(5) An expression used in this section and in the Insolvency Act 1986 (c.45) has the same meaning in this section as in that Act.

28 Surrender of premises licence

(1) Where the holder of a premises licence wishes to surrender his licence he may give the relevant licensing authority a notice to that effect.

(2) The notice must be accompanied by the premises licence or, if that is not practicable, by a statement of the reasons for the failure to provide the licence.

(3) Where a notice of surrender is given in accordance with this section, the premises licence lapses on receipt of the notice by the authority.

(4) This section is subject to section 50 (which makes provision for the reinstatement in certain circumstances of a licence surrendered under this section).

Provisional statement

29 Application for a provisional statement where premises being built, etc.

(1) This section applies to premises which –
   (a) are being or are about to be constructed for the purpose of being used for one or more licensable activities, or
   (b) are being or are about to be extended or otherwise altered for that purpose (whether or not they are already being used for that purpose).

(2) A person may apply to the relevant licensing authority for a provisional statement if –
   (a) he is interested in the premises, and
   (b) where he is an individual, he is aged 18 or over.

(3) In this Act 'provisional statement' means a statement issued under section 31(2) or (3)(c).

(4) Subsection (2) is subject to regulations under –
   (a) section 54 (form etc. of applications etc.);
   (b) section 55 (fees to accompany applications etc.).

(5) An application under this section must also be accompanied by a schedule of works.

(6) A schedule of works is a document in the prescribed form which includes –
   (a) a statement made by or on behalf of the applicant including particulars of the premises to which the application relates and of the licensable activities for which the premises are to be used,
   (b) plans of the work being or about to be done at the premises, and
   (c) such other information as may be prescribed.

(7) For the purposes of this Part, in relation to any premises in respect of which an application for a provisional statement has been made, references to the work being satisfactorily completed are to work at the premises being completed in a manner which substantially complies with the schedule of works accompanying the application.

30 Advertisement of application for provisional statement

(1) This section applies where an application is made under section 29.

(2) The duty to make regulations imposed on the Secretary of State by section 17(5) (advertisement etc. of application) applies in relation to an application under section 29 as it applies in relation to an application under section 17.

(3) Regulations made under section 17(5)(a) by virtue of subsection (2) may, in particular, require advertisements to contain a statement in the prescribed form describing the effect of section 32 (restriction on representations following issue of a provisional statement).

31 Determination of application for provisional statement

(1) This section applies where the relevant licensing authority –
  (a) receives a provisional statement application, and
  (b) is satisfied that the applicant has complied with any requirement imposed on him by virtue of section 30.

(2) Where no relevant representations are made, the authority must issue the applicant with a statement to that effect.

(3) Where relevant representations are made, the authority must –
  (a) hold a hearing to consider them, unless the authority, the applicant and each person who has made such representations agree that a hearing is unnecessary,
  (b) determine whether, on the basis of those representations and the provisional statement application, it would consider it necessary to take any steps under section 18(3)(b) if, on the work being satisfactorily completed, it had to decide whether to grant a premises licence in the form described in the provisional statement application, and
  (c) issue the applicant with a statement which –
    (i) gives details of that determination, and
    (ii) states the authority's reasons for its decision as to the steps (if any) that it would be necessary to take under section 18(3)(b).

(4) The licensing authority must give a copy of the provisional statement to –
  (a) each person who made relevant representations, and
  (b) the chief officer of police for each police area in which the premises are situated.

(5) In this section 'relevant representations' means representations –
  (a) which are about the likely effect on the licensing objectives of the grant of a premises licence in the form described in the provisional statement application, if the work at the premises was satisfactorily completed, and
  (b) which meet the requirements of subsection (6).

(6) The requirements are –
  (a) that the representations are made by an interested party or responsible authority within the period prescribed under section 17(5)(c) by virtue of section 30,
  (b) that the representations have not been withdrawn, and
  (c) in the case of representations made by an interested party (who is not also a responsible authority), that they are not, in the opinion of the relevant licensing authority, frivolous or vexatious.

(7) Where the authority determines for the purposes of subsection (6)(c) that any representations are frivolous or vexatious, it must notify the person who made them of the reasons for its determination.

(8) In this section 'provisional statement application' means an application made in accordance with section 29.

32 Restriction on representations following provisional statement

(1) This section applies where a provisional statement has been issued in respect of any premises ('the relevant premises') and a person subsequently applies for a premises licence in respect of –
  (a) the relevant premises or a part of them, or
  (b) premises that are substantially the same as the relevant premises or a part of them.

(2) Where –
  (a) the application for the premises licence is an application for a licence in the same form as the licence described in the application for the provisional statement, and
  (b) the work described in the schedule of works accompanying the application for that statement has been satisfactorily completed,

representations made by a person ('the relevant person') in respect of the application for the premises licence are excluded representations for the purposes of section 18(6)(d) if subsection (3) applies.

(3) This subsection applies if –
  (a) given the information provided in the application for the provisional statement, the relevant person could have made the same, or substantially the same, representations about that application but failed to do so, without reasonable excuse, and
  (b) there has been no material change in circumstances relating either to the relevant premises or to the area in the vicinity of those premises since the provisional statement was made.

Duty to notify certain changes

33 Notification of change of name or address

(1) The holder of a premises licence must, as soon as is reasonably practicable, notify the relevant licensing authority of any change in –
  (a) his name or address,
  (b) unless the designated premises supervisor has already notified the authority under subsection (4), the name or address of that supervisor.

(2) Subsection (1) is subject to regulations under section 55(1) (fee to accompany application).

(3) A notice under subsection (1) must also be accompanied by the premises licence (or the appropriate part of the licence) or, if that is not practicable, by a statement of the reasons for the failure to produce the licence (or part).

(4) Where the designated premises supervisor under a premises licence is not the holder of the licence, he may notify the relevant licensing authority under this subsection of any change in his name or address.

(5) Where the designated premises supervisor gives a notice under subsection (4), he must, as soon as is reasonably practicable, give the holder of the premises licence a copy of that notice.

(6) A person commits an offence if he fails, without reasonable excuse, to comply with this section.

(7) A person guilty of an offence under subsection (6) is liable on summary conviction to a fine not exceeding level 2 on the standard scale.

Variation of licences

34 Application to vary premises licence

(1) The holder of a premises licence may apply to the relevant licensing authority for variation of the licence.

(2) Subsection (1) is subject to regulations under –
  (a) section 54 (form etc. of applications etc.);
  (b) section 55 (fees to accompany applications etc.).

(3) An application under this section must also be accompanied by the premises licence (or the appropriate part of that licence) or, if that is not practicable, by a statement of the reasons for the failure to provide the licence (or part).

(4) This section does not apply to an application within section 37(1) (application to vary licence to specify individual as premises supervisor).

(5) The duty to make regulations imposed on the Secretary of State by subsection (5) of section 17 (advertisement etc. of application) applies in relation to applications under this section as it applies in relation to applications under that section.

35 Determination of application under section 34

(1) This section applies where the relevant licensing authority –
  (a) receives an application, made in accordance with section 34, to vary a premises licence, and
  (b) is satisfied that the applicant has complied with any requirement imposed on him by virtue of subsection (5) of that section.

(2) Subject to subsection (3) and section 36(6), the authority must grant the application.

(3) Where relevant representations are made, the authority must –
  (a) hold a hearing to consider them, unless the authority, the applicant and each person who has made such representations agree that a hearing is unnecessary, and
  (b) having regard to the representations, take such of the steps mentioned in subsection (4) (if any) as it considers necessary for the promotion of the licensing objectives.

(4) The steps are –
  (a) to modify the conditions of the licence;
  (b) to reject the whole or part of the application;

and for this purpose the conditions of the licence are modified if any of them is altered or omitted or any new condition is added.

(5) In this section 'relevant representations' means representations which –
  (a) are about the likely effect of the grant of the application on the promotion of the licensing objectives, and
  (b) meet the requirements of subsection (6).

(6) The requirements are –
  (a) that the representations are made by an interested party or responsible authority within the period prescribed under section 17(5)(c) by virtue of section 34(5),
  (b) that they have not been withdrawn, and
  (c) in the case of representations made by an interested party (who is not also a responsible authority), that they are not, in the opinion of the relevant licensing authority, frivolous or vexatious.

(7) Subsections (2) and (3) are subject to sections 19, 20 and 21 (which require certain conditions to be included in premises licences).

36 Supplementary provision about determinations under section 35

(1) Where an application (or any part of an application) is granted under section 35, the relevant licensing authority must forthwith give a notice to that effect to –
  (a) the applicant,
  (b) any person who made relevant representations in respect of the application, and
  (c) the chief officer of police for the police area (or each police area) in which the premises are situated.

(2) Where relevant representations were made in respect of the application, the notice under subsection (1) must state the authority's reasons for its decision as to the steps (if any) to take under section 35(3)(b).

(3) The notice under subsection (1) must specify the time when the variation in question takes effect.

That time is the time specified in the application or, if that time is before the applicant is given that notice, such later time as the relevant licensing authority specifies in the notice.

(4) Where an application (or any part of an application) is rejected under section 35, the relevant licensing authority must forthwith give a notice to that effect stating its reasons for rejecting the application to –
  (a) the applicant,
  (b) any person who made relevant representations in respect of the application, and
  (c) the chief officer of police for the police area (or each police area) in which the premises are situated.

(5) Where the relevant licensing authority determines for the purposes of section 35(6)(c) that any representations are frivolous or vexatious, it must notify the person who made them of the reasons for that determination.

(6) A licence may not be varied under section 35 so as –
  (a) to extend the period for which the licence has effect, or
  (b) to vary substantially the premises to which it relates.

(7) In discharging its duty under subsection (2) or (3)(b) of that section, a licensing authority may vary a premises licence so that it has effect subject to different conditions in respect of –
  (a) different parts of the premises concerned;
  (b) different licensable activities.

(8) In this section 'relevant representations' has the meaning given in section 35(5).

37 Application to vary licence to specify individual as premises supervisor

(1) The holder of a premises licence may –
  (a) if the licence authorises the supply of alcohol, or
  (b) if he has applied under section 34 to vary the licence so that it authorises such supplies,

apply to vary the licence so as to specify the individual named in the application ('the proposed individual') as the premises supervisor.

(2) Subsection (1) is subject to regulations under –
  (a) section 54 (form etc. of applications etc.);
  (b) section 55 (fees to accompany applications etc.).

(3) An application under this section must also be accompanied by –
  (a) a form of consent in the prescribed form given by the proposed individual, and
  (b) the premises licence (or the appropriate part of that licence) or, if that is not practicable, a statement of the reasons for the failure to provide the licence (or part).

(4) The holder of the premises licence must give notice of his application –

(a) to the chief officer of police for the police area (or each police area) in which the premises are situated, and

(b) to the designated premises supervisor (if there is one),

and that notice must state whether the application is one to which section 38 applies.

(5) Where a chief officer of police notified under subsection (4) is satisfied that the exceptional circumstances of the case are such that granting the application would undermine the crime prevention objective, he must give the relevant licensing authority a notice stating the reasons why he is so satisfied.

(6) The chief officer of police must give that notice within the period of 14 days beginning with the day on which he is notified of the application under subsection (4).

38 Circumstances in which section 37 application given interim effect

(1) This section applies where an application made in accordance with section 37, in respect of a premises licence which authorises the supply of alcohol, includes a request that the variation applied for should have immediate effect.

(2) By virtue of this section, the premises licence has effect during the application period as if it were varied in the manner set out in the application.

(3) For this purpose 'the application period' means the period which –

(a) begins when the application is received by the relevant licensing authority, and

(b) ends –

(i) if the application is granted, when the variation takes effect,

(ii) if the application is rejected, at the time the rejection is notified to the applicant, or

(iii) if the application is withdrawn before it is determined, at the time of the withdrawal.

39 Determination of section 37 application

(1) This section applies where an application is made, in accordance with section 37, to vary a premises licence so as to specify a new premises supervisor ('the proposed individual').

(2) Subject to subsection (3), the relevant licensing authority must grant the application.

(3) Where a notice is given under section 37(5) (and not withdrawn), the authority must –

(a) hold a hearing to consider it, unless the authority, the applicant and the chief officer of police who gave the notice agree that a hearing is unnecessary, and

(b) having regard to the notice, reject the application if it considers it necessary for the promotion of the crime prevention objective to do so.

(4) Where an application under section 37 is granted or rejected, the relevant licensing authority must give a notice to that effect to –
(a) the applicant,
(b) the proposed individual, and
(c) the chief officer of police for the police area (or each police area) in which the premises are situated.

(5) Where a chief officer of police gave a notice under subsection (5) of that section (and it was not withdrawn), the notice under subsection (4) of this section must state the authority's reasons for granting or rejecting the application.

(6) Where the application is granted, the notice under subsection (4) must specify the time when the variation takes effect.
That time is the time specified in the application or, if that time is before the applicant is given that notice, such later time as the relevant licensing authority specifies in the notice.

40 Duty of applicant following determination under section 39

(1) Where the holder of a premises licence is notified under section 39(4), he must forthwith –
(a) if his application has been granted, notify the person (if any) who has been replaced as the designated premises supervisor of the variation, and
(b) if his application has been rejected, give the designated premises supervisor (if any) notice to that effect.

(2) A person commits an offence if he fails, without reasonable excuse, to comply with subsection (1).

(3) A person guilty of an offence under subsection (2) is liable on summary conviction to a fine not exceeding level 3 on the standard scale.

41 Request to be removed as designated premises supervisor

(1) Where an individual wishes to cease being the designated premises supervisor in respect of a premises licence, he may give the relevant licensing authority a notice to that effect.

(2) Subsection (1) is subject to regulations under section 54 (form etc. of notices etc.).

(3) Where the individual is the holder of the premises licence, the notice under subsection (1) must also be accompanied by the premises licence (or the appropriate part of the licence) or, if that is not practicable, by a statement of the reasons for the failure to provide the licence (or part).

(4) In any other case, the individual must no later than 48 hours after giving the notice under subsection (1) give the holder of the premises licence –
  (a) a copy of that notice, and
  (b) a notice directing the holder to send to the relevant licensing authority within 14 days of receiving the notice –
    (i) the premises licence (or the appropriate part of the licence), or
    (ii) if that is not practicable, a statement of the reasons for the failure to provide the licence (or part).

(5) A person commits an offence if he fails, without reasonable excuse, to comply with a direction given to him under subsection (4)(b).

(6) A person guilty of an offence under subsection (5) is liable on summary conviction to a fine not exceeding level 3 on the standard scale.

(7) Where an individual –
  (a) gives the relevant licensing authority a notice in accordance with this section, and
  (b) satisfies the requirements of subsection (3) or (4),

he is to be treated for the purposes of this Act as if, from the relevant time, he were not the designated premises supervisor.

(8) For this purpose 'the relevant time' means –
  (a) the time the notice under subsection (1) is received by the relevant licensing authority, or
  (b) if later, the time specified in the notice.

Transfer of premises licence

42 Application for transfer of premises licence

(1) Subject to this section, any person mentioned in section 16(1) (applicant for premises licence) may apply to the relevant licensing authority for the transfer of a premises licence to him.

(2) Where the applicant is an individual he must be aged 18 or over.

(3) Subsection (1) is subject to regulations under –
  (a) section 54 (form etc. of applications etc.);
  (b) section 55 (fees to accompany applications etc.).

(4) An application under this section must also be accompanied by the premises licence or, if that is not practicable, a statement of the reasons for the failure to provide the licence.

(5) The applicant must give notice of his application to the chief officer of police for the police area (or each police area) in which the premises are situated.

(6) Where a chief officer of police notified under subsection (5) is satisfied that the exceptional circumstances of the case are such that granting the application would undermine the crime prevention objective, he must

give the relevant licensing authority a notice stating the reasons why he is so satisfied.

(7) The chief officer of police must give that notice within the period of 14 days beginning with the day on which he is notified of the application under subsection (5).

43 Circumstances in which transfer application given interim effect

(1) Where –
- (a) an application made in accordance with section 42 includes a request that the transfer have immediate effect, and
- (b) the requirements of this section are met,

then, by virtue of this section, the premises licence has effect during the application period as if the applicant were the holder of the licence.

(2) For this purpose 'the application period' means the period which –
- (a) begins when the application is received by the relevant licensing authority, and
- (b) ends –
  - (i) when the licence is transferred following the grant of the application, or
  - (ii) if the application is rejected, when the applicant is notified of the rejection, or
  - (iii) when the application is withdrawn.

(3) Subject to subsections (4) and (5), an application within subsection (1)(a) may be made only with the consent of the holder of the premises licence.

(4) Where a person is the holder of the premises licence by virtue of an interim authority notice under section 47, such an application may also be made by that person.

(5) The relevant licensing authority must exempt the applicant from the requirement to obtain the holder's consent if the applicant shows to the authority's satisfaction –
- (a) that he has taken all reasonable steps to obtain that consent, and
- (b) that, if the application were one to which subsection (1) applied, he would be in a position to use the premises during the application period for the licensable activity or activities authorised by the premises licence.

(6) Where the relevant licensing authority refuses to exempt an applicant under subsection (5), it must notify the applicant of its reasons for that decision.

44 Determination of transfer application

(1) This section applies where an application for the transfer of a licence is made in accordance with section 42.

(2) Subject to subsections (3) and (5), the authority must transfer the licence in accordance with the application.

(3) The authority must reject the application if none of the conditions in subsection (4) applies.

(4) The conditions are –
- (a) that section 43(1) (applications given interim effect) applies to the application,
- (b) that the holder of the premises licence consents to the transfer,
- (c) that the applicant is exempted under subsection (6) from the requirement to obtain the holder's consent to the transfer.

(5) Where a notice is given under section 42(6) (and not withdrawn), and subsection (3) above does not apply, the authority must –
- (a) hold a hearing to consider it, unless the authority, the applicant and the chief officer of police who gave the notice agree that a hearing is unnecessary, and
- (b) having regard to the notice, reject the application if it considers it necessary for the promotion of the crime prevention objective to do so.

(6) The relevant licensing authority must exempt the applicant from the requirement to obtain the holder's consent if the applicant shows to the authority's satisfaction –
- (a) that he has taken all reasonable steps to obtain that consent, and
- (b) that, if the application were granted, he would be in a position to use the premises for the licensable activity or activities authorised by the premises licence.

(7) Where the relevant licensing authority refuses to exempt an applicant under subsection (6), it must notify the applicant of its reasons for that decision.

45 Notification of determination under section 44

(1) Where an application under section 42 is granted or rejected, the relevant licensing authority must give a notice to that effect to –
- (a) the applicant, and
- (b) the chief officer of police for the police area (or each police area) in which the premises are situated.

(2) Where a chief officer of police gave a notice under subsection (6) of that section (and it was not withdrawn), the notice under subsection (1) of this section must state the licensing authority's reasons for granting or rejecting the application.

(3) Where the application is granted, the notice under subsection (1) must specify the time when the transfer takes effect.
That time is the time specified in the application or, if that time is before the applicant is given that notice, such later time as the relevant licensing authority specifies in the notice.

(4) The relevant licensing authority must also give a copy of the notice given under subsection (1) –
- (a) where the application is granted –
  - (i) to the holder of the licence immediately before the application was granted, or
  - (ii) if the application was one to which section 43(1) applied, to the holder of the licence immediately before the application was made (if any),
- (b) where the application is rejected, to the holder of the premises licence (if any).

46 Duty to notify designated premises supervisor of transfer

(1) This section applies where –
- (a) an application is made in accordance with section 42 to transfer a premises licence in respect of which there is a designated premises supervisor, and
- (b) the applicant and that supervisor are not the same person.

(2) Where section 43(1) applies in relation to the application, the applicant must forthwith notify the designated premises supervisor of the application.

(3) If the application is granted, the applicant must forthwith notify the designated premises supervisor of the transfer.

(4) A person commits an offence if he fails, without reasonable excuse, to comply with this section.

(5) A person guilty of an offence under subsection (4) is liable on summary conviction to a fine not exceeding level 3 on the standard scale.

Interim authority notices

47 Interim authority notice following death etc. of licence holder

(1) This section applies where –
- (a) a premises licence lapses under section 27 in a case within subsection (1)(a), (b) or (c) of that section (death, incapacity or insolvency of the holder), but
- (b) no application for transfer of the licence has been made by virtue of section 50 (reinstatement of licence on transfer following death etc.).

(2) A person who –
 (a) has a prescribed interest in the premises concerned, or
 (b) is connected to the person who held the premises licence immediately before it lapsed ('the former holder'),
 may, during the initial seven day period, give to the relevant licensing authority a notice (an 'interim authority notice') in respect of the licence.
(3) Subsection (2) is subject to regulations under –
 (a) section 54 (form etc. of notices etc.);
 (b) section 55 (fees to accompany applications etc.).
(4) Only one interim authority notice may be given under subsection (2).
(5) For the purposes of subsection (2) a person is connected to the former holder of the premises licence if, and only if –
 (a) the former holder has died and that person is his personal representative,
 (b) the former holder has become mentally incapable and that person acts for him under a power of attorney created by an instrument registered under section 6 of the Enduring Powers of Attorney Act 1985 (c.29), or
 (c) the former holder has become insolvent and that person is his insolvency practitioner.
(6) Where an interim authority notice is given in accordance with this section –
 (a) the premises licence is reinstated from the time the notice is received by the relevant licensing authority, and
 (b) the person who gave the notice is from that time the holder of the licence.
(7) But the premises licence lapses again –
 (a) at the end of the initial seven day period unless before that time the person who gave the interim authority notice has given a copy of the notice to the chief officer of police for the police area (or each police area) in which the premises are situated;
 (b) at the end of the interim authority period, unless before that time a relevant transfer application is made to the relevant licensing authority.
(8) Nothing in this section prevents the person who gave the interim authority notice from making a relevant transfer application.
(9) If –
 (a) a relevant transfer application is made during the interim authority period, and
 (b) that application is rejected or withdrawn,
 the licence lapses again at the time of the rejection or withdrawal.
(10) In this section –
 'becomes insolvent' is to be construed in accordance with section 27;

'initial seven day period', in relation to a licence which lapses as mentioned in subsection (1), means the period of seven days beginning with the day after the day the licence lapses;
'insolvency practitioner', in relation to a person, means a person acting as an insolvency practitioner in relation to him (within the meaning of section 388 of the Insolvency Act 1986 (c.45));
'interim authority period' means the period beginning with the day on which the interim authority notice is received by the relevant licensing authority and ending –
- (a) two months after that day, or
- (b) if earlier, when it is terminated by the person who gave the interim authority notice notifying the relevant licensing authority to that effect;

'mentally incapable' has the same meaning as in section 27(1)(b); and
'relevant transfer application' in relation to the premises licence, is an application under section 42 which is given interim effect by virtue of section 43.

48 Cancellation of interim authority notice following police objections

(1) This section applies where –
- (a) an interim authority notice by a person ('the relevant person') is given in accordance with section 47,
- (b) the chief officer of police for the police area (or each police area) in which the premises are situated is given a copy of the interim authority notice before the end of the initial seven day period (within the meaning of that section), and
- (c) that chief officer (or any of those chief officers) is satisfied that the exceptional circumstances of the case are such that a failure to cancel the interim authority notice would undermine the crime prevention objective.

(2) The chief officer of police must no later than 48 hours after he receives the copy of the interim authority notice give the relevant licensing authority a notice stating why he is so satisfied.

(3) Where a notice is given by the chief officer of police (and not withdrawn), the authority must –
- (a) hold a hearing to consider it, unless the authority, the relevant person and the chief officer of police agree that a hearing is unnecessary, and
- (b) having regard to the notice given by the chief officer of police, cancel the interim authority notice if it considers it necessary for the promotion of the crime prevention objective to do so.

(4) An interim authority notice is cancelled under subsection (3)(b) by the licensing authority giving the relevant person a notice stating that it is cancelled and the authority's reasons for its decision.

(5) The licensing authority must give a copy of a notice under subsection (4) to the chief officer of police for the police area (or each police area) in which the premises are situated.

(6) The premises licence lapses if, and when, a notice is given under subsection (4).
This is subject to paragraph 7(5) of Schedule 5 (reinstatement of premises licence where appeal made against cancellation of interim authority notice).

(7) The relevant licensing authority must not cancel an interim authority notice after a relevant transfer application (within the meaning of section 47) is made in respect of the premises licence.

49 Supplementary provision about interim authority notices

(1) On receipt of an interim authority notice, the relevant licensing authority must issue to the person who gave the notice a copy of the licence and a copy of the summary (in each case certified by the authority to be a true copy).

(2) The copies issued under this section must be copies of the premises licence and summary in the form in which they existed immediately before the licence lapsed under section 27, except that they must specify the person who gave the interim authority notice as the person who is the holder.

(3) This Act applies in relation to a copy issued under this section as it applies in relation to an original licence or summary.

(4) Where a person becomes the holder of a premises licence by virtue of section 47, he must (unless he is the designated premises supervisor under the licence) forthwith notify the supervisor (if any) of the interim authority notice.

(5) A person commits an offence if he fails, without reasonable excuse, to comply with subsection (4).

(6) A person guilty of an offence under subsection (5) is liable on summary conviction to a fine not exceeding level 3 on the standard scale.

Transfer following death etc. of licence holder

50 Reinstatement of licence on transfer following death etc. of holder

(1) This section applies where –
   (a) a premises licence lapses by virtue of section 27 (death, incapacity or insolvency etc. of the holder), but no interim authority notice has effect, or
   (b) a premises licence lapses by virtue of section 28 (surrender).

(2) For the purposes of subsection (1)(a) an interim authority notice ceases to have effect when it is cancelled under section 48 or withdrawn.

(3) Notwithstanding the lapsing of the licence, a person mentioned in section 16(1) (who, in the case of an individual, is aged 18 or over) may apply under section 42 for the transfer of the licence to him provided that the application –
   (a) is made no later than seven days after the day the licence lapsed, and
   (b) is one to which section 43(1)(a) applies.

(4) Where an application is made in accordance with subsection (3), section 43(1)(b) must be disregarded.

(5) Where such an application is made, the premises licence is reinstated from the time the application is received by the relevant licensing authority.

(6) But the licence lapses again if, and when –
   (a) the applicant is notified of the rejection of the application, or
   (b) the application is withdrawn.

(7) Only one application for transfer of the premises licence may be made in reliance on this section.

Review of licences

51 Application for review of premises licence

(1) Where a premises licence has effect, an interested party or a responsible authority may apply to the relevant licensing authority for a review of the licence.

(2) Subsection (1) is subject to regulations under section 54 (form etc. of applications etc.).

(3) The Secretary of State must by regulations under this section –
   (a) require the applicant to give a notice containing details of the application to the holder of the premises licence and each responsible authority within such period as may be prescribed;
   (b) require the authority to advertise the application and invite representations about it to be made to the authority by interested parties and responsible authorities;
   (c) prescribe the period during which representations may be made by the holder of the premises licence, any responsible authority or any interested party;
   (d) require any notice under paragraph (a) or advertisement under paragraph (b) to specify that period.

(4) The relevant licensing authority may, at any time, reject any ground for review specified in an application under this section if it is satisfied –

(a) that the ground is not relevant to one or more of the licensing objectives, or
(b) in the case of an application made by a person other than a responsible authority, that –
(i) the ground is frivolous or vexatious, or
(ii) the ground is a repetition.

(5) For this purpose a ground for review is a repetition if –
(a) it is identical or substantially similar to –
(i) a ground for review specified in an earlier application for review made in respect of the same premises licence and determined under section 52, or
(ii) representations considered by the relevant licensing authority in accordance with section 18, before it determined the application for the premises licence under that section, or
(iii) representations which would have been so considered but for the fact that they were excluded representations by virtue of section 32, and
(b) a reasonable interval has not elapsed since that earlier application for review or the grant of the licence (as the case may be).

(6) Where the authority rejects a ground for review under subsection (4)(b), it must notify the applicant of its decision and, if the ground was rejected because it was frivolous or vexatious, the authority must notify him of its reasons for making that decision.

(7) The application is to be treated as rejected to the extent that any of the grounds for review are rejected under subsection (4).
Accordingly the requirements imposed under subsection (3)(a) and (b) and by section 52 (so far as not already met) apply only to so much (if any) of the application as has not been rejected.

52 Determination of application for review

(1) This section applies where –
(a) the relevant licensing authority receives an application made in accordance with section 51,
(b) the applicant has complied with any requirement imposed on him under subsection (3)(a) or (d) of that section, and
(c) the authority has complied with any requirement imposed on it under subsection (3)(b) or (d) of that section.

(2) Before determining the application, the authority must hold a hearing to consider it and any relevant representations.

(3) The authority must, having regard to the application and any relevant representations, take such of the steps mentioned in subsection (4) (if any) as it considers necessary for the promotion of the licensing objectives.

(4) The steps are –
  (a) to modify the conditions of the licence;
  (b) to exclude a licensable activity from the scope of the licence;
  (c) to remove the designated premises supervisor;
  (d) to suspend the licence for a period not exceeding three months;
  (e) to revoke the licence;

and for this purpose the conditions of the licence are modified if any of them is altered or omitted or any new condition is added.

(5) Subsection (3) is subject to sections 19, 20 and 21 (requirement to include certain conditions in premises licences).

(6) Where the authority takes a step mentioned in subsection (4)(a) or (b), it may provide that the modification or exclusion is to have effect for only such period (not exceeding three months) as it may specify.

(7) In this section 'relevant representations' means representations which –
  (a) are relevant to one or more of the licensing objectives, and
  (b) meet the requirements of subsection (8).

(8) The requirements are –
  (a) that the representations are made –
    (i) by the holder of the premises licence, a responsible authority or an interested party, and
    (ii) within the period prescribed under section 51(3)(c),
  (b) that they have not been withdrawn, and
  (c) if they are made by an interested party (who is not also a responsible authority), that they are not, in the opinion of the relevant licensing authority, frivolous or vexatious.

(9) Where the relevant licensing authority determines that any representations are frivolous or vexatious, it must notify the person who made them of the reasons for that determination.

(10) Where a licensing authority determines an application for review under this section it must notify the determination and its reasons for making it to –
  (a) the holder of the licence,
  (b) the applicant,
  (c) any person who made relevant representations, and
  (d) the chief officer of police for the police area (or each police area) in which the premises are situated.

(11) A determination under this section does not have effect –
  (a) until the end of the period given for appealing against the decision, or
  (b) if the decision is appealed against, until the appeal is disposed of.

53 Supplementary provision about review

(1) This section applies where a local authority is both –
  (a) the relevant licensing authority, and
  (b) a responsible authority,
  in respect of any premises.
(2) The authority may, in its capacity as a responsible authority, apply under section 51 for a review of any premises licence in respect of the premises.
(3) The authority may, in its capacity as licensing authority, determine that application.

General provision

54 Form etc. of applications and notices under Part 3

In relation to any application or notice under this Part, regulations may prescribe –
  (a) its form;
  (b) the manner in which it is to be made or given;
  (c) information and documents that must accompany it.

55 Fees

(1) Regulations may –
  (a) require applications under any provision of this Part (other than section 51) or notices under section 47 to be accompanied by a fee, and
  (b) prescribe the amount of the fee.
(2) Regulations may also require the holder of a premises licence to pay the relevant licensing authority an annual fee.
(3) Regulations under subsection (2) may include provision prescribing –
  (a) the amount of the fee, and
  (b) the time at which any such fee is due.
(4) Any fee which is owed to a licensing authority under subsection (2) may be recovered as a debt due to the authority.

Production of licence, rights of entry, etc.

56 Licensing authority's duty to update licence document

(1) Where –
  (a) the relevant licensing authority, in relation to a premises licence, makes a determination or receives a notice under this Part,
  (b) a premises licence lapses under this Part, or

(c) an appeal against a decision under this Part is disposed of,

the relevant licensing authority must make the appropriate amendments (if any) to the licence and, if necessary, issue a new summary of the licence.

(2) Where a licensing authority is not in possession of the licence (or the appropriate part of the licence) it may, for the purposes of discharging its obligations under subsection (1), require the holder of a premises licence to produce the licence (or the appropriate part) to the authority within 14 days from the date on which he is notified of the requirement.

(3) A person commits an offence if he fails, without reasonable excuse, to comply with a requirement under subsection (2).

(4) A person guilty of an offence under subsection (3) is liable on summary conviction to a fine not exceeding level 2 on the standard scale.

57 Duty to keep and produce licence

(1) This section applies whenever premises in respect of which a premises licence has effect are being used for one or more licensable activities authorised by the licence.

(2) The holder of the premises licence must secure that the licence or a certified copy of it is kept at the premises in the custody or under the control of –

(a) the holder of the licence, or

(b) a person who works at the premises and whom the holder of the licence has nominated in writing for the purposes of this subsection.

(3) The holder of the premises licence must secure that –

(a) the summary of the licence or a certified copy of that summary, and

(b) a notice specifying the position held at the premises by any person nominated for the purposes of subsection (2),

are prominently displayed at the premises.

(4) The holder of a premises licence commits an offence if he fails, without reasonable excuse, to comply with subsection (2) or (3).

(5) A constable or an authorised person may require the person who, by virtue of arrangements made for the purposes of subsection (2), is required to have the premises licence (or a certified copy of it) in his custody or under his control to produce the licence (or such a copy) for examination.

(6) An authorised person exercising the power conferred by subsection (5) must, if so requested, produce evidence of his authority to exercise the power.

(7) A person commits an offence if he fails, without reasonable excuse, to produce a premises licence or certified copy of a premises licence in accordance with a requirement under subsection (5).

(8) A person guilty of an offence under this section is liable on summary conviction to a fine not exceeding level 2 on the standard scale.

(9) In subsection (3) the reference to the summary of the licence is a reference to the summary issued under section 23 or, where one or more summaries have subsequently been issued under section 56, the most recent summary to have been so issued.

(10) Section 58 makes provision about certified copies of documents for the purposes of this section.

58 Provision supplementary to section 57

(1) Any reference in section 57 to a certified copy of any document is a reference to a copy of that document which is certified to be a true copy by –

  (a) the relevant licensing authority,

  (b) a solicitor or notary, or

  (c) a person of a prescribed description.

(2) Any certified copy produced in accordance with a requirement under section 57(5) must be a copy of the document in the form in which it exists at the time.

(3) A document which purports to be a certified copy of a document is to be taken to be such a copy, and to comply with the requirements of subsection (2), unless the contrary is shown.

59 Inspection of premises before grant of licence etc.

(1) In this section 'relevant application' means an application under –

  (a) section 17 (grant of licence),

  (b) section 29 (provisional statement),

  (c) section 34 (variation of licence), or

  (d) section 51 (review of licence).

(2) A constable or an authorised person may, at any reasonable time before the determination of a relevant application, enter the premises to which the application relates to assess –

  (a) in a case within subsection (1)(a), (b) or (c), the likely effect of the grant of the application on the promotion of the licensing objectives, and

  (b) in a case within subsection (1)(d), the effect of the activities authorised by the premises licence on the promotion of those objectives.

(3) An authorised person exercising the power conferred by this section must, if so requested, produce evidence of his authority to exercise the power.

(4) A constable or an authorised person exercising the power conferred by this section in relation to an application within subsection (1)(d) may, if necessary, use reasonable force.

(5) A person commits an offence if he intentionally obstructs an authorised person exercising a power conferred by this section.

(6) A person guilty of an offence under this section is liable on summary conviction to a fine not exceeding level 2 on the standard scale.

APPENDIX A2

Licensing Act 2003, Schedule 1, Part 1 – Provision of regulated entertainment: general definitions

1 The provision of regulated entertainment

(1) For the purposes of this Act the 'provision of regulated entertainment' means the provision of –
  (a) entertainment of a description falling within paragraph 2, or
  (b) entertainment facilities falling within paragraph 3,
  where the conditions in sub-paragraphs (2) and (3) are satisfied.
(2) The first condition is that the entertainment is, or entertainment facilities are, provided –
  (a) to any extent for members of the public or a section of the public,
  (b) exclusively for members of a club which is a qualifying club in relation to the provision of regulated entertainment, or for members of such a club and their guests, or
  (c) in any case not falling within paragraph (a) or (b), for consideration and with a view to profit.
(3) The second condition is that the premises on which the entertainment is, or entertainment facilities are, provided are made available for the purpose, or for purposes which include the purpose, of enabling the entertainment concerned (whether of a description falling within paragraph 2(1) or paragraph 3(2)) to take place.
  To the extent that the provision of entertainment facilities consists of making premises available, the premises are to be regarded for the purposes of this sub-paragraph as premises 'on which' entertainment facilities are provided.
(4) For the purposes of sub-paragraph (2)(c), entertainment is, or entertainment facilities are, to be regarded as provided for consideration only if any charge –
  (a) is made by or on behalf of –
    (i) any person concerned in the organisation or management of that entertainment, or
    (ii) any person concerned in the organisation or management of those facilities who is also concerned in the organisation or

management of the entertainment within paragraph 3(2) in which those facilities enable persons to take part, and
(b) is paid by or on behalf of some or all of the persons for whom that entertainment is, or those facilities are, provided.

(5) In sub-paragraph (4), 'charge' includes any charge for the provision of goods or services.

(6) For the purposes of sub-paragraph (4)(a), where the entertainment consists of the performance of live music or the playing of recorded music, a person performing or playing the music is not concerned in the organisation or management of the entertainment by reason only that he does one or more of the following –
(a) chooses the music to be performed or played,
(b) determines the manner in which he performs or plays it,
(c) provides any facilities for the purposes of his performance or playing of the music.

(7) This paragraph is subject to Part 2 of this Schedule (exemptions).

2 Entertainment

(1) The descriptions of entertainment are –
(a) a performance of a play,
(b) an exhibition of a film,
(c) an indoor sporting event,
(d) a boxing or wrestling entertainment,
(e) a performance of live music,
(f) any playing of recorded music,
(g) a performance of dance,
(h) entertainment of a similar description to that falling within paragraph (e), (f) or (g),

where the entertainment takes place in the presence of an audience and is provided for the purpose, or for purposes which include the purpose, of entertaining that audience.

(2) Any reference in sub-paragraph (1) to an audience includes a reference to spectators.

(3) This paragraph is subject to Part 3 of this Schedule (interpretation).

3 Entertainment facilities

(1) In this Schedule, 'entertainment facilities' means facilities for enabling persons to take part in entertainment of a description falling within sub-paragraph (2) for the purpose, or for purposes which include the purpose, of being entertained.

(2) The descriptions of entertainment are –
(a) making music,

(b) dancing,
(c) entertainment of a similar description to that falling within paragraph (a) or (b).

(3) This paragraph is subject to Part 3 of this Schedule (interpretation).

4 Power to amend Schedule

The Secretary of State may by order amend this Schedule for the purpose of modifying –

(a) the descriptions of entertainment specified in paragraph 2, or
(b) the descriptions of entertainment specified in paragraph 3,

and for this purpose 'modify' includes adding, varying or removing any description.

APPENDIX A3

Licensing Act 2003, Schedule 4 – Personal licence: relevant offences

1 An offence under this Act.

2 An offence under any of the following enactments –
  (a) Schedule 12 to the London Government Act 1963 (c. 33) (public entertainment licensing);
  (b) the Licensing Act 1964 (c. 26);
  (c) the Private Places of Entertainment (Licensing) Act 1967 (c. 19);
  (d) section 13 of the Theatres Act 1968 (c. 54);
  (e) the Late Night Refreshment Houses Act 1969 (c. 53);
  (f) section 6 of, or Schedule 1 to, the Local Government (Miscellaneous Provisions) Act 1982 (c. 30);
  (g) the Licensing (Occasional Permissions) Act 1983 (c. 24);
  (h) the Cinemas Act 1985 (c. 13);
  (i) the London Local Authorities Act 1990 (c. vii).

3 An offence under the Firearms Act 1968 (c. 27).

4 An offence under section 1 of the Trade Descriptions Act 1968 (c. 29) (false trade description of goods) in circumstances where the goods in question are or include alcohol.

5 An offence under any of the following provisions of the Theft Act 1968 (c. 60) –
  (a) section 1 (theft);
  (b) section 8 (robbery);
  (c) section 9 (burglary);
  (d) section 10 (aggravated burglary);
  (e) section 11 (removal of articles from places open to the public);
  (f) section 12A (aggravated vehicle-taking), in circumstances where subsection (2)(b) of that section applies and the accident caused the death of any person;
  (g) section 13 (abstracting of electricity);
  (h) section 15 (obtaining property by deception);
  (i) section 15A (obtaining a money transfer by deception);
  (j) section 16 (obtaining pecuniary advantage by deception);
  (k) section 17 (false accounting);
  (l) section 19 (false statements by company directors etc.);

(m) section 20 (suppression, etc. of documents);
(n) section 21 (blackmail);
(o) section 22 (handling stolen goods);
(p) section 24A (dishonestly retaining a wrongful credit);
(q) section 25 (going equipped for stealing etc.).

6 An offence under section 7(2) of the Gaming Act 1968 (c. 65) (allowing child to take part in gaming on premises licensed for the sale of alcohol).

7 An offence under any of the following provisions of the Misuse of Drugs Act 1971 (c. 38) –
(a) section 4(2) (production of a controlled drug);
(b) section 4(3) (supply of a controlled drug);
(c) section 5(3) (possession of a controlled drug with intent to supply);
(d) section 8 (permitting activities to take place on premises).

8 An offence under either of the following provisions of the Theft Act 1978 (c. 31) –
(a) section 1 (obtaining services by deception);
(b) section 2 (evasion of liability by deception).

9 An offence under either of the following provisions of the Customs and Excise Management Act 1979 (c. 2) –
(a) section 170 (disregarding subsection (1)(a)) (fraudulent evasion of duty etc.);
(b) section 170B (taking preparatory steps for evasion of duty).

10 An offence under either of the following provisions of the Tobacco Products Duty Act 1979 (c. 7) –
(a) section 8G (possession and sale of unmarked tobacco);
(b) section 8H (use of premises for sale of unmarked tobacco).

11 An offence under the Forgery and Counterfeiting Act 1981 (c. 45) (other than an offence under section 18 or 19 of that Act).

12 An offence under the Firearms (Amendment) Act 1988 (c. 45).

13 An offence under any of the following provisions of the Copyright, Designs and Patents Act 1988 (c. 48) –
(a) section 107(1)(d)(iii) (public exhibition in the course of a business of article infringing copyright);
(b) section 107(3) (infringement of copyright by public performance of work etc.);
(c) section 198(2) (broadcast etc. of recording of performance made without sufficient consent);
(d) section 297(1) (fraudulent reception of transmission);
(e) section 297A(1) (supply etc. of unauthorised decoder).

14 An offence under any of the following provisions of the Road Traffic Act 1988 (c. 52) –
(a) section 3A (causing death by careless driving while under the influence of drink or drugs);

(b) section 4 (driving etc. a vehicle when under the influence of drink or drugs);

(c) section 5 (driving etc. a vehicle with alcohol concentration above prescribed limit).

15 An offence under either of the following provisions of the Food Safety Act 1990 (c. 16) in circumstances where the food in question is or includes alcohol –

(a) section 14 (selling food or drink not of the nature, substance or quality demanded);

(b) section 15 (falsely describing or presenting food or drink).

16 An offence under section 92(1) or (2) of the Trade Marks Act 1994 (c. 26) (unauthorised use of trade mark, etc. in relation to goods) in circumstances where the goods in question are or include alcohol.

17 An offence under the Firearms (Amendment) Act 1997 (c. 5).

18 A sexual offence, within the meaning of section 161(2) of the Powers of Criminal Courts (Sentencing) Act 2000 (c. 6).

19 A violent offence, within the meaning of section 161(3) of that Act.

20 An offence under section 3 of the Private Security Industry Act 2001 (c. 12) (engaging in certain activities relating to security without a licence).

APPENDIX A4

Summary of spent convictions under the Rehabilitation of Offenders Act 1974

Section 114 of the Licensing Act 2003 provides that:

> For the purposes of this Part [relating to personal licences] a conviction for a relevant offence or a foreign offence must be disregarded if it is spent for the purposes of the Rehabilitation of Offenders Act 1974.

SUMMARY OF REHABILITATION OF OFFENDERS ACT 1974
(see Act for full details)

Sentence	*Becomes Spent After*
*Imprisonment of between 6 months and 2 years	10 years
*Imprisonment or youth custody of up to 6 months	7 years
Borstal training	7 years
*A fine or other sentence not otherwise covered in this table.	5 years
For an absolute discharge	6 months
For a probation order	5 years or 2 years, if under 18 years of age at the time of conviction, or until the order expires (whichever is the longer)
Conditional discharge or bind over	1 year (or until Order expires, whichever is the longer)
Disqualification (Driving)	For period of disqualification
Remand Home, Attendance Centre or Approved School Order	Period of the Order and a further year after the Order expires
Hospital Order under the Mental Health Act	Period of the Order and a further 2 years after it expires.
*Cashiering, discharge with ignominy or dismissal from the Armed Forces.	10 years
*Dismissal from the Armed Forces	7 years

*Detention by the Armed Forces	5 years
Detention by direction of the Home Secretary:	
For a period exceeding 6 months but not exceeding 30 months (Armed Forces):	5 years
Detention of less than 6 months.	3 years

Note: (i) A sentence of more than 2 years' imprisonment can never become spent.
(ii) If you were under 18 years of age on the date of conviction, please halve the period in the right hand column for the sentences marked with an *.

APPENDIX B

Extracts from Secretary of State's Guidance (July 2004)

APPENDIX B1

Chapter 5 – Premises licences

5.1 This Chapter provides advice about best practice for the administration of the processes for issuing, varying, transferring and reviewing premises licences and other associated procedures.

Licensable activities

5.2 A premises licence authorises the use of any premises, (which is defined in the 2003 Act as a vehicle, vessel or moveable structure or any place or a part of any premises), for licensable activities described and defined in section 1(1) of and Schedules 1 and 2 to the 2003 Act. The licensable activities are:

- the sale by retail of alcohol;
- the supply of alcohol by or on behalf of a club to, or to the order of, a member of the club;
- the provision of regulated entertainment; and
- the provision of late night refreshment.

5.3 Schedule 1 to the 2003 Act, which is reproduced for convenience at Annex A, sets out what constitutes the provision of regulated entertainment and identifies those activities which are not to be regarded as the provision of regulated entertainment and, as a consequence, are exempt from the regulated entertainment aspects of the licensing regime. Schedule 2, which is reproduced at Annex B, sets out what constitutes the provision of late night refreshment and identifies those activities which are not to be regarded as the provision of late night refreshment and, as a consequence, are exempt from the late night refreshment aspects of the licensing regime.

Small venues providing dancing and amplified or unamplified music

5.4 In addition, subsections (1) and (2) of section 177 of the 2003 Act provide that where

- a premises licence or club premises certificate authorises the supply of alcohol for consumption on the premises and the provision of

'music entertainment' (live music or dancing or facilities enabling people to take part in those activities),
- the relevant premises are used primarily for the supply of alcohol for consumption on the premises, and
- the premises have a permitted capacity limit of not more than 200 persons any conditions relating to the provision of the music entertainment imposed on the premises licence or club premises certificate by the licensing authority, other than those set out by the licence or certificate which are consistent with the operating schedule, will be suspended except where they were imposed as being necessary for public safety or the prevention of crime and disorder or both.

5.5 In addition, subsection (4) of section 177 provides that where
- a premises licence or club premises certificate authorises the provision of music entertainment (live music and dancing), and
- the premises have a capacity limit of not more than 200 persons

then, during the hours of 8am and midnight, if the premises are being used for the provision of unamplified live music or the facilities enabling people to take part in such entertainment, but no other description of regulated entertainment, any conditions imposed on the licence by the licensing authority, again other than those which are consistent with the operating schedule, which relate to the provision of that music entertainment will be suspended.

5.6 Section 177 can be disapplied in relation to any condition of a premises licence or club premises certificate following a review of the licence or certificate. This means that conditions attached to the existing premises licence relating to the provision of music entertainment can be given effect at the relevant times or that new conditions may also be imposed as an outcome of the review process.

5.7 Accordingly, those seeking to take advantage of the exemption relating to both amplified and unamplified music entertainment need to be aware that they must hold a premises licence or club premises certificate covering the supply of alcohol for consumption on the premises and the type of regulated music entertainment involved. Examples of premises used 'primarily' for the supply of alcohol for consumption on the premises would include public houses and some qualifying club premises, but would not normally include, for example, a restaurant. For the 'unamplified' music exemption, any premises appropriately licensed are included, including restaurants. The area to which the 200 'capacity limit' applies concerns the area covered by the premises licence or club premises certificate and not just to part of those premises unless separately licensed.

Wholesale of alcohol

5.8 The wholesale of alcohol to the general public was not licensable prior to the coming into force of the 2003 Act. Licensing authorities will want to have particular regard to the definition of 'sale by retail' given in section 192 of the 2003 Act. Sales which are made to traders for the purpose of their trade (including, for example, another wholesaler) or holders of club premises certificates, premises licences, personal licences or premises users who have given temporary event notices for the purpose of making sales authorised by those permissions or notices, are not licensable. But a sale otherwise made to a member of the public in wholesale quantities is now a licensable activity and subject to the provisions of the 2003 Act.

Internet and mail order sales

5.9 In considering applications for premises licences involving internet or mail order sales, where the place where the sale of alcohol takes place is different to the place from which the alcohol is appropriated to the contract, i.e. specifically selected for the particular purchaser, section 190 provides that the sale of alcohol is to be treated as taking place at the place where the alcohol is appropriated to the contract. Thus, for the purposes of the 2003 Act, the sale is treated as being made at the premises from which the alcohol is appropriated to the contract and such premises will be the premises for which an authorisation under the 2003 Act is required for that licensable activity. This would mean, for example, that a call centre would not be the premises for which the appropriate licence is required, but the warehouse where the alcohol is stored and specifically selected for and despatched to the purchaser would be.

Regulated entertainment

5.10 Schedule 1 to the 2003 Act sets out what constitutes the provision of regulated entertainment and defines for these purposes both entertainment and entertainment facilities. Subject to the conditions, definitions and the exemptions in Schedule 1, descriptions of entertainment to be regulated by the 2003 Act are:

- a performance of a play
- an exhibition of a film
- an indoor sporting event
- a boxing or wrestling entertainment (indoor and outdoor)
- a performance of live music
- any playing of recorded music

- a performance of dance
- entertainment of a similar description to that falling within the performance of live music, the playing of recorded music and the performance of dance

but only where the entertainment takes place in the presence of an audience and is provided for the purpose (or for purposes which include the purpose) of entertaining that audience.

5.11 Subject to the conditions, definitions and the exemptions in Schedule 1, entertainment facilities means facilities for enabling persons to take part in entertainment consisting of:

- making music
- dancing
- entertainment of a similar description to making music or for dancing.

These facilities must be provided for the purpose of, or purposes including the purpose of, being entertained. It is important to note that this is a more limited list in the 2003 Act than all the descriptions of entertainment in the 2003 Act. Accordingly, the provision of a juke box where members of the public could self-select background music for their own enjoyment is not an entertainment facility. Entertainment facilities include, for example, a karaoke machine provided for the use of and entertainment of customers in a public house or a dance floor provided for use by the public in a nightclub. Musical instruments made available for use by the public at premises for the purpose of them being entertained would constitute an entertainment facility.

5.12 In carrying out their functions, licensing authorities will need to consider whether an activity constitutes the provision of regulated entertainment. Schedule 1 governs the assessment of this. Activities which do not involve the provision of entertainment to others are not licensable under the 2003 Act. For example, the following activities do not amount to regulated entertainment under the regime:

- education – teaching students to perform music or to dance;
- activities which involve participation as acts of worship in a religious context;
- the demonstration of a product – for example, a guitar – in a music shop; or
- the rehearsal of a play or rehearsal of a performance of music to which the public are not admitted.

Much of this involves the simple application of common sense and this Guidance cannot give examples of every eventuality or possible activity. It is only when a licensing authority is satisfied that activities amount to entertainment or the provision of entertainment facilities that it should go on to consider the qualifying conditions, definitions and exemptions in Schedule 1 to see if a provision of regulated entertainment is involved and, as a result, there is a licensable activity to be governed by the provisions of the 2003 Act.

5.13 There are a number of other entertainments, which are not themselves licensable activities, for which live or recorded music may be incidental to the main attraction or performance and therefore not licensable (see below). For example, stand-up comedy is not a licensable activity and musical accompaniment incidental to the main performance would not make it a licensable activity.

5.14 It should be noted that there is nothing in the legislation to prevent shops, stores and supermarkets proposing the inclusion of regulated entertainment in their premises licences. For example, many shops may decide to present a variety of entertainment at Christmas and other festive times or more generally in support of promotional events.

Pub games

5.15 Games commonly played in pubs and social and youth clubs like pool, darts, table tennis and billiards may fall within the definition of indoor sports in Schedule 1, but normally they would not be played for the entertainment of spectators but for the private enjoyment of the participants. As such, they would not normally constitute the provision of regulated entertainment, and the facilities provided (even if a pub provides them with a view to profit) do not fall within the limited list of entertainment facilities in that Schedule (see paragraph 5.11 above). It is only when such games take place in the presence of an audience and are provided to, at least in part, entertain that audience, for example, a darts championship competition, that the activity would become licensable.

Private events

5.16 Private events can involve licensable activities where certain conditions pertain. Entertainment at a private event to which the public are not admitted becomes regulated entertainment, and therefore licensable, only if it is provided for consideration **and** with a view to profit. Accordingly, a mere charge to those attending a private event to cover the costs of the entertainment, and for no other purpose, would not make the entertainment licensable as this would not be with a view to profit. The fact that a profit might inadvertently be made would be irrelevant as long as there had not been an intention to make a profit. Furthermore, Schedule 1 to the 2003 Act makes it clear that in relation to entertainment facilities, before an activity becomes regarded as being provided for consideration, a charge has to be made by a person concerned with the organisation or the management of the entertainment or the entertainment facilities who is also concerned in the organisation or management of the entertainment in which those facilities enable persons to take part and it is paid by or on behalf of some or all of the persons for whom that entertainment is, or those facilities are, provided. This means that, for example, a wedding reception for invited guests (at which no charge intended to generate a profit is made to those guests) at which a live band plays and dancing takes place is not regulated entertainment where the organiser or manager of those facilities is not also concerned in the organisation or management of the entertainment and therefore not a licensable activity. Similarly, for example, a party organised in a private house by and for friends at which music and dancing is provided and a charge or contribution is made solely to cover the costs of the entertainment is not a licensable event. Furthermore, any charge made by musicians or other performers or their agents to the organiser of a private event does not make that entertainment licensable unless the guests attending are themselves charged for the entertainment with a view to achieving a profit as explained above.

5.17 A private event – for example, a wedding reception – held in a separate room of a public house or a hotel would normally be an event which needs to be covered by the premises licence held by the public house or hotel. For such events, the management of the premises would normally be making available entertainment facilities (for example, a dance floor) and the premises (the room) for the performance of music for the entertainment of those attending. This would unquestionably be done for a charge and with a view to profit.

Incidental music

5.18 The incidental performance of live music and incidental playing of recorded music may not be regarded as the provision of regulated entertainment activities under the 2003 Act in certain circumstances. This is where they are incidental to another activity which is not itself entertainment or the provision of entertainment facilities. This exemption does not extend to the provision of other forms of regulated entertainment. Whether or not music of this kind is 'incidental' to other activities is expected to be judged on a case by case basis and there is no definition in the 2003 Act. It will ultimately be for the courts to decide whether music is 'incidental' in the individual circumstances of any case. In the first instance, the operator of the premises concerned must decide whether or not he considers that he needs a premises licence. One factor that is expected to be relevant is 'volume'. Common sense dictates that live or recorded music played at volumes which predominate over other activities at a venue could rarely be regarded as incidental to those activities. So, for example, a juke box played in a public house at moderate levels would normally be regarded as incidental to the other activities there, but one played at high volume would not benefit from this exemption. Stand-up comedy is not regulated entertainment and musical accompaniment incidental to the main performance would not make it a licensable activity. But there are likely to be some circumstances which occupy a greyer area. In cases of doubt, operators should seek the advice of the licensing authority, particularly with regard to their policy on enforcement.

Spontaneous music, singing and dancing

5.19 The spontaneous performance of music, singing or dancing does not amount to the provision of regulated entertainment and is not a licensable activity. The relevant part of the 2003 Act to consider in this context is paragraph 1(3) of Schedule 1 to the Act. This states that the second condition which must apply before an activity constitutes the provision of regulated entertainment is that the premises (meaning 'any place') at which the entertainment is, or entertainment facilities are, provided are made available for the purpose, or purposes which include the purpose, of enabling the entertainment concerned to take place. In the case of genuinely spontaneous music (including singing) and dancing, the place where the entertainment takes place will not have been made available to those taking part for that purpose.

Late night refreshment

5.20 Schedule 2 to the 2003 Act provides a more precise definition of what constitutes the provision of late night refreshment than that which has existed in earlier legislation. Licensing authorities, in Greater London particularly, should note the differences. For example, shops, stores and supermarkets selling food that is immediately consumable from 11.00pm will not be licensable as providing late night refreshment unless they are selling hot food or hot drink. The legislation will impact on those premises such as night cafés and take away food outlets where people may gather at any time from 11.00pm and until 5.00am giving rise to the possibility of disorder and disturbance. The licensing regime will not catch premises only selling immediately consumable food, such as, bread, milk or cold sandwiches in all night grocers' shops and which do not tend to attract these problems.

5.21 Some premises provide hot food or hot drink between 11.00pm and 5.00am by means of vending machines established on the premises for that purpose. The supply of hot drink by a vending machine will not be a licensable activity and is exempt under the 2003 Act so long as the machine is one to which the public have access and it is operated by members of the public without any involvement of the staff on the premises with the payment being inserted in the machine. However, this exemption does not apply to hot food. Premises supplying hot food for a charge by vending machine will be licensable when the food has been heated for the purposes of supply, even though no staff on the premises may have been involved in the transaction.

5.22 It is not expected that the provision of late night refreshment as a secondary activity in licensed premises open for other purposes such as public houses, cinemas or nightclubs or casinos should give rise to a need for significant additional conditions. The Secretary of State considers that the key licensing objectives in connection with late night refreshment are the prevention of crime and disorder and public nuisance, and it is expected that both will normally have been adequately covered in the conditions relating to the other licensable activities on such premises.

5.23 The supply of hot drink which consists of or contains alcohol is exempt under the 2003 Act as late night refreshment because it is caught by the provisions relating to the sale or supply of alcohol.

5.24 The supply of hot food or hot drink free of charge is not a licensable activity. However, where any charge is made for either admission to the premises or for some other item in order to obtain the hot food or hot drink, this will not be regarded as 'free of charge'. Supplies by a registered charity or anyone authorised by a registered charity are also exempt. Similarly, supplies made on vehicles – other than when they are permanently or temporarily parked – are also exempt.

5.25 Supplies of hot food or hot drink at the appropriate time are exempt from the provisions of the 2003 Act if there is no admission to the public to the premises involved and they are supplies to:

- a member of a recognised club supplied by the club;
- persons staying overnight in a hotel, guest house, lodging house, hostel, a caravan or camping site or any other premises whose main purpose is providing overnight accommodation;
- an employee supplied by a particular employer (e.g. a staff canteen);
- a person who is engaged in a particular profession or who follows a particular vocation (e.g. a tradesman carrying out work at particular premises);
- a guest of any of the above.

Premises

5.26 In determining whether any premises falls to be licensed, the following parts of the 2003 Act are relevant:

- section 1 which outlines the licensable activities;
- Part 3 which outlines provisions relating to premises licences;
- Part 4 which outlines provisions for qualifying clubs;
- section 173 which provides that activities in certain locations are not licensable;
- section 174 which provides that premises may be exempted on grounds of national security;
- section 175 which provides that minor raffles and tombolas involving prizes of alcohol are not to be treated as licensable if certain conditions are fulfilled;
- section 176 which prohibits the sale of alcohol at motorway service areas; and restricts the circumstances in which alcohol may be sold at garages;
- section 189 which makes special provision regarding the licensing of vessels, vehicles and moveable structures;
- section 190 which provides that where the place where a contract for the sale of alcohol is made is different from the place where the alcohol is appropriated to the contract then for the purposes of the Act the sale of alcohol is to be treated as taking place where the alcohol is appropriated to the contract;
- section 191 which defines 'alcohol' for the purposes of the Act;
- section 192 which defines the meaning of 'sale by retail' for the purposes of the Act;
- section 193 which defines among other things 'premises', 'vehicle', 'vessel' and 'wine'; and
- Schedules 1 and 2 which define provision of regulated entertainment and late night refreshment.

5.27 Section 191 provides the meaning of 'alcohol' for the purposes of the 2003 Act, and it should be noted that a wide variety of foodstuffs contain alcohol but generally in a highly diluted form when measured against the volume of the product. For the purposes of the Act, the sale or supply of alcohol which is of a strength not exceeding 0.5 per cent ABV (alcohol by volume) at the time of the sale or supply in question is not a licensable activity. However, where the foodstuff contains alcohol at greater strengths, for example, as with some alcoholic jellies, the sale would be a licensable activity.

Garages

5.28 Section 176 of the 2003 Act provides that no authority (premises licence, club premises certificate or temporary event notice) under the Act will have effect to authorise the sale or supply of alcohol on or from certain premises. This section of the Act has the effect of restricting the ability to use premises for the sale or supply of alcohol, among other things, if they are used **primarily** as a garage or form part of premises which are **primarily** so used. Premises are used as a garage if they are used for one or more of the following:

- the retailing of petrol;
- the retailing of derv;
- the sale of motor vehicles; and
- the maintenance of motor vehicles.

The 2003 Act therefore largely maintains the position which existed under the Licensing Act 1964. It is for the licensing authority to decide in the light of the facts whether or not any premises is used primarily as a garage. Such decisions under the 1964 Act have most recently not been based on an examination of the gross or net turnover of income from non-qualifying products and other products. The approach to establishing primary use so far approved by the courts has been based on an examination of the intensity of use by customers of the premises. For example, if a garage shop in any rural area is used more intensely by customers purchasing other products than by customers purchasing non-qualifying products or services, it may be eligible to seek authority to sell or supply alcohol.

Relevant licensing authority

5.29 Premises licences are issued by the licensing authority in which the premises are situated or in the case of premises straddling an area boundary, the licensing authority in whose area the greater or greatest part of the premises is situated or where the premises is located equally in two or more areas, the applicant may choose. In the rare cases where such premises exist, it will be important that the licensing authorities concerned maintain close contact about the grant of the premises licence, inspection, enforcement and other licensing functions in respect of these premises.

Authorised persons, interested parties and responsible authorities

5.30 In section 13, the 2003 Act defines three key groups that have important roles in the context of applications, inspection, enforcement and reviews of premises licences.

5.31 The first group – 'authorised persons' – are bodies empowered by the Act to carry out inspection and enforcement roles. The police are not included because they are separately empowered by the Act to carry out their duties. In respect of all premises, the authorised persons include officers of the licensing authority, fire authority inspectors, inspectors locally responsible for the enforcement of the Health and Safety at Work etc. Act 1974, and environmental health officers. Local authority officers will most commonly have responsibility for the enforcement of health and safety legislation. But in connection with certain premises, the Health and Safety Executive have this responsibility. In respect of vessels, authorised persons also include an inspector or a surveyor of ships appointed under section 256 of the Merchant Shipping Act 1995. These would normally be officers acting on behalf of the Maritime and Coastguard Agency. The Secretary of State may also prescribe other authorised persons by means of regulations. Details of any such secondary legislation may be viewed on the DCMS website.

5.32 The second group – 'interested parties' – are the bodies or individuals who are entitled to make representations to licensing authorities on applications for the grant, variation or review of premises licences. In addition, interested parties may themselves seek a review of a premises licence. This group includes:

- a person living in the vicinity of the premises in question;
- a body representing persons living in that vicinity, for example, a residents' association;
- a person involved in a business in the vicinity of the premises in question; and
- a body representing persons involved in such businesses, for example, a trade association.

Any of these individuals or groups may specifically request a representative to make his, her or its representation on his, her or its behalf. For example, a legal representative, a friend, a Member of Parliament, a Member of the National Assembly for Wales, or a local ward councillor could all act in such a capacity. In the case of the last of these, it would be expected that any councillor who is also a member of the licensing committee and who is making such representations on behalf of the interested party would disqualify him or herself from any involvement in the decision-making process affecting the premises licence in question. In addition, it is expected that 'individuals involved in business' will be given its widest possible interpretation, including partnerships, and need not be confined to those engaged in trade and commerce. It is also expected that the expression can be held to embrace the functions of charities, churches and medical practices.

5.33 It is for the licensing authority to determine in the first instance whether or not representations are relevant representations. This may involve determining whether they have, as a matter of fact, been made by an interested party and whether or not, for example, an individual making a representation resides or is involved in business 'in the vicinity' of the premises concerned. However, licensing authorities should be aware that their initial decision on this issue could be subject to legal challenge in the courts. Whether or not an individual resides 'in the vicinity of' the licensed premises is ultimately a matter of fact to be decided by the courts, but initially licensing authorities must decide if the individual or body making a representation qualifies as an interested party. In making their initial decision, licensing authorities should consider, for example, whether the individual's residence or business is likely to be directly affected by disorder and disturbance occurring or potentially occurring on those premises or immediately outside the premises. Where a representation concerns 'cumulative impact', the licensing authority may be unable to consider this factor and would probably need to examine issues such as the proximity of the residence or business. In essence, it is expected that the decision will be approached with common sense and individuals living and working in the neighbourhood or area immediately surrounding the premises will be able to make representations.

5.34 Licensing authorities should consider providing advice on their websites about how any interested party can make representations to them.

5.35 The third group – 'responsible authorities' – includes public bodies that must be fully notified of applications and that are entitled to make representations to the licensing authority in relation to the application for the grant, variation or review of a premises licence. All representations made by responsible authorities are relevant representations if they concern the effect of the application on the licensing objectives. For all premises, these include the chief officer of police; the local fire authority; the local enforcement agency for the Health and Safety at Work etc. Act 1974 (which may be the local authority in certain circumstances, and the Health and Safety Executive in others); the local authority with responsibility for environmental health; the local planning authority; any body that represents those who are responsible for, or interested in, matters relating to the protection of children from harm and is recognised by the licensing authority for that area as being competent to advise it on such matters; and any licensing authority, other than the relevant licensing authority, in whose area part of the premises are situated.

5.36 In respect of the protection of children from harm, it is expected that the body recognised by the licensing authority to be competent to advise will have been indicated in the statement of licensing policy. This is important as applications for premises licences have to be copied to the responsible authorities by the applicant in order for them to make any representations they think are relevant. In many licensing authority areas, it is expected that the body recognised by the licensing authority to be competent in this regard will be the Area Child Protection Committee. However, in some areas, the Committee's involvement may not be practical and in these circumstances the licensing authority is expected to nominate another body, for example, the local authority social services department.

5.37 In relation to a vessel, but no other premises, responsible authorities also include navigation authorities within the meaning of section 221(1) of the Water Resources Act 1991 that have statutory functions in relation to the waters where the vessel is usually moored or berthed or any waters where it is proposed to be navigated at a time when it is used for licensable activities; the Environment Agency; the British Waterways Board; and the Secretary of State. The provision of the Secretary of State as a responsible authority in this case means the Secretary of State for Transport who in practice acts through the Maritime and Coastguard Agency, an executive agency of central Government, which has no formal legal existence.

5.38 The Maritime and Coastguard Agency is the lead responsible authority for public safety, including fire safety, issues affecting passenger vessels. The safety regime for passenger vessels is enforced under the Merchant Shipping Acts by the Maritime and Coastguard Agency who operate a passenger ship certification scheme. Fire authorities, the Health and Safety Executive and local authority health and safety inspectors should normally be able to make 'nil' returns in respect of passenger vessels and rely on the Maritime and Coastguard Agency to make any necessary representations in respect of this licensing objective. Merchant shipping legislation does not, however, apply to permanently moored vessels. So, for example, restaurant ships moored on the Thames Embankment, with permanent shore connections will require consideration by the other responsible authorities concerned with public safety, including fire safety.

5.39 The Secretary of State for Culture, Media and Sport may prescribe other responsible authorities by means of regulations. Any such secondary legislation may be viewed at the DCMS website. The Secretary of State expects to prescribe Crime and Disorder Reduction Partnerships in due course.

Applications for premises licences

5.40 Any person (if an individual aged 18 or over) who is carrying on or who proposes to carry on a business which involves the use of premises (which includes any place including one in the open air) for licensable activities may apply for a premises licence either on a permanent basis or for a time-limited period. 'A person' in this context includes, for example, a business or a partnership. Licensing authorities should not require the nomination of an individual to hold the licence. It is not for the licensing authority to decide who is the most appropriate person to hold the licence. For example, in respect of most leased public houses, a tenant may run or propose to run the business at the premises in agreement with a pub owning company. Both would be eligible to apply for the appropriate licence and it is for these businesses or individuals to agree contractually amongst themselves who should do so. It is not for the licensing authority to interfere in that decision. However, in the case of a managed public house, the pub operating company should apply for the licence as the manager (an employee) would not be entitled to do so. Similarly, with cinema chains, the normal holder of the premises licence would be the company owning the cinema and not the cinema manager (an employee of the main company).

5.41 In considering joint applications (which is likely to be a rare occurrence), it must be stressed that under section 16(1)(a) of the 2003 Act each applicant must be carrying on a business which involves the use of the premises for licensable activities at the premises. In the case of public houses, this would be easier for a tenant to demonstrate than for a pub owning company that is not itself carrying on licensable activities. The Secretary of State recommends that where licences are to be held by businesses, it is desirable that this should be a single business to avoid any lack of clarity in terms of accountability.

5.42 Where a public house is owned or a tenancy is held jointly by a husband and wife or other partnerships of a similar nature and both actively involve themselves in the business of carrying on licensable activities at the premises, it is entirely possible for the husband and wife or the partners to apply jointly as applicant for the premises licence, even if they are not formally partners in business terms. This is unlikely to lead to the same issues of clouded accountability that could arise where two separate businesses apply jointly for the licence. If the application is granted, the premises licence would identify the holder as comprising both names and any subsequent applications, for example for a variation of the licence, need to be made jointly. Applicants would need to consider whether, in these circumstances, a joint application provides sufficient flexibility for their business or whether a single application, coupled with the flexible provisions in the 2003 Act in respect of transfer and interim authorities, is a preferable course.

5.43 A wide range of other individuals and bodies set out in section 16 of the 2003 Act may apply for premises licences. They include, for example, Government Departments, local authorities, hospitals, schools, charities or police forces. In addition to the bodies listed in section 16, the Secretary of State may prescribe by regulations other bodies that may so apply and any such secondary legislation may be viewed on the DCMS website.

5.44 There is nothing in the 2003 Act which prevents an application being made for a premises licence at premises for which a premises licence is already held. For example, a premises licence authorising the sale of alcohol may be held by one individual and another individual could apply for a premises licence in respect of the same premises or part of those premises which would authorise regulated entertainment. This also ensures that one business could not seek premises licences, for example, for all potential circus sites in England and Wales and thereby prevent other circuses from using those sites even though they had the permission of the landowner. Similarly, there is nothing to stop a temporary event notice being given for a premises in respect of which a premises licence is in force.

5.45 An application for a premises licence must be made in the prescribed form to the relevant licensing authority and be copied to each of the appropriate responsible authorities (applications for premises which are not vessels are not, for example, to be sent to the Maritime and Coastguard Agency). The application must be accompanied by:

- the required fee (details of fees may be viewed on the DCMS website);
- an operating schedule (see below);
- a plan of the premises in a prescribed form to which the application relates; and
- if the application involves the supply of alcohol, a form of consent from the individual who is to be specified in the licence as the designated premises supervisor.

Regulations containing provisions on fees and the prescribed form of applications and plans may be viewed on the DCMS website.

The operating schedule

5.46 The operating schedule will form part of the completed application form for a premises licence. An operating schedule should include information which is necessary to enable any responsible authority or interested party to assess whether the steps to be taken to promote licensing objectives are satisfactory. For example, it should include a description of the style and character of the business to be conducted on the premises (for example, a supermarket, or a cinema with six screens and a bar, or a restaurant, or a public house with two bars, a dining area and a garden open to customers). Where alcohol is being sold for consumption on the premises in public houses, bars and nightclubs, it would also be valuable to know the extent to which seating is to be provided because research has shown that the amount of seating can be relevant to the prevention of crime and disorder. It should also indicate the type of activities available on the premises, whether licensable under the 2003 Act or not. While 'a performance of dance' with the exception of morris dancing is a licensable activity, the type of dancing, which is unaffected by the licensing requirement, may give rise to issues concerning the steps needed to protect children from harm and more generally conditions which would be appropriate. An operating schedule should therefore describe the type of dancing in broad terms and disclose if the dancing involves striptease or lap-dancing. Similarly, if dancing is to take place, it should be clear whether this would involve dancing by members of the public or by professional performers or both and in what setting. If music is to be provided, it is important that clear indication is given of the type of music to be provided. In the case of passenger vessels, it will also be valuable for the area within any vessel where licensable activities will be taking place to be described. This type of information is essential so that responsible authorities and interested parties can form a proper view as to what measures may be necessary to ensure public safety and prevent public nuisance. An operating schedule must also set out the following details:

- the relevant licensable activities to be conducted on the premises;
- the times during which it is proposed that the relevant licensable activities are to take place (including the times during each day of the week, during particular holiday periods and during particular seasons, if it is likely that the times would be different during different parts of the year);
- any other times when the premises are to be open to the public;
- where the licence is required only for a limited period, that period;
- where the licensable activities include the supply of alcohol, the name and address of the individual to be specified as the designated premises supervisor;
- where the licensable activities include the supply of alcohol, whether the alcohol will be supplied for consumption on or off the premises or both;
- the steps which the applicant proposes to take to promote the licensing objectives.

Examples of specimen operating schedules may be viewed on the DCMS website. Other details to be included in the operating schedule will be set out in regulations made from time to time by the Secretary of State which may be viewed on the DCMS website.

Steps to promote the licensing objectives

5.47 In preparing an operating schedule, the Secretary of State recommends that applicants should be aware of the expectations of the licensing authority and the responsible authorities about the steps that are necessary for the promotion of the licensing objectives. This does not mean that applicants must check their operating schedules with responsible authorities before submitting them, but when uncertain, the responsible authorities can provide expert advice on matters relating to the licensing objectives. For example, the best source of advice on crime prevention is the local police. In preparing operating schedules, applicants should have regard to statements of licensing policy published by the licensing authority for their area. All parties are expected to work together in partnership to ensure that the licensing objectives are promoted collectively. Licensing authorities and responsible authorities are therefore expected so far as possible to publish material about the promotion of the licensing objectives and to ensure that applicants can readily access advice about these matters. To minimise the burden on licensing authorities and applicants, it may be sensible for applicants to seek the views of the key responsible authorities before formally submitting applications and having completed drafts of their own operating schedules (after considering the effect on the four licensing objectives). For example, on matters relating to crime and disorder, the police and local authority community safety officers, and local community groups, might be consulted and on matters relating to noise, local environmental health officers might be consulted. Such co-operative effort should minimise the number of disputes which arise in respect of operating schedules. Where there are no disputes, the steps that applicants propose to take to promote the licensing objectives that they have set out in the operating schedule will very often translate directly into conditions that will be attached to premises licences with the minimum of fuss.

5.48 Where permission is to be sought for regulated entertainment involving the provision of live music or other cultural activity, applicants may wish to consider consulting the local authority arts officer or local representatives of the Musicians' Union before completing their operating schedule.

5.49 The steps to be taken should be both realistic and within the control of the applicant and management of the premises. If a licence is granted with conditions attached requiring the implementation of such steps, the conditions will be enforceable in law and it will be a criminal offence to fail to comply with them (under section 136 of the 2003 Act). As such, it would be wholly inappropriate to impose conditions outside the control of those responsible for the running of the premises.

5.50 In respect of some premises, it is entirely possible that no measures will be needed to promote one or more of the licensing objectives, for example, because they are adequately dealt with by other existing legislation. It is however important that all operating schedules should be precise and clear about the measures that it is proposed to take to promote each of the licensing objectives and in particular, the protection of children from harm.

5.51 Further advice on the steps that the Secretary of State would expect to be needed to promote the licensing objectives is given below.

Advertising applications

5.52 Regulations governing the advertising of applications for the grant or variation or review of premises licences will be contained in secondary legislation made by the Secretary of State and can be viewed on the DCMS website. They include the requirement that a brief summary of the application setting out matters such as the proposed licensable activities and the proposed hours of opening should be clearly displayed on an A3 size notice immediately on or outside the premises for the period during which representations may be made, together with information about where the details of the application may be viewed. So far as possible, as well as putting in place arrangements for interested parties to view a record of the application in the licensing register as described in Schedule 3 to the 2003 Act, it is expected that licensing authorities will also include these details on their websites. Charges made for copies of the register should not exceed the cost of preparing such copies.

Casinos and bingo clubs

5.53 Casinos and bingo clubs are the subject of separate legislation with regard to the licensing of gaming – the Gaming Act 1968. When granting, varying or reviewing licences authorising the sale of alcohol for consumption on such premises and/or the provision of regulated entertainment and/or late night refreshment at such premises, licensing authorities should not duplicate any conditions imposed by virtue of such legislation. Where applicants wish to carry on activities licensable under the 2003 Act, they will need to prepare and submit an operating schedule, but in detailing the steps to be taken in promoting the four licensing objectives the applicant may refer to the statutory conditions in respect of his gaming licence where relevant. In addition, any conditions which are attached to premises licences should not prevent the holder from complying with the requirements of the 1968 Act and its supporting regulations.

5.54 In considering applications for premises licences, licensing authorities and responsible authorities should note:

- the licensing of such premises for gaming remains the responsibility of magistrates, meeting as gaming licensing committees, who have the power to impose such restrictions on the hours during which gaming will be permitted to take place on such premises as appear to them to be necessary for the purpose of preventing disturbance or annoyance to the occupiers of other premises in the vicinity and, in the case of casinos, restrictions limiting the purposes, other than gaming, for which such premises may be used.
- licences under Part II of the Gaming Act 1968 fall to be renewed annually and renewal may be refused if, among other things, the holder of the licence applying for such renewal is not a fit and proper person to be the holder of a licence under the 1968 Act. Such a licence may also be cancelled, or a certificate of consent issued by the Gaming Board for Great Britain revoked, on similar grounds.
- such premises are regulated by the Gaming Board for Great Britain which issues guidelines for the casino and bingo club industries, and failure to comply is taken into account in assessing whether holders of licences under Part II of the 1968 Act have acted in a fit and proper manner. The Gaming Board's current guidelines may be viewed on its website: **www.gbgb.org.uk**.
- under the provisions of the 1968 Act, such premises may operate only as private clubs, with participation in the gaming (and in practice admission to the premises) restricted to members (and only then when at least 24 hours has elapsed since an application for membership) and their bona fide guests. The principal purpose of casinos and bingo clubs is gaming and the sale of alcohol is incidental to that purpose and similarly, sales may only be made to members and their bona fide guests.
- the provision of entertainment in such premises is incidental to gaming and in determining whether to permit casinos to provide entertainment of a type that constitutes regulated entertainment under the 2003 Act, gaming licensing committees should take into account guidance contained in the Gambling Circular 7 dated 5 August 2002 issued by the Gambling and National Lottery Division of the DCMS. The circular may be viewed on the DCMS

website. The Secretary of State accordingly considers that the licensing objectives will have been or will be in the main adequately considered by gaming licensing committees in respect of an application for gaming licences and duplication of conditions should be avoided when considering applications under the 2003 Act where relevant representations have been made.

Designated sports grounds, designated sports events and major outdoor sports stadia

5.55 Outdoor sports stadia are the subject of separate legislation with regard to health and safety and fire safety. When granting, varying or reviewing premises licences, licensing authorities should not therefore duplicate any conditions relating to such legislation. The sports events taking place at such outdoor stadia do not fall within the definition of the provision of regulated entertainment under the 2003 Act; with the exception of boxing and wrestling matches. No premises licence should therefore seek to impose times when such events that are not licensable under the 2003 Act may take place. Consideration of applications for premises licences should be limited to those activities that are licensable under the 2003 Act; i.e. the sale of alcohol, the provision of regulated entertainment and the provision of late night refreshment.

5.56 Major stadia will often have several bars and restaurants, including bars generally open to all spectators as well as bars and restaurants to which members of the public do not have free access. Alcohol will also be supplied in private boxes and viewing areas. A premises licence may make separate arrangements for public and private areas or for restaurant areas on the same premises. It may also designate areas where alcohol may not be consumed at all or at particular times. History demonstrates that certain sports events are more likely than others to give rise to concerns about the safety of, and disorder among, spectators. Premises licences can and should make different provision for different sports events where licensable activities take place because of that history. Further details are provided in Chapter 6 of this Guidance. Because of the issues of crowd control that arise in and around such grounds, it is expected that licensing authorities will give considerable weight to the views of the local chief officer of police when representations are made concerning licensable activities, such as the sale of alcohol, taking place at such premises.

Sports stadia with roofs that open and close

5.57 Under the provisions of the 2003 Act, major sports grounds with roofs that open and close, such as the Millennium Stadium in Cardiff, are not within the definition of an 'indoor sporting event' for the purposes of the Act. As a result events taking place in such stadia do not come within the descriptions of entertainment for the purposes of the provision of regulated entertainment and are not licensable for this purpose under the 2003 Act.

Vessels

5.58 The 2003 Act applies in relation to a vessel (which includes a ship or a boat) which is not permanently moored or berthed as if it were premises situated in a place where it is usually moored or berthed. The relevant licensing authority for considering an application for a premises licence in respect of a vessel is therefore the licensing authority for the area in which it is usually moored or berthed. However, an activity is not a licensable activity if it takes place aboard a vessel engaged on an international journey. An 'international journey' means a journey from a place in the United Kingdom to an immediate destination outside the United Kingdom or a journey from outside the United Kingdom to an immediate destination in the United Kingdom. A vessel that is permanently moored or berthed is premises situated at that place.

5.59 Where a premises licence is sought in connection with a vessel which will be navigated whilst licensable activities take place, the licensing authority should be concerned, following the receipt of relevant representations, with the promotion of the licensing objectives on-board the vessel. It should not focus on matters relating to safe navigation or operation of the vessel, the general safety of passengers or emergency provision, all of which are subject to regulations which must be met before the vessel is issued with its Passenger Certificate and Safety Management Certificate. It is expected that, if the Maritime and Coastguard Agency is satisfied that the vessel complies with Merchant Shipping Standards for a passenger ship, the premises will normally be accepted as meeting the public safety objective of the regime. In respect of other public safety aspects of the application, representations made by the Maritime and Coastguard Agency on behalf of the Secretary of State should be given particular weight.

International airports and International ports

5.60 Under the 2003 Act, the Secretary of State may designate a port, hoverport or airport, if it appears to the Secretary of State that there is a substantial amount of international traffic, so that an activity is not a licensable activity if it is carried on at such designated locations. The Secretary of State may also preserve existing designations made under earlier legislation. Details of the ports, hoverports and airports so designated may be viewed on the DCMS website.

5.61 Where a port has been designated by the Secretary of State, the areas at the ports which are 'airside' or 'wharfside' are included in the exemption in the 2003 Act from the licensing regime. These are areas to which the non-travelling public do not have access and are subject to stringent bye-laws, and the exemption is to enable the provision of refreshment of all kinds to travellers at all times of the day and night. Other parts of designated ports, hoverports and airports are subject to the normal licensing controls.

Vehicles

5.62 Under the 2003 Act, alcohol may not be sold on a **moving** vehicle and the vehicle may not be licensed for that purpose. However, licensing authorities may consider applications in respect of a vehicle for the sale of alcohol when it is parked or stationary. For example, mobile bars could sell alcohol at special events as long as they were parked. Any permission granted would relate solely to the place where the vehicle is parked and where sales are to take place.

5.63 It should also be noted that the provision of any entertainment or entertainment facilities on premises consisting of or forming part of any vehicle while it is in motion and not permanently or temporarily parked is not to be regarded as a regulated entertainment for the purposes of the 2003 Act. For example, a band performing on a moving float in a parade would not require a premises licence if performances only take place while the vehicle is in motion.

Trains and aircraft

5.64 Under the 2003 Act, railway vehicles and aircraft engaged on journeys are exempted from the licensing regime. However, licensing authorities should note that some defunct aircraft and railway carriages are used as restaurants and bars, remaining in a fixed position. Licensing authorities may consider applications made in respect of such premises and they are subject to the provisions of the 2003 Act. It should also be noted that under the 2003 Act, the sale of alcohol to a minor anywhere in England and Wales has been made a criminal offence. Until the 2003 Act came into force, such sales were only offences if they took place on licensed premises. This is no longer the case. Accordingly, the sale of alcohol aboard a train or aircraft to a minor is now a criminal offence.

Considering applications for new and major variations of premises licences

5.65 A major variation is one that does not relate simply to a change of the name or address of someone named in the licence or an application to vary the licence to specify a new individual as the designated premises supervisor. The approach taken in the 2003 Act to applications for new and major variations is based on five main policy aims. These are that:

- the main purpose of the licensing regime is to promote the licensing objectives;
- applicants for premises licences or for major variations of such licences are expected to conduct a thorough risk assessment with regard to the licensing objectives when preparing their applications. This risk assessment will inform any necessary steps to be set out in an operating schedule to promote the four licensing objectives;
- operating schedules, which form part of an application, should be considered by professional experts in the areas concerned, such as the police and environmental health officers, when applications for premises licences and club premises certificates are copied to them by applicants;
- local residents and businesses are free to raise relevant representations, which relate to the promotion of the licensing objectives, about the proposals contained in an application; and
- the role of a licensing authority is primarily to regulate the carrying on of the licensable activity when there are differing specific interests in those activities to ensure that the licensing objectives are promoted in the wider interests of the community.

When considering applications, it is expected that licensing authorities will seek to uphold these policy aims.

5.66 When a licensing authority receives an application for a new or a major variation of a premises licence, it must determine whether the application has been made properly in accordance with section 17 of the 2003 Act, and in accordance with regulations made by the Secretary of State under sections 17(4), 17(5), 54 and 55 of the Act. This means that the licensing authority must consider among other things whether the application has been properly advertised in accordance with the regulations.

5.67 Where an application has been lawfully made and provided that no responsible authority (for example, the chief officer of police or an environmental health authority) makes a representation about an application and no interested party seeks to do so, then no hearing would be required and the application **must** be granted in the terms sought, subject only to conditions which are consistent with the operating schedule and relevant mandatory conditions in the Act. This should be undertaken as a simple administrative process by the licensing authority's officials by whom the proposals contained in the operating schedule to promote the licensing objectives should be translated into clear and understandable conditions consistent with the proposals in the operating schedule. In these circumstances, it is expected and particularly important that licensing authorities do not attempt to second-guess the views of the professional and expert consultees, for example, those of the police, the fire authority and environmental health authority. Accordingly, if operating schedules are prepared efficiently, often in consultation with responsible authorities, it is expected that the likelihood of hearings being necessary following relevant representations would be significantly reduced.

5.68 Where a representation concerning the licensing objectives is lodged by a responsible authority about a proposed operating schedule it is relevant and the licensing authority's discretion will be engaged. It will also be engaged if an interested party makes relevant representations to the licensing authority, i.e. those which are not frivolous or vexatious and which relate to the licensing objectives (see paragraphs 5.70 – 5.77 below). A hearing will be required for the licensing authority to consider the representations, at which the parties should be invited to comment upon the representations made and if necessary, to provide clarification of their own representations. The need for a hearing can only be dispensed with by the agreement of the licensing authority, the applicant and all of the parties who made relevant representations. The hearing process must meet the requirements of regulations made by the Secretary of State and which may be viewed on the DCMS website. As a matter of practice, licensing authorities should seek to focus the hearing on the steps needed to promote the particular licensing objective which has given rise to the specific representation and avoid straying into undisputed areas. A responsible authority or interested party may choose to rely on their written representation which gave rise to the hearing. They may not add further representations to those disclosed to the applicant prior to the hearing, but they may amplify their existing representation. In determining the application with a view to promoting the licensing objectives in the overall interests of the local community, the licensing authority must give appropriate weight to:

- the representations (including supporting information) presented by all the parties;

- this Guidance;
- its own statement of licensing policy; and
- the steps that are necessary to promote the licensing objectives.

5.69 The determination should be given forthwith and reasons provided to support the determination. This is important not least in anticipation of an appeal by any of the parties. After considering all the relevant issues, it is open to the licensing authority to grant the application subject to such conditions that are consistent with the operating schedule, and these can be modified to such an extent that the licensing authority considers necessary for the promotion of the licensing objectives. Any conditions so imposed must be necessary for the promotion of the licensing objectives. There is no power for the licensing authority to attach a condition which is merely aspirational: it must be necessary. For example, conditions may not be attached which relate solely to the health of customers rather than their direct physical safety. Alternatively, the licensing authority may refuse the application on the grounds that refusal is necessary for the promotion of the licensing objectives. It may also refuse to specify a designated premises supervisor and/or only allow certain requested licensable activities.

5.70 Where a representation is made under the provisions of the 2003 Act by an interested party (for example, a local business or a resident living in the vicinity of the premises), there is a preliminary stage at which the licensing authority must consider whether the representation is relevant. This is dealt with in more detail below. If the licensing authority decides it is not relevant, a hearing would not be required in relation to that representation and in the absence of representations from other interested parties or responsible authorities, the application must be granted. The aggrieved interested party whose representation is not regarded as 'relevant' may challenge the licensing authority's decision by way of judicial review.

5.71 With regard to applications to vary the hours during which alcohol may be sold in shops, stores and supermarkets, the Secretary of State recommends that the norm should be for such premises to be free to provide sales of alcohol for consumption off the premises at any times when the retail outlet is open for shopping unless there are very good reasons for restricting those hours. Where representations are received from the police, for example, in the case of some shops known to be a focus of disorder and disturbance because youths gather there, a limitation may be necessary.

5.72 In the context of variations, which may involve structural alteration to or change of use of the building, it should be noted that the decision of the licensing authority will not exempt an applicant from the need to apply for building control where appropriate.

Relevant, vexatious and frivolous representations

5.73 A representation would only be 'relevant' if it relates to the likely effect of the grant of the licence on the promotion of at least one of the licensing objectives. A representation that fails to do this is not 'relevant' for the purposes of the 2003 Act. It is not intended, for example, that the consideration of the application should be a re-run of the planning application which would have considered a wider range of matters. Premises licences authorise the activities within the scope of the 2003 Act that it is proposed should take place on the premises. For example, a representation from a local businessman which argued that his business would be commercially damaged by the new business for which an application is being made under Part 3 of the 2003 Act would not be relevant. On the other hand, a representation to the effect that nuisance caused by the new business would deter customers from entering the local area and the steps proposed by the applicant to control that nuisance are inadequate would amount to relevant representations and must be considered provided the other conditions necessary to be a relevant representation were fulfilled.

5.74 After a premises licence has been granted or varied, a complaint relating to a general (crime and disorder) situation in a town centre would generally not be regarded as relevant if it cannot be positively tied or linked by a causal connection to particular premises which would allow for a proper review of its licence. For instance, a geographic cluster of complaints, including along transport routes related to an individual public house and its closing time could give grounds for a review of an existing licence as well as direct incidents of crime and disorder around a particular public house. In this context, it should be noted that the 'cumulative impact' on the licensing objectives of a concentration of multiple licensed premises may only give rise to a relevant representation when an application for the grant or variation of a premises licence is being considered: it cannot give rise to a relevant representation after a licence has been granted or varied when a review of a licence may be sought. A review must relate specifically to a particular premises licence relating to an individual premises, and by its nature 'cumulative impact' relates to the indirect effect of a concentration of many premises. Identifying one for a review by reason of cumulative impact on the licensing objectives would inevitably be arbitrary.

5.75 It is for the licensing authority to determine on its merits whether any representation by an interested party is frivolous or vexatious. The interested party making representations may not consider the matter to be frivolous or vexatious, but the test is whether the licensing authority is of the opinion they are frivolous or vexatious. The licensing authority must determine this and make the decision on the basis of what might ordinarily be considered to be vexatious or frivolous. Vexation may arise because of disputes between rival businesses and local knowledge will therefore be invaluable in considering such matters. Frivolous representations would be essentially categorised by a lack of seriousness. A trivial complaint may not always be frivolous, but it would have to be pertinent in order to be relevant. An interested party aggrieved by a rejection of his representations on these grounds may challenge the authority's decision by way of judicial review.

5.76 Decisions as to whether representations are relevant should not be made on the basis of any political judgement which would undermine a natural approach to the issue. This may be difficult for ward councillors receiving complaints from residents within their own wards. If consideration is not to be delegated, contrary to the recommendation in this Guidance, an assessment should be prepared by officials for consideration by the sub-committee before any decision is taken that necessitates a hearing; i.e. the decision would be that the representations are relevant. Any ward councillor who considers that his own interests are such that he is unable to consider the matter independently should disqualify himself.

5.77 The Secretary of State recommends that in borderline cases, the benefit of the doubt should be given to the interested party making the representation. The subsequent hearing would then provide an opportunity for the person or body making the representation to amplify and clarify it. If it then emerged, for example, that the representation should not be supported, the licensing authority could decide not to take any action in respect of the application for the grant or variation of a premises licence.

Transfers of premises licences

5.78 The 2003 Act provides for any person who may apply for a premises licence, which includes a business, to apply for the transfer of a premises licence to him, her or it. Notice of the application has to be given to the chief officer of police. Where an applicant is an individual he or she must be 18 years old or over. A transfer of a premises licence would often arise when a business involving licensable activities is sold to a new owner. A transfer of the licence only changes the identity of the holder of the licence and does not alter the licence in any other way.

5.79 In the vast majority of cases, it is expected that a transfer will be a very simple administrative process and section 43 of the 2003 Act provides a mechanism whereby the transfer can be given immediate effect on the receiving of an application by the licensing authority until it is formally determined or withdrawn. This is to ensure that there should be no interruption to normal business at the premises. If the police raise no objection about the application, the licensing authority must transfer the licence in accordance with the application, amend the licence accordingly and return it to the new holder.

5.80 In exceptional circumstances where the chief officer of police believes the transfer may undermine the crime prevention objective, the police may object to the transfer. Such objections are expected to be rare and arise because the police have evidence that the business or individuals seeking to hold the licence or business or individuals linked to such persons are involved in crime (or disorder). For example, the police would rightly seek to prevent a company having a licence transferred to it in respect of licensed premises if they had evidence that the premises may be used to launder money obtained from drugs crime. Where an objection is made, the licensing authority must hold a hearing at which the authority will consider the objection. The authority's consideration would be confined to the issue of the crime prevention objective and the hearing should not be permitted to stray into other extraneous matters. The burden would be on the police to demonstrate to the authority that there were good grounds for believing that the transfer of the licence would undermine the crime prevention objective. The licensing authority must give clear and comprehensive reasons for its eventual determination in anticipation of a possible appeal by either party.

5.81 It is stressed that such objections (and therefore such hearings) should only arise in truly exceptional circumstances. If the licensing authority believes that the police are using this mechanism to vet transfer applicants routinely and to seek hearings as a fishing expedition to inquire into applicants' backgrounds, it is expected that they would raise the matter immediately with the chief officer of police.

Applications to change the designated premises supervisors

5.82 Paragraphs 4.18 to 4.23 above cover designated premises supervisors and applications to vary a premises licence covering sales of alcohol by specifying a new designated premises supervisor.

Provisional statements

5.83 Where premises are being or are about to be constructed for the purpose of being used for one or more licensable activities, or are being or about to be extended or otherwise altered for that purpose, the necessary investment may not be committed unless investors have some assurance not only that the project has appropriate planning permission but that they have some degree of assurance that a premises licence covering the desired licensable activities would be granted for the premises when the building work is completed.

5.84 The 2003 Act does not define the words 'otherwise altered', but the alteration must relate to the purpose of being used for one or more licensable activities. For example, a premises licence should indicate the whole of or part of the premises which are licensed for one or more licensable activity. If the building is to be altered to allow a previously unlicensed area to be used for a licensable activity, a provisional statement may be sought in respect of the additional area.

5.85 It is open to any person falling within section 16 of the 2003 Act to apply for a premises licence before new premises are constructed or extended or changed. Nothing in the 2003 Act prevents such an application. This would be possible where clear plans of the proposed structure exist and an operating schedule is capable of being completed about the activities to take place there, the time at which such activities will take place, the proposed hours of opening, where the applicant wishes the licence to have effect for a limited period, that period, the steps to be taken to promote the licensing objectives, and where the sale of alcohol is involved, whether supplies are proposed to be for consumption on or off the premises (or both) and the name of the designated premises supervisor the applicant wishes to specify. On granting such an application, the authority of the licence would not have immediate effect but the licensing authority would include in the licence the date upon which it would have effect. A provisional statement will therefore normally only be required when the information described above is not available.

5.86 The 2003 Act therefore provides for a person, if an individual aged 18 or over, who has an interest in the premises to apply for a 'provisional statement'. A provisional statement does not have limited duration but with the potential for there to be material changes over time, the longer there is a delay before a premises licence is applied for the greater potential for representations made in respect of an application for a premises licence not to be excluded. 'Person' in this context includes a business. The applicant could be a firm of architects or a construction company or a financier. The application would include the particulars of the premises, describe the work to be done and the licensable activities that it is planned would take place at the completed premises. Plans would also be included. The application must be advertised and notified to responsible authorities in a similar way to the arrangements for applications for premises licences and as set out in regulations. Responsible authorities and interested parties may make representations. Where no representations are made, a provisional statement must be issued to that effect. Where relevant representations are made, a hearing must be arranged by the licensing authority to consider them. The need for a hearing can be dispensed with only by agreement of the licensing authority, the applicant for the provisional statement and all the parties who made relevant representations.

5.87 When a hearing is held, the licensing authority must decide whether, if the premises were constructed or altered in the way proposed in the schedule of works and if a premises licence was sought for those premises, it would consider it necessary for the promotion of the licensing objectives to attach conditions to the licence, to rule out any of the licensable activities applied for, to refuse to specify the person nominated as premises supervisor, or to reject the application. It will then issue the applicant with a provisional statement setting out the details of that decision together with its reasons. The licensing authority must copy the provisional statement to each person who made relevant representations and the chief officer of police for the area in which the premises is situated. The licensing authority should give full and comprehensive reasons for its decision. This is important in anticipation of an appeal by any aggrieved party.

5.88 When a person applies for a premises licence in respect of premises (or part of the premises or premises which are substantially the same) for which a provisional statement has been made, representations by responsible authorities and interested parties will be excluded in certain circumstances. These are where:

- the application for a licence is in the same form as the licence described in the provisional statement; and
- the work in the schedule of works has been satisfactorily completed;
- given the information provided in the application for a provisional statement, the responsible authority or interested party could have made the same, or substantially the same, representations about the application then but failed to do so without reasonable excuse; and
- there has been no material change in the circumstances relating either to the premises or to the area in the vicinity of those premises since the provisional statement was made.

5.89 Licensing authorities should exclude representations in these circumstances. It will be important for investment and employment opportunities in their areas for provisional statements to function properly by providing a limited assurance. But it should be recognised that a great deal of time may pass between the issue of a provisional statement and the completion of a premises in accordance with a schedule of works. Genuine and material changes in circumstances may arise during the intervening years.

5.90 It should be noted that any decision of the licensing authority on an application for a provisional statement would not relieve an applicant of the need to apply for building control.

5.91 A provisional statement may not be sought or given for a vessel, a vehicle or a moveable structure (see section 189 of the 2003 Act).

Interim authorities

5.92 The 2003 Act provides special arrangements for the continuation of permissions under a premises licence when the holder of a licence dies suddenly or becomes bankrupt or mentally incapable. In the normal course of events, the licence would lapse in such circumstances. Because there may also be some time before, for example, the deceased person's estate can be dealt with or an administrative receiver appointed this could have a damaging effect on those with interests in the premises, such as an owner or lessor, as well as for employees working at the premises in question; and could bring unnecessary disruption to customers' plans. The Act therefore provides for the licence to be capable of being reinstated in a discrete period of time in certain circumstances.

5.93 These circumstances arise only where a premises licence has lapsed owing to the death, incapacity or insolvency of the holder. In such circumstances, an 'interim authority' notice may be given to the licensing authority within seven days beginning the day after the licence lapsed. It should also be copied to the chief officer of police. The premises licence would lapse until such a notice is given and carrying on licensable activities in that time would be unlawful. Such activity will be an offence as an unauthorised licensable activity under section 136(1)(a) of the 2003 Act, to which there is a 'defence of due diligence' provided in section 139. This may be relevant where, for example, the manager of particular premises is wholly unaware for a period of time that the premises licence holder has died. As soon as an interim authority notice is given within the seven day period, the business may continue to carry on any licensable activities permitted by the premises licence.

5.94 An interim notice may only be given either by a person with a prescribed interest in the premises as set out by the Secretary of State in regulations which may be viewed on the DCMS website; or by a person connected to the former holder of the licence (normally a personal representative of the former holder or a person with power of attorney or where someone has become insolvent that persons insolvency practitioner).

5.95 The effect of giving the notice is to reinstate the premises licence as if the person giving the notice is the holder of the licence and thereby allow licensable activities to continue to take place pending a formal application for transfer. The maximum period for which an interim authority notice may have effect is two months.

5.96 The interim authority notice ceases to have effect unless by the end of the initial 7 day period a copy of the notice has been given to the chief officer of police. Within 48 hours of the giving of the copy of the notice, and if satisfied that in the exceptional circumstances of the case failure to cancel the interim authority would undermine the crime prevention objective, the police may give a notice to that effect to the licensing authority. In such circumstances, the licensing authority must hold a hearing to consider the objection notice and cancel the interim authority notice if it determines that it is necessary to do so for the promotion of the crime prevention objective.

5.97 In respect of these matters, it is expected that licensing authorities will be alert to the urgency of the circumstances and the need to consider the objection quickly.

5.98 It should also be noted that by virtue of section 50 of the 2003 Act where the premises licence lapses (because of death, incapacity or insolvency of the holder etc.) or by its surrender, but no interim authority notice has effect, a person who may apply for the grant of a premises licence under section 16(1) may apply within 7 days of the lapse for the transfer of the licence to him with immediate effect pending the determination of the application – causing the licence to be reinstated from the point at which the transfer application was received by the licensing authority. The person applying for the transfer must copy his application to the chief officer of police.

Reviews

5.99 The proceedings set out in the 2003 Act for reviewing premises licences represent a key protection for the community where problems associated with crime and disorder, public safety, public nuisance or the protection of children from harm are occurring. It is the existence of these procedures which should, in general, allow licensing authorities to apply a light touch bureaucracy to the grant and variation of premises licences by providing a review mechanism when concerns relating to the licensing objectives arise later in respect of individual premises.

5.100 At any stage, following the grant of a premises licence, a responsible authority, such as the police or the fire authority, or an interested party, such as a resident living in the vicinity of the premises, may ask the licensing authority to review the licence because of a matter arising at the premises in connection with any of the four licensing objectives. In addition, a review of the licence will normally follow any action by the police to close down the premises for up to 24 hours on grounds of disorder or noise nuisance as a result of a notice of magistrates' court's determination sent to the licensing authority. Licensing authorities may not initiate their own reviews of premises licences. Officers of the local authority who are specified as responsible authorities under the 2003 Act, such as environmental health officers, may however request reviews on any matter which relates to the promotion of one or more of the licensing objectives.

5.101 Representations made by a department of the local authority which is a responsible authority should be treated by the licensing authority in precisely the same way that they would treat representations made by any other body or individual.

5.102 In every case, the representation must relate to particular premises for which a premises licence is in existence and must be relevant to the promotion of the licensing objectives. Representations must be in writing and may be amplified at the subsequent hearing or may stand in their own right. Additional representations which do not amount to an amplification of the original representation may not be made at the hearing.

5.103 It is important to recognise that the promotion of the licensing objectives relies heavily on a partnership between licence holders, authorised persons, interested parties and responsible authorities in pursuit of common aims. It is therefore equally important that reviews are not used to drive a wedge between these groups in a way that would undermine the benefits of cooperation. It would therefore be good practice for authorised persons and responsible authorities to give licence holders early warning of their concerns about problems identified at the premises concerned and of the need for improvement. It is expected that a failure to respond to such warnings would lead to a decision to request a review.

5.104 Where the request originates with an interested party – e.g. a local resident, residents' association, local business or trade association – the licensing authority must first consider whether the complaint made is not relevant, vexatious, frivolous or repetitious. Relevance, vexation and frivolousness were dealt with in paragraphs 5.73 – 5.77 above. A repetitious representation is one that is identical or substantially similar to:

- a ground for review specified in an earlier application for review made in respect of the same premises licence which has already been determined; or
- representations considered by the licensing authority when the premises licence was first granted; or
- representations which would have been made when the application for the premises licence was first made and which were

excluded then by reason of the prior issue of a provisional statement; and

- in addition to the above grounds, a reasonable interval has not elapsed since that earlier review or the grant of the licence.

5.105 Licensing authorities are expected to be aware of the need to prevent attempts to review licences merely as a second bite of the cherry following the failure of representations to persuade the licensing authority on earlier occasions. It is for licensing authorities themselves to judge what should be regarded as a reasonable interval in these circumstances. However, the Secretary of State recommends that more than one review originating from an interested party should not be permitted within a period of twelve months on similar grounds save in compelling circumstances or where it arises following a closure order.

5.106 Following receipt of a request for a review from a responsible authority or an interested party or in accordance with the closure procedures described in Part 8 of the 2003 Act, the licensing authority must arrange a hearing. The arrangements for the hearing must follow the provisions set out by the Secretary of State in regulations. The details may be viewed on the DCMS website. The Secretary of State considers it particularly important that the premises licence holder is fully aware of the representations made in respect of the premises, any evidence supporting the representations and that he or his legal representatives has therefore been able to prepare a response.

Powers of a licensing authority on the determination of a review

5.107 The 2003 Act provides a range of powers for the licensing authority on determining a review that it may exercise where it considers them necessary for the promotion of the licensing objectives.

5.108 The licensing authority may decide that no action is necessary if it finds that the review does not require it to take any steps necessary to promote the licensing objectives. In addition, there is nothing to prevent a licensing authority issuing an informal warning to the licence holder and/or to recommend improvement within a particular period of time. It is expected that licensing authorities will regard such warnings as an important mechanism for ensuring that the licensing objectives are effectively promoted and that warnings should be issued in writing to the holder of the licence. However, where responsible authorities like the police or environmental health officers have already issued warnings requiring improvement – either orally or in writing – that have failed as part of their own stepped approach to concerns, licensing authorities should not merely repeat that approach.

5.109 Where the licensing authority considers that action under its statutory powers are necessary, it may take any of the following steps:

- to modify the conditions of the premises licence (which includes adding new conditions or any alteration or omission of an existing condition), for example, by reducing the hours of opening or by requiring door supervisors at particular times;
- to exclude a licensable activity from the scope of the licence, for example, to exclude the performance of live music or playing of recorded music (where it is not within the incidental live and recorded music exemption);
- to remove the designated premises supervisor, for example, because they consider that the problems are the result of poor management;
- to suspend the licence for a period not exceeding three months;
- to revoke the licence.

5.110 In deciding which of these powers to invoke, it is expected that licensing authorities should so far as possible seek to establish the cause or causes of the concerns which the representations identify. The remedial action taken should generally be directed at these causes and should always be no more than a necessary and proportionate response. For example, licensing authorities should be alive to the possibility that the removal and replacement of the designated premises supervisor may be sufficient to remedy a problem where the cause of the identified problem directly relates to poor management decisions made by that individual. Equally, it may emerge that poor management is a direct reflection of poor company practice or policy and the mere removal of the designated premises supervisor may be an inadequate response to the problems presented. Indeed, where subsequent review hearings are generated by representations, it should be rare merely to remove a succession of designated premises supervisors as this would be a clear indication of deeper problems which impact upon the licensing objectives.

5.111 Licensing authorities should also note that modifications of conditions and exclusions of licensable activities may be imposed either permanently or for a temporary period of up to three months. Accordingly temporary changes or suspension of the licence for up to three months may be imposed. This could impact on the business holding the licence financially and would only be expected to be pursued as a necessary means of promoting the licensing objectives. Accordingly, a licence could be suspended for a weekend as a means of deterring the holder from allowing the problems that gave rise to the review to happen again. However, it will always be important that any detrimental financial impact that may result from a licensing authority's decision is necessary and proportionate to the promotion of the licensing objectives in the circumstances that gave rise to the application for a review.

Reviews arising in connection with crime

5.112 A number of reviews may arise in connection with crime that is not directly connected with licensable activities. For example, reviews may arise because of drugs problems at the premises or money laundering by criminal gangs or the sale of contraband or stolen goods there or the sale of firearms. Licensing authorities do not have the power to judge the criminality or otherwise of any issue. This is a matter for the courts of law. The role of the licensing authority when determining such a review is not therefore to establish the guilt or innocence of any individual but to ensure that the crime prevention objective is promoted. Reviews are part of the regulatory process introduced by the 2003 Act and they are not part of criminal law and procedure. Some reviews will arise after the conviction in the criminal courts of certain individuals but not all. In any case, it is for the licensing authority to determine whether the problems associated with the alleged crimes are taking place on the premises and affecting the promotion of the licensing objectives. Where a review follows a conviction, it would also not be for the licensing authority to attempt to go behind any finding of the courts, which should be treated as a matter of undisputed evidence before them.

5.113 Where the licensing authority is conducting a review on the ground that the premises have been used for criminal purposes, its role is solely to determine what steps are necessary to be taken in connection with the premises licence for the promotion of the crime prevention objective. It is important to recognise that certain criminal activity or associated problems may be taking place or have taken place despite the best efforts of the licensee and the staff working at the premises and despite full compliance with the conditions attached to the licence. In such circumstances, the licensing authority is still empowered to take any necessary steps to remedy the problems. The licensing authority's duty is to take steps with a view to the promotion of the licensing objectives in the interests of the wider community and not those of the individual holder of the premises licence.

5.114 As explained above, it is not the role of a licensing authority to determine the guilt or innocence of individuals charged with licensing or other offences committed on licensed premises. There is therefore no reason why representations giving rise to a review of a premises licence need be delayed pending the outcome of any criminal proceedings. As stated above, at the conclusion of a review, it will be for the licensing authority to determine on the basis of the application for the review and any relevant representations made, what action needs to be taken for the promotion of the licensing objectives in respect of the licence in question, regardless of any subsequent judgment in the courts about the behaviour of individuals.

5.115 There is certain criminal activity that may arise in connection with licensed premises, which the Secretary of State considers should be treated particularly seriously. These are the use of the licensed premises:

- for the sale and distribution of Class A drugs and the laundering of the proceeds of drugs crime;
- for the sale and distribution of illegal firearms;
- for the evasion of copyright in respect of pirated or unlicensed films and music, which does considerable damage to the industries affected;
- for the purchase and consumption of alcohol by minors which impacts on the health, educational attainment, employment prospects and propensity for crime of young people;
- for prostitution or the sale of unlawful pornography;
- by organised groups of paedophiles to groom children;
- as the base for the organisation of criminal activity, particularly by gangs;
- for the organisation of racist activity or the promotion of racist attacks;
- for unlawful gaming and gambling; and
- for the sale of smuggled tobacco and alcohol.

5.116 It is envisaged that licensing authorities, the police and other law enforcement agencies, which are responsible authorities, will use the review procedures effectively to deter such activities and crime. Where reviews arise and the licensing authority determines that the crime prevention objective is being undermined through the premises being used to further crimes, it is expected that revocation of the licence – even in the first instance – should be seriously considered. We would also encourage liaison with the local Crime and Disorder Reduction Partnership.

5.117 It should be noted that it is unlawful to discriminate or to refuse service on grounds of race or by displaying racially discriminatory signs on the premises. Representations made about such activity from responsible authorities or interested parties would be relevant to the promotion of the crime prevention objective and justifiably give rise to a review.

Right of freeholders etc. to be notified of licensing matters

5.118 A person (which will include a business or company) with a property interest in any premises situated in the licensing authority's area may give notice of his interest to the authority using a prescribed form and on payment of a fee prescribed by the Secretary of State. Details of fees and forms will be available on the DCMS website. It is entirely at the discretion of such persons whether they choose to register or not. It is not a legal requirement. Those who may take advantage of this arrangement include the freeholder or leaseholder, a legal mortgagee in respect of the premises, a person in occupation of the premises or any other person prescribed by the Secretary of State. Any regulations regarding individuals so prescribed will also be viewable on the DCMS website. The notice will have effect for 12 months but a new notice can be given every year. Whilst the notice has effect, if any change relating to the premises concerned has been made to the licensing register (which the licensing authority has a duty to keep under section 8 of the 2003 Act), the licensing authority must notify the person who registered an interest of the matter to which the change relates. The person will also be notified of their right under section 8 to request a copy of the information contained in any entry in the register. In cases relating to interim authority notices (see above), it is important that such communications are dealt with promptly.

AWP (Amusements with prizes) machines

5.119 Licensing authorities should note that Schedule 6 (minor and consequential amendments) to the 2003 Act amends the Gaming Act 1968 in respect of the grant of 'section 34 permits' for AWP (amusements with prizes) machines in premises licensed for the sale of alcohol for consumption on the premises. On the bringing into force of this amendment, responsibility for the grant of these permits will transfer from the licensing justices to the relevant licensing authority. This is not a 'licensing function' under the 2003 Act and the authority for the grant or refusal of such permits will continue to derive from Schedule 9 to the 1968 Act. Local authorities already have responsibility for the grant of permits for AWP machines on other premises and therefore will be aware of the issues that surround them. The following guidance under this sub-heading does not therefore form part of the Guidance issued under section 182 of the 2003 Act in this document but is provided merely to assist licensing authorities in understanding their new responsibility for AWP machines in connection with premises licensed for the sale of alcohol for consumption on those premises.

5.120 Permits last for a minimum period of three years but may be issued for longer periods. The current fee for the grant or renewal of a permit under section 34 of the 1968 Act is £32.

5.121 The Secretary of State recommends that applicants for permits be advised that they may make applications by post and that provided the fee has been paid, they need not attend a hearing unless notified to do so. Applicants to licensing authorities must be holders of premises licences authorising the sale of alcohol for consumption on the premises. It has been the practice for a number of years for companies who rent or lease machines to licence holders to make application for the grant and renewal of permits, and where such applications are made the company should make it clear that the application is made on behalf of, and with the agreement of, the premises licence holder. In the absence of such information, the application should be postponed for the premises licence holder's consent to be notified.

5.122 Licensing authorities are not permitted to attach conditions on the grant of a section 34 permit other than a condition limiting the number of machines authorised under it. The Secretary of State also recommends that licensing authorities should not require applicants to provide a plan of the premises indicating where the machines are to be sited.

5.123 It is recommended that licensing authorities should indicate that its licensing committee and sub-committees will be prepared to grant permits authorising up to two machines without a hearing. If licensing authorities consider it appropriate, they may choose, at their discretion, not to hold hearings in respect of applications concerning larger numbers of such machines.

5.124 There is no requirement under the 1968 Act for the police to be notified of an application.

5.125 Some licensing authorities may be concerned that children are able to play machines authorised under a permit in licensed premises. Parliament has, however, placed no restrictions on the age at which such machines may be played (other than those in amusement arcades). It is therefore a matter for the discretion of the premises licence holder and any adults accompanying the children concerned whether they are entitled to play such machines. In the case of premises used exclusively or primarily for the consumption of alcohol, all children under the age of 16 will only be lawfully permitted entry to the premises if accompanied by adults. The British Amusement Catering Trade Association (BACTA), the gaming machines trade representative body, have a code of practice in respect of children and gaming machines to which their members are expected to adhere.

5.126 Under paragraph 10A of Schedule 9 to the Gaming Act 1968, all such machines must be located in a bar of the premises. The 2003 Act amends this paragraph in respect of the meaning of 'bar' and licensing authorities should note that 'bar' in this context means any place which, by virtue of the premises licence, may be used for the supply of alcohol, and which is exclusively or mainly used for the supply and consumption of alcohol.

Large scale temporary events requiring premises licences

5.127 Licensing authorities should note that a premises licence may be sought for a short, discrete period. The 2003 Act also provides for the giving of temporary event notices. These are dealt with later in this Guidance. Temporary event notices are subject to various conditions and limitations. These concern:

- duration – they are limited to events lasting for up to 96 hours (this relates to the period during which licensable activities may be carried on, and does not relate to preparation and setting up time, packing away or clearing up time);
- scale – they cannot involve the presence of more than 499 people at any one time;
- use of the same premises – the same premises cannot be used on more than 12 occasions in any calendar year, but are subject to the overall aggregate of 15 days irrespective of the number of occasions on which they have been used; and
- the number of notices given by one individual within a given period of time – a personal licence holder is limited to 50 notices in one year, and any other person to five notices in the same period.

5.128 If these conditions are not fulfilled, a temporary event at which licensable activities are to take place may not be a permitted temporary activity carried on under the authority of a temporary event notice but would require a premises licence, if the premises or place at which the event is to take place is currently unlicensed for the activity or activities involved. The procedures for applying for and granting such a licence are identical to those for an unlimited duration premises licence except that it should be stated on the application that the period of the licence will be limited. Licensing authorities should note that they should clearly specify on such a licence when it comes into force and when the permission ends. Where the sale of alcohol is involved, there will need to be a designated premises supervisor specified who must be a personal licence holder.

5.129 Temporary events may range from relatively small local events, like fairs, which may last for four or five days, to major pop festivals lasting only one day. Despite the temporary duration of such major events, they can attract huge crowds of more than 100,000 and the risks to public safety and to crime and disorder as well as public nuisance may be considerable. Licensing authorities are expected to make clear in local publicity that they should be given early notice of such major events to allow responsible authorities to discuss operating schedules with the organisers well before a formal application is submitted. Many of these events will give rise to special considerations in respect of public safety. Operating schedules should therefore reflect an awareness of these matters and in particular, advice given in the following documents will be relevant:

- The Event Safety Guide – A guide to health, safety and welfare at music and similar events (HSE 1999)('The Purple Book') ISBN 0 7176 2453 6
- Managing Crowds Safely (HSE 2000) ISBN 0 7176 1834 X
- 5 Steps to Risk Assessment: Case Studies (HSE 1998) ISBN 07176 15804
- The Guide to Safety at Sports Grounds (The Stationery Office, 1997) ('The Green Guide') ISBN 0 11 300095 2
- Safety Guidance for Street Arts, Carnival, Processions and Large Scale Performances published by the Independent Street Arts Network, copies of which may be obtained through **www.streetartsnetwork.org.uk/pages/publications.htm**.

APPENDIX B2

Annex D – Conditions relating to the prevention of crime and disorder

It should be noted in particular that it is unlawful under the 2003 Act:

- **knowingly to sell or supply or attempt to sell or supply alcohol to a person who is drunk**
- **knowingly to allow disorderly conduct on licensed premises**
- **for the holder of a premises licence or a designated premises supervisor knowingly to keep or to allow to be kept on licensed premises any goods that have been imported without payment of duty or which have otherwise been unlawfully imported**
- **to allow the presence of children under 16 who are not accompanied by an adult between midnight and 5am at any premises licensed for the sale of alcohol for consumption on the premises, and at any time in premises used exclusively or primarily for the sale and consumption of alcohol**

Conditions enforcing these arrangements are therefore unnecessary.

General

When applicants for premises licences or club premises certificates are preparing their operating schedules or club operating schedules, when responsible authorities are considering such applications and when licensing authorities are considering applications following the receipt of any relevant representations from a responsible authority or interested party, the following options should be considered as measures which, if necessary, would promote the prevention of crime and disorder.

Whether or not any risk assessment shows these options to be necessary in the individual circumstances of any premises will depend on a range of factors including the nature and style of the venue, the activities being conducted there, the location of the premises and the anticipated clientele of the business involved. It should also be borne in mind that club premises operate under codes of discipline to ensure the good order and behaviour of members.

Necessary conditions for the licence or certificate will also depend on local knowledge of the premises.

Under no circumstances should the following measures be regarded as standard conditions to be automatically imposed in all cases. They are designed to provide a range of possible conditions drawn from experience relating to differing situations and to offer guidance.

Any individual preparing an operating schedule is at liberty to volunteer any measure, such as those described below, as a step he or she intends to take to promote the licensing objectives. When incorporated into the licence or certificate as a condition, they become enforceable under the law and a breach of such a condition could give rise to prosecution.

Text/Radio pagers

Text and radio pagers connecting premises licence holders, designated premises supervisors, managers of premises and clubs to the local police can provide for rapid response by the police to situations of disorder which may be endangering the customers and staff on the premises.

Such pagers provide two-way communication, both enabling licence holders, managers, designated premises supervisors and clubs to report incidents to the police, and enabling the police to warn those operating a large number of other premises of potential trouble-makers or individuals suspected of criminal behaviour who are about in a particular area. Pager systems can also be used by licence holders, door supervisors, managers, designated premises supervisors and clubs to warn each other of the presence in an area of such people.

The Secretary of State recommends that text or radio pagers should be considered appropriate necessary conditions for public houses, bars and nightclubs operating in city and town centre leisure areas with a high density of licensed premises. Following individual consideration of the particular circumstances of the venue, such conditions may also be appropriate and necessary in other areas for the prevention of crime and disorder.

It is recommended that a condition requiring the text/radio pager links to the police should include the following elements:

- a requirement that the text/pager equipment is kept in working order at all times;
- a requirement that the pager link be activated, made available to and monitored by the designated premises supervisor or a responsible member of staff at all times that the premises are open to the public;
- a requirement that any police instructions/directions are complied with whenever given; and
- a requirement that all instances of crime or disorder are reported via the text/radio pager link by the designated premises supervisor or a responsible member of staff to an agreed police contact point.

Door supervisors

Conditions relating to the provision of door supervisors and security teams may be valuable in:

- preventing the admission and ensuring the departure from the premises of the drunk and disorderly, without causing further disorder;
- keeping out excluded individuals (subject to court bans or imposed by the licence holder);
- searching and excluding those suspected of carrying illegal drugs, or carrying offensive weapons; and
- maintaining orderly queuing outside of venues prone to such queuing.

Where door supervisors conducting security activities are to be a condition of a licence, which means that they would have to be registered with the Security Industry Authority, conditions may also need to deal with the number of such supervisors, the displaying of name badges, the carrying of proof of registration, where and at what times they should be stationed on the premises, and whether at least one female supervisor should be available (for example, if female customers are to be the subject of body searches). Door supervisors also have a role to play in ensuring public safety (see Annex E).

Bottle bans

Glass bottles may be used as weapons inflicting more serious harm during incidents of disorder. A condition can prevent sales of drinks in glass bottles for consumption on the premises.

It is recommended that a condition requiring that no sales of beverages in glass bottles for consumption on the premises should be expressed in clear terms and include the following elements:

- no bottles containing beverages of any kind, whether open or sealed, shall be given to customers on the premises whether at the bar or by staff service away from the bar;
- no customers carrying open or sealed bottles shall be admitted to the premises at any time that the premises are open to the public (**note:** this needs to be carefully worded where off-sales also take place);

In appropriate circumstances, the condition could include exceptions, for example, as follows:

- but bottles containing wine may be sold for consumption with a table meal by customers who are seated in an area set aside from the main bar area for the consumption of food.

Plastic containers and toughened glass

Glasses containing drinks may be used as weapons during incidents of disorder and in untoughened form, can cause very serious injuries. Consideration could therefore be given to conditions requiring either the use of plastic containers or toughened glass which inflicts less severe injuries where considered necessary. Location and style of the venue and the activities carried on there would be particularly important in assessing whether a condition is necessary. For example, the use of glass containers on the terraces of some outdoor sports grounds may obviously be of concern, and similar concerns may also apply to indoor sports events such as boxing matches. Similarly, the use of such plastic containers or toughened glass during the televising of live sporting events, such as international football matches, when high states of excitement and emotion fuelled by alcohol might arise, may be a necessary condition.

It should be noted that the use of plastic or paper drinks containers and toughened glass may also be relevant as measures necessary to promote public safety (see Annex E).

CCTV

The presence of CCTV cameras can be an important means of deterring and detecting crime at and immediately outside licensed premises. Conditions should not just consider a requirement to have CCTV on the premises, but also the precise siting of each camera, the requirement to maintain cameras in working order, and to retain recordings for an appropriate period of time.

The police should provide individuals conducting risk assessments when preparing operating schedules with advice on the use of CCTV to prevent crime.

Open containers not to be taken from the premises

Drinks purchased in licensed premises or clubs may be taken from those premises for consumption elsewhere. Where premises are licensed for the sale of alcohol for consumption off the premises that would be entirely lawful. However, consideration should be given to a condition preventing the taking of alcoholic and other drinks from the premises in open containers (e.g. glasses and opened bottles). This may again be necessary to prevent the use of these containers as offensive weapons in surrounding streets after individuals have left the premises.

Restrictions on drinking areas

It may be necessary to restrict the areas where alcoholic drinks may be consumed in premises after they have been purchased from the bar. An example would be at a sports ground where the police consider it necessary to prevent the consumption of alcohol on the terracing of sports grounds during particular sports events. Such conditions should not only specify these areas, but indicate the circumstances in which the ban would apply and times at which it should be enforced.

Capacity limits

Although most commonly made a condition of a licence on public safety grounds, consideration should also be given to conditions which set capacity limits for licensed premises or clubs where it may be necessary to prevent overcrowding which can lead to disorder and violence. Where such a condition is considered necessary, consideration should also be given to whether door supervisors would be needed to ensure that the numbers are appropriately controlled.

Proof of age cards

It is unlawful for children under 18 to attempt to buy alcohol just as it is unlawful to sell or supply alcohol to them. To prevent such crimes, it may be necessary to require a policy to be applied at certain licensed premises requiring the production of 'proof of age' before such sales are made. This should not be limited to recognised 'proof of age' cards, but allow for the production of other proof, such as photo-driving licences, student cards and passports. The Secretary of State strongly supports the PASS accreditation system (see paragraph 12.8 of the Guidance) which aims to approve and accredit various proof of age schemes that are in existence. This ensures that such schemes maintain high standards, particularly in the area of integrity and security, and where appropriate and necessary, conditions may refer directly to PASS accredited proof of age cards, photo-driving licences and passports.

It should be noted that many adults in England and Wales do not currently carry any proof of age. This means that the wording of any condition will require careful thought. For example, the requirement might be to ensure sight of evidence of age from any person appearing to those selling or supplying alcohol to be under the age of 18 and who is attempting to buy alcohol. This would ensure that most minors – even those looking older – would need to produce proof of age appropriately before making such a purchase. Under such an arrangement only a minority of adults might be affected, but for the majority there would be no disruption to their normal activity, for example, when shopping in a supermarket.

Crime prevention notices

It may be necessary at some premises for notices to be displayed which warn customers of the prevalence of crime which may target them. Some premises may be reluctant to volunteer the display of such notices for commercial reasons. For example, in certain areas, a condition attached to a premises licence or club premises certificate might require the displaying of notices at the premises which warn customers about the need to be aware of pick-pockets or bag snatchers, and to guard their property. Similarly, it may be necessary for notices to be displayed which advise customers not to leave bags unattended because of concerns about terrorism. Consideration could be given to a condition requiring a notice to display the name of a contact for customers if they wish to report concerns.

Drinks promotions

Standardised conditions should not be attached to premises licences or club premises certificates which promote fixed prices for alcoholic drinks. It is also likely to be unlawful for licensing authorities or police officers to promote voluntary arrangements of this kind. This can risk creating cartels. Using conditions to control the prices of alcoholic drinks in an area may also breach competition law. Conditions tailored to the individual circumstances of particular premises which address **irresponsible** drinks promotions may be permissible provided they are necessary for the promotion of the licensing objectives, but licensing authorities should take their own legal advice before a licence or certificate is granted in that form. Judgements may be subjective, and on occasions, there will be a very fine line between responsible and irresponsible promotions but an even greater distinction to whether the promotion in question can be subject to the imposition of a condition. It is therefore vital that such matters are considered objectively in the context of the licensing objectives and with the benefit of appropriate legal advice.

In addition, when considering any relevant representations which demonstrate a clear causal link between sales promotions or discounting and levels of crime and disorder on or in the vicinity of the premises, it would be appropriate for the licensing authority to consider whether the imposition of a new condition prohibiting irresponsible sales promotions or discounting of prices of alcoholic beverages is necessary at those premises. However, before pursuing any form of restrictions at all, licensing authorities should take their own legal advice.

Signage

It may be necessary for the normal hours under the terms of the premises licence or club premises certificate at which licensable activities are permitted to take place to be displayed on or immediately outside the premises so that it is clear if breaches of the terms of the licence or certificate are taking place.

Similarly, it may be necessary for any restrictions on the admission of children to be displayed on or immediately outside the premises so that the consequences of breaches of these conditions would also be clear and to deter those who might seek admission in breach of those conditions.

Large capacity venues used exclusively or primarily for the 'vertical' consumption of alcohol (HVVDs)

Large capacity 'vertical drinking' premises, sometimes called High Volume Vertical Drinking establishments (HVVDs), are premises with exceptionally high capacities, used primarily or exclusively for the sale and consumption of alcohol, and have little or no seating for patrons.

Where necessary and appropriate, conditions can be attached to premises licences for the promotion of the prevention of crime and disorder at such premises (if not volunteered by the venue operator and following representations on such grounds) which require adherence to:

- a prescribed capacity;
- an appropriate ratio of tables and chairs to customers based on the capacity; and
- the presence of SIA registered security teams to control entry for the purpose of compliance with the capacity limit.

APPENDIX B3

Annex E – Conditions relating to public safety (including fire safety)

It should be noted that conditions relating to public safety should be those which are necessary, in the particular circumstances of any individual premises or club premises, and should not duplicate other requirements of the law. Equally, the attachment of conditions to a premises licence or club premises certificate will not in any way relieve employers of the statutory duty to comply with the requirements of other legislation including the Health and Safety at Work etc. Act 1974, associated regulations and especially the requirements under the Management of Health and Safety at Work Regulations 1999 and the Fire Precautions (Workplace) Regulations 1997 to undertake risk assessments. Employers should assess the risks, including risks from fire, and take measures necessary to avoid and control these risks. Conditions enforcing those requirements would therefore be unnecessary.

General

When applicants for premises licences or club premises certificates are preparing their operating schedules or club operating schedules, responsible authorities are considering such applications and licensing authorities are considering applications following the receipt of relevant representations from a responsible authority or interested party, the following options should be considered as measures that, if necessary, would promote public safety. Additional matters relating to cinemas and theatres are considered in Annex F. It should also be recognised that special issues may arise in connection with outdoor and large scale events.

Whether or not any risk assessment shows any of the measures to be necessary in the individual circumstances of any premises will depend on a range of factors including the nature and style of the venue, the activities being conducted there, the location of the premises and the anticipated clientele of the business involved.

Necessary conditions for the licence or certificate will also depend on local knowledge of the premises.

In addition, to considering the points made in this Annex, those preparing operating schedules or club operating schedules, licensing authorities and responsible authorities should consider:

- Model National and Standard Conditions for Places of Public Entertainment and Associated Guidance ISBN 1 904031 11 0 (Entertainment Technology Press – ABTT Publications)
- The Event Safety Guide – A guide to health, safety and welfare at music and similar events (HSE 1999)('The Purple Book') ISBN 0 7176 2453 6
- Managing Crowds Safely (HSE 2000) ISBN 0 7176 1834 X
- 5 Steps to Risk Assessment: Case Studies (HSE 1998) ISBN 07176 15804
- The Guide to Safety at Sports Grounds (The Stationery Office, 1997) ('The Green Guide') ISBN 0 11 300095 2
- Safety Guidance for Street Arts, Carnival, Processions and Large Scale Performances published by the Independent Street Arts Network, copies of which may be obtained through: **www.streetartsnetwork.org.uk/pages/publications.htm**
- The London District Surveyors Association's 'Technical Standards for Places of Public Entertainment' ISBN 0 9531229 2 1

The following British Standards should also be considered:

- BS 5588 Part 6 (regarding places of assembly)
- BS 5588 Part 9 (regarding ventilation and air conditioning systems)
- BS 5588 Part 9 (regarding means of escape for disabled people)
- BS 5839 (fire detection, fire alarm systems and buildings)
- BS 5266 (emergency lighting systems)

However, in consulting these texts, which were prepared prior to the coming into force of the Licensing Act 2003, those creating operating schedules or club operating schedules, licensing authorities and responsible authorities should again note that under no circumstances should any conditions be regarded as standard for all premises.

Any individual preparing an operating schedule or club operating schedule is at liberty to volunteer any measure, such as those described below, as a step he or she intends to take to promote the licensing objectives. When incorporated into the licence or certificate as a condition, they become enforceable under the law and a breach of such a condition could give rise to prosecution.

Disabled people

In certain premises where existing legislation does not provide adequately for the safety of the public, consideration might also be given to conditions that ensure that:

- when disabled people are present, adequate arrangements exist to enable their safe evacuation in the event of an emergency; and
- disabled people on the premises are made aware of those arrangements.

Escape routes

It may be necessary to include conditions relating to the maintenance of all escape routes and exits including external exits. These might be expressed in terms of the need to ensure that such exits are kept unobstructed, in good order with non-slippery and even surfaces, free of trip hazards and clearly identified. In restaurants and other premises where chairs and tables are provided this might also include ensuring that internal gangways are kept unobstructed.

In certain premises where existing legislation does not provide adequately for the safety of the public, consideration might also be given to conditions that ensure that:

- all exits doors are easily openable without the use of a key, card, code or similar means;
- doors at such exits are regularly checked to ensure that they function satisfactorily and a record of the check kept;
- any removable security fastenings are removed whenever the premises are open to the public or occupied by staff;
- all fire doors are maintained effectively self-closing and shall not be held open other than by approved devices (for example, electromagnetic releases operated by smoke detectors);
- fire resisting doors to ducts, service shafts, and cupboards shall be kept locked shut; and
- the edges of the treads of steps and stairways are maintained so as to be conspicuous.

Safety checks

In certain premises where existing legislation does not provide adequately for the safety of the public or club members and guests, consideration might also be given to conditions that ensure that:

- safety checks are carried out before the admission of the public; and
- details of such checks are kept in a Log-book.

Curtains, hangings, decorations and upholstery

In certain premises where existing legislation does not provide adequately for the safety of the public or club members and guests, consideration might also be given to conditions that ensure that:

- hangings, curtains and temporary decorations are maintained in a flame-retardant condition;
- any upholstered seating meets on a continuous basis the pass criteria for smouldering ignition source 0, flaming ignition source 1 and crib ignition source 5 when tested in accordance with section 5 of BS 5852:1990;
- curtains, hangings and temporary decorations are arranged so as not to obstruct exits, fire safety signs or fire-fighting equipment; and
- temporary decorations are not used without prior notification to the licensing authority/fire authority.

Accommodation limits

In certain premises where existing legislation does not provide adequately for the safety of the public or club members and guests, consideration might also be given to conditions that ensure that:

- arrangements are made to ensure that any capacity limit imposed under the premises licence or club premises certificate are not exceeded; and
- the licence holder, a club official, manager or designated premises supervisor should be aware of the number of people on the premises and required to inform any authorised person on request.

Fire action notices

In certain premises where existing legislation does not provide adequately for the safety of the public or club members and guests, consideration might also be given to conditions that ensure that:

- notices detailing the actions to be taken in the event of fire or other emergencies, including how the fire brigade should be summoned, are prominently displayed and protected from damage and deterioration.

Outbreaks of fire

In certain premises where existing legislation does not provide adequately for the safety of the public or club members and guests, consideration might also be given to conditions that ensure that:

- the fire brigade must be called at once to any outbreak of fire, however slight, and the details recorded in a Fire Log-book.

Loss of water

In certain premises where existing legislation does not provide adequately for the safety of the public or club members and guests, consideration might also be given to conditions that ensure that:

- the local Fire Control Centre are notified as soon as possible if the water supply to any hydrant, hose reel, sprinkler, drencher or other fire extinguishing installation is cut off or restricted.

Access for emergency vehicles

In certain premises where existing legislation does not provide adequately for the safety of the public or club members and guests, consideration might also be given to conditions that ensure that:

- access for emergency vehicles is kept clear and free from obstruction.

First aid

In certain premises where existing legislation does not provide adequately for the safety of the public or club members and guests, consideration might also be given to conditions that ensure that:

- adequate and appropriate supply of first aid equipment and materials is available on the premises;
- if necessary, at least one suitably trained first-aider shall be on duty when the public are present; and if more than one suitably trained first-aider that their respective duties are clearly defined.

Lighting

In certain premises where existing legislation does not provide adequately for the safety of the public or club members and guests, consideration might also be given to conditions that ensure that:

- in the absence of adequate daylight, the lighting in any area accessible to the public, members or guests shall be fully in operation when they are present;
- fire safety signs are adequately illuminated;
- emergency lighting is not altered;
- emergency lighting batteries are fully charged before the admission of the public, members or guests; and
- in the event of the failure of normal lighting, where the emergency lighting battery has a capacity of one hour, arrangements are in place to ensure that the public, members or guests leave the premises within 20

minutes unless within that time normal lighting has been restored and the battery is being re-charged; and, if the emergency lighting battery has a capacity of three hours, the appropriate period by the end of which the public should have left the premises is one hour.

Temporary electrical installations

In certain premises where existing legislation does not provide adequately for the safety of the public or club members and guests, consideration might also be given to conditions that ensure that:

- temporary electrical wiring and distribution systems are not provided without [notification to the licensing authority at least ten days before commencement of the work] [prior inspection by a suitable qualified electrician];
- temporary electrical wiring and distribution systems shall comply with the recommendations of BS 7671 or where applicable BS 7909; and
- where they have not been installed by a competent person, temporary electrical wiring and distribution systems are inspected and certified by a competent person before they are put to use.

With regard to the first bullet above, it should be recognised that ten days notice may not be possible where performances are supported by outside technical teams. For example, where temporary electrical installations are made in theatres for television show performances. In such circumstances, the key requirement is that conditions where necessary should ensure that temporary electrical installations are only undertaken by competent qualified persons, for example, employed by the television company.

Indoor sports entertainments

In certain premises where existing legislation does not provide adequately for the safety of the public or club members and guests, consideration might also be given to conditions that ensure that:

- if necessary, an appropriately qualified medical practitioner is present throughout a sports entertainment involving boxing, wrestling, judo, karate or other sports entertainment of a similar nature;
- where a ring is involved, it is constructed and supported by a competent person and inspected by a competent authority and any material used to form the skirt around the ring is flame-retardant;
- at any wrestling or other entertainments of a similar nature members of the public do not occupy any seat within 2.5 metres of the ring; and
- at water sports entertainments, staff adequately trained in rescue and life safety procedures are stationed and remain within the vicinity of the water

at all material times (see also Managing Health and Safety in Swimming Pools issued jointly by the Health and Safety Commission and Sport England).

Alterations to the premises

Premises should not be altered in such a way as to make it impossible to comply with an existing licence condition without first seeking a variation of the premises licence proposing the deletion of the condition relating to public safety in question. The applicant will need to propose in a new operating schedule reflecting the proposed alteration to the premises how he or she intends to take alternative steps to promote the public safety objective. The application for variation will enable the responsible authorities with expertise in safety matters to consider whether the proposal is acceptable.

Special effects

The use of special effects in venues of all kinds being used for regulated entertainment is increasingly common and can present significant risks. Any special effects or mechanical installation should be arranged and stored so as to minimise any risk to the safety of the audience, the performers and staff.

Specials effects which should be considered include:

- dry ice machines and cryogenic fog;
- smoke machines and fog generators;
- pyrotechnics, including fireworks;
- real flame;
- firearms;
- motor vehicles;
- strobe lighting;
- lasers (see HSE Guide The Radiation Safety of lasers used for display purposes [HS(G)95] and BS EN 60825: Safety of laser products);
- explosives and highly flammable substances.

In certain circumstances, it may be necessary to require that certain special effects are only used with the prior notification of the licensing authority or [inspection by] the fire authority.

APPENDIX B4

Annex G – Conditions relating to the prevention of public nuisance

It should be noted that provisions of the Environmental Protection Act 1990 and the Noise Act 1996 provide some protection to the general public from the effects of noise nuisance. In addition, the provisions in Part 8 of the Licensing Act 2003 enable a senior police officer to close down instantly for up to 24 hours licensed premises and premises carrying on temporary permitted activities that are causing nuisance resulting from noise emanating from the premises. These matters should be considered before deciding whether or not conditions are necessary for the prevention of public nuisance.

General

When applicants for premises licences or club premises certificates are preparing their operating schedules or club operating schedules, responsible authorities are considering such applications and licensing authorities are considering applications following the receipt of relevant representations from a responsible authority or interested party, the following options should be considered as measures that, if necessary, would promote the prevention of public nuisance.

Whether or not any risk assessment shows them to be necessary in the individual circumstances of any premises will depend on a range of factors including the nature and style of the venue, the activities being conducted there, the location of the premises and the anticipated clientele of the business involved.

Necessary conditions for licences and certificates will also depend on local knowledge of the premises.

Hours

The hours during which the premises are permitted to be open to the public or to members and their guests can be restricted (other than where they are protected by the transitional provisions of the Licensing Act 2003) by the conditions of a premises licence or a club premises certificate for the prevention of public nuisance. But this must be balanced by the potential impact on disorder which results from artificially early fixed closing times.

Restrictions could be necessary on the times when certain licensable activities take place even though the premises may be open to the public at such times. For example, the playing of recorded music after a certain time might be prohibited, even though other licensable activities are permitted to continue.

Restrictions might be necessary on the parts of premises that might be used for certain licensable activities at certain times. For example, while the provision of regulated entertainment might be permitted while the premises is open to the public or members and their guests, regulated entertainment might not be permitted in garden areas of the premises after a certain time.

Noise and vibration

In certain premises where existing legislation does not provide adequately for the prevention of public nuisance, consideration might be given to conditions that ensure that:

- noise or vibration does not emanate from the premises so as to cause a nuisance to nearby properties. This might be achieved by a simple requirement to keep doors and windows at the premises closed, or to use noise limiters on amplification equipment used at the premises;
- prominent, clear and legible notices are displayed at all exits requesting the public to respect the needs of local residents and to leave the premises and the area quietly;
- the use of explosives, pyrotechnics and fireworks of a similar nature which could cause disturbance in surrounding areas are restricted; and
- the placing of refuse – such as bottles – into receptacles outside the premises takes place at times that will minimise the disturbance to nearby properties.

Noxious smells

In certain premises where existing legislation does not provide adequately for the prevention of public nuisance, consideration might be given to conditions that ensure that:

- noxious smells from licensed premises are not permitted so as to cause a nuisance to nearby properties and the premises are properly vented.

Light pollution

In certain premises where existing legislation does not provide adequately for the prevention of public nuisance, consideration might be given to conditions that ensure that:

- flashing or particularly bright lights on or outside licensed premises do not cause a nuisance to nearby properties. Any such condition needs to be balanced against the benefits to the prevention of crime and disorder of bright lighting in certain places.

APPENDIX B5

Annex H – Conditions relating to the protection of children from harm

It should be noted that it is unlawful under the 2003 Act to permit unaccompanied children under the age of 16 to be present on premises exclusively or primarily used for supply of alcohol for consumption on those premises under the authorisation of a premises licence, club premises certificate or a temporary event notice when open for the purposes of being used for the supply of alcohol for consumption there. In addition, it is an offence to permit the presence of children under 16 who are not accompanied by an adult between midnight and 5am at all premises supplying alcohol for consumption on those premises under the authorisation of any premises licence, club premises certificate or temporary event notice. Conditions duplicating these provisions are, therefore, unnecessary.

Access for children to licensed premises – in general

Restrictions on the access of children under 18 to premises where licensable activities are being carried on should be made where it is necessary to protect children from harm. Precise policy and details will be a matter for individual licensing authorities. Conditions attached to premises licences and club premises certificates may reflect the concerns of responsible authorities and interested parties who have made representations but only where the licensing authority considers it necessary to protect children from harm. Whilst applications in relation to premises licences and club premises certificates must be judged by licensing authorities on their individual merits and characteristics, the Secretary of State recommends (unless there are circumstances justifying the contrary) that:

- for any premises with known associations (having been presented with evidence) with or likely to give rise to heavy or binge or underage drinking, drugs, significant gambling, or any activity or entertainment (whether regulated entertainment or not) of a clearly adult or sexual nature, there should be a strong presumption against permitting any access at all for children under 18 years. Applicants wishing to allow access for children to premises where these associations may be relevant, when preparing operating schedules or club operating schedules or

variations of those schedules for the purposes of obtaining or varying a premises licence or club premises certificate should:
- explain their reasons; and
- outline in detail the steps that they intend to take to protect children from harm on such premises.

- for any premises, not serving alcohol for consumption on the premises, but where the public are allowed on the premises after 11.00pm in the evening, there should be a presumption against the presence of children under the age of 12 unaccompanied by adults after that time. Applicants wishing to allow access when preparing operating schedules or variations of those schedules or club operating schedules for the purposes of obtaining or varying a premises licence or club premises certificate should:
  - explain their reasons; and
  - outline in detail the steps that they intend to take to protect children from harm on such premises.
- in any other case, subject to the premises licence holder's or club's discretion, the expectation would be for unrestricted access for children subject to the terms of the 2003 Act. An operating schedule or club operating schedule should indicate any decision for the premises to exclude children completely, which would mean there would be no need to detail in the operating schedule steps that the applicant proposes to take to promote the protection of children from harm. Otherwise, where entry is to be permitted, the operating schedule should outline the steps to be taken to promote the protection of children from harm while on the premises.

Age Restrictions – specific

Under the 2003 Act a wide variety of licensable activities could take place at various types of premises and at different times of the day and night. Whilst it may be appropriate to allow children unrestricted access at particular times and when certain activities are not taking place, licensing authorities following relevant representations made by responsible authorities and interested parties will need to consider a range of conditions that are to be tailored to the particular premises and their activities where these are necessary. Licensing authorities are expected to consider:

- the hours of day during which age restrictions should and should not apply. For example, the fact that adult entertainment may be presented at premises after 8.00pm does not mean that it would be necessary to impose age restrictions for earlier parts of the day;
- types of event or activity in respect of which no age restrictions may be needed, for example;
  - family entertainment; or
  - non-alcohol events for young age groups, such as under 18s dances,

- Similarly, types of event or activity which give rise to a more acute need for age restrictions than normal, for example;
  - during 'Happy Hours' or on drinks promotion nights;
  - during activities outlined in the first bullet point in the first paragraph above.

Age restrictions – cinemas

The Secretary of State considers that, in addition to the mandatory condition imposed by virtue of section 20, requiring the admission of children to films to be restricted in accordance with recommendations given either by a body designated under section 4 of the Video Recordings Act 1984 or by the licensing authority itself, conditions restricting the admission of children to film exhibitions should include:

- a condition that where the licensing authority itself is to make recommendations on the admission of children to films, the cinema or venue operator must submit any film to the authority that it intends to exhibit 28 days before it is proposed to show it. This is to allow the authority time to classify it so that the premises licence holder is able to adhere to any age restrictions then imposed;
- a condition that when films are classified, by either the film classification body as specified in the licence or the licensing authority, they should be classified in the following way:
  - U – Universal. Suitable for audiences aged four years and over
  - PG – Parental Guidance. Some scenes may be unsuitable for young children.
  - 12A – Passed only for viewing by persons aged 12 years or older or persons younger than 12 when accompanied by an adult.
  - 15 – Passed only for viewing by persons aged 15 years and over.
  - 18 – Passed only for viewing by persons aged 18 years and over.
- that conditions specify that immediately before each exhibition at the premises of a film passed by the British Board of Film Classification there shall be exhibited on screen for at least five seconds in such a manner as to be easily read by all persons in the auditorium a reproduction of the certificate of the Board or, as regards a trailer advertising a film, of the statement approved by the Board indicating the classification of the film;
- a condition that when a licensing authority has made a recommendation on the restriction of admission of children to a film, notices are required to be displayed both inside and outside the premises so that persons entering can readily be made aware of the classification attached to any film or trailer. Such a condition might be expressed in the following terms:

  > "Where a programme includes a film recommended by the licensing authority as falling into the 12A, 15 or 18 category no person appearing to

be under the age of 12 and unaccompanied, or under 15 or 18 as appropriate, shall be admitted to any part of the programme; and the licence holder shall display in a conspicuous position a notice in the following terms –
PERSONS UNDER THE AGE OF [INSERT APPROPRIATE AGE] CANNOT BE ADMITTED TO ANY PART OF THE PROGRAMME
Where films of different categories form part of the same programme, the notice shall refer to the oldest age restriction.
This condition does not apply to members of staff under the relevant age while on-duty provided that the prior written consent of the person's parent or legal guardian has first been obtained."

Theatres

The admission of children to theatres, as with other licensed premises, is not expected to normally be restricted unless it is necessary to promote the licensing objective of the protection of children from harm. However, theatres may be the venue for a wide range of activities. The admission of children to the performance of a play is expected to normally be left to the discretion of the licence holder and no condition restricting the access of children to plays should be attached. However, theatres may also present entertainment including, for example, variety shows, incorporating adult entertainment. A condition restricting the admission of children in such circumstances may be necessary. Entertainment may also be presented at theatres specifically for children (see below).

Licensing authorities are also expected to consider whether a condition should be attached to a premises licence which requires the presence of a sufficient number of adult staff on the premises to ensure the well being of children present on the premises during any emergency (See Annex F).

Performances especially for children

Where performances are presented especially for unaccompanied children in theatres and cinemas conditions are anticipated to be needed which require:

- an attendant to be stationed in the area(s) occupied by the children, in the vicinity of each exit, provided that on each level occupied by children the minimum number of attendants on duty should be one attendant per 50 children or part thereof.

Licensing authorities are expected, having regard to any representations made by responsible authorities on the issue, to also consider whether or not standing should be allowed. For example, there may be reduced risk for children in the stalls than at other levels or areas in the building.

Children in performances

There are many productions each year that are one-off shows where the cast is made up almost entirely of children. They may be taking part as individuals or as part of a drama club, stage school or school group. The age of those involved may range from 5 to 18. The Children (Performances) Regulations 1968 as amended set out requirements for children performing in a show. Licensing authorities should familiarise themselves with the requirements of these Regulations and not duplicate any of these requirements. However, if it is necessary to consider imposing conditions, in addition to these requirements, for the promotion of the protection of children from harm then the licensing authority should consider the matters outlined below.

- **Venue** – the backstage facilities should be large enough to accommodate safely the number of children taking part in any performance.
- **Fire safety** – all chaperones and production crew on the show should receive instruction on the fire procedures applicable to the venue prior to the arrival of the children.
- **Special effects** – it may be inappropriate to use certain special effects, including smoke, dry ice, rapid pulsating or flashing lights, which may trigger adverse reactions especially with regard to children.
- **Care of children** – theatres, concert halls and similar places are places of work and may contain a lot of potentially dangerous equipment. It is therefore important that children performing at such premises are kept under adult supervision at all times including transfer from stage to dressing room and anywhere else on the premises. It is also important that the children can be accounted for at all times in case of an evacuation or emergency.

The Portman Group Code of Practice on the Naming, Packaging and Promotion of Alcoholic Drinks

The Portman Group operates, on behalf of the alcohol industry, a Code of Practice on the Naming, Packaging and Promotion of Alcoholic Drinks. The Code seeks to ensure that drinks are packaged and promoted in a socially responsible manner and only to those who are 18 years old or older. Complaints about products under the Code are considered by an Independent Complaints Panel and the Panel's decisions are published on the Portman Group's website, in the trade press and in an annual report. If a product's packaging or point-of-sale advertising is found to be in breach of the Code, the Portman Group may issue a Retailer Alert Bulletin to notify retailers of the decision and ask them not to replenish stocks of any such product or to display such point-of-sale material, until the decision has been complied with. The Code is an important mechanism in protecting children from harm because it addresses the naming, marketing and promotion of alcohol products sold in licensed premises in a manner which may appeal to or attract minors.

Where appropriate and necessary, consideration can be given to attaching conditions to premises licences and club premises certificates that require compliance with the Portman Group's Retailer Alert Bulletins.

Proof of Age cards

Proof of age cards are discussed under Annex D in connection with the prevention of crime and disorder. However, where necessary and appropriate, a requirement for the production of proof of age cards before any sale of alcohol is made could be attached to any premises licence or club premises certificate for the protection of children from harm. Any such requirement should not be limited to recognised 'proof of age' cards, but allow for the production of other proof, such as photo-driving licences and passports. The Secretary of State strongly supports the PASS accreditation system (see paragraph 12.8 of the Guidance) which aims to approve and accredit various proof of age schemes that are in existence. This ensures that such schemes maintain high standards, particularly in the area of integrity and security, and where appropriate and necessary, conditions may refer directly to PASS accredited proof of age cards, photo-driving licences, student cards and passports. As for conditions relating to crime and disorder, it should be noted that many adults in England and Wales do not currently carry any proof of age. This means that the wording of any condition will require careful thought. For example, the requirement might be to ensure sight of evidence of age from any person appearing to those engaged in selling or supplying alcohol to be under the age of 18 and who is attempting to buy alcohol. This would ensure that most minors – even those looking older – would need to produce proof of age appropriately before making such a purchase. Under such an arrangement only a minority of adults might be affected, but for the majority there would be no disruption to their normal activity, for example, when shopping in a supermarket.

Proof of age cards can also ensure that appropriate checks are made where the presence of children is restricted by age at certain times, such as 16.

APPENDIX C

Sample clauses

APPENDIX C1

Obtaining seller's consent to transfer of premises licence

The Seller shall on [or] [within 5 working days after] the date of this Agreement hand over to the Buyer a consent signed by 'X' [the Licence Holder of the Premises Licence for the Property] consenting to the transfer of the Premises Licence to [the Buyer] [Y [the person nominated by the Buyer to be the new Licence Holder]] such consent to be in the form annexed to this Agreement

Alternatively where the buyer is applying to the licensing authority for a transfer of the premises licence with immediate effect :

The Seller shall on [or] [within 5 working days after] the date of this Agreement hand over to the Buyer a consent signed by 'X' [the Licence Holder of the Premises Licence for the Property] consenting to the transfer of the Premises Licence with immediate effect to [the Buyer] [the person nominated by the Buyer to be the new Licence Holder] such consent to be in the form annexed to this Agreement

Drafting Notes: 'Premises Licence' needs to be defined and form of consent needs to be annexed to the agreement.

APPENDIX C2

Contract conditional on transfer of premises licence

Agreement conditional on transfer of Premises Licence

(1) This Agreement is conditional upon the transfer of the Premises Licence to [the Buyer] [Y [the person nominated by the Buyer to be the new Licence Holder]]

(2) The Buyer shall [on] [within [ ] working days of] the date of this Agreement apply to the Licensing Authority for a transfer of the Premises Licence to [the Buyer] [Y [the person nominated by the Buyer to be the new Licence Holder]] and shall use [his best] [all reasonable] endeavours to obtain the transfer of the Premises Licence by the Completion Date [but this obligation shall not extend to the Buyer appealing against any rejection of the application to transfer the Premises Licence by the Licensing Authority] and the Buyer shall keep the Seller informed of the progress of the Buyer's application to transfer the Premises Licence

(3) The Seller shall use [his best] [all reasonable] endeavours to assist the Buyer to obtain the transfer of the Premises Licence

(4) If the transfer of the Premises Licence has not taken place by the [Completion Date] then completion of the sale and purchase shall take place [on the date of the transfer of the Premises Licence] [within [ ] working days of the transfer of the Premises Licence being notified to the Buyer] who shall forthwith notify the Seller of such transfer

(5) If the Premises Licence has not been transferred to the Buyer by [ ] ('the Longstop Date') either party may rescind this Agreement by written notice to that effect to the other party whereupon this Agreement shall become null and void but without prejudice to any claim by either party against the other for any antecedent breach of the terms of this Agreement [Provided That in the event that there is an appeal against the Licensing Authority's rejection of the application to transfer the Premises Licence which has yet to be determined the Longstop Date shall be extended to [ ] working days after determination of such appeal]

Drafting Notes:

Define: 'Premises Licence'; 'Licensing Authority'; 'Completion Date'.

Note also that this clause will be unnecessary if the buyer applies for a transfer with immediate effect. However if the buyer wishes to have certainty as to the transfer of the premises licence then the contract will need to be conditional on the outcome of the application for the transfer.

A seller may wish the buyer to appeal against any rejection of the application. On the other hand the buyer may wish to review his chances of success before lodging any appeal.

APPENDIX C3

Contract conditional on grant of new premises licence

(1) This Agreement is conditional upon the grant to the Buyer [or his nominee] of a Premises Licence for the Property [which is subject only to such conditions as are acceptable to the Buyer [acting reasonably]] [which is subject only to such conditions as are listed in the schedule] [which is subject only to such conditions as would be acceptable to a reasonable buyer]

(2) The Buyer shall [on] [within [ ] working days of] the date of this Agreement apply to the Licensing Authority for the Premises Licence and shall use [his best] [all reasonable] endeavours to obtain the Premises Licence by the Completion Date [but this obligation shall not extend to the Buyer appealing against any rejection of the application for the Premises Licence by the Licensing Authority or against any conditions attached to the Premises Licence] [and this obligation shall extend to the Buyer appealing against any rejection of the application for the Premises Licence by the Licensing Authority or against any conditions attached to the Premises Licence if so required by the Seller] and the Buyer shall keep the Seller informed of the progress of the Buyer's application for the Premises Licence and the decision of the Licensing Authority

(3) The Seller shall use [his best] [all reasonable] endeavours to assist the Buyer to obtain the Premises Licence

(4) If the grant of the Premises Licence has not taken place by the [Completion Date] then completion of the sale and purchase shall take place [on the date of the grant of the Premises Licence] [within [ ] working days of the grant of the Premises Licence] [or within [ ] days of a determination that the grant of the Premises Licence is not subject to unreasonable conditions in accordance with the provisions of clause [5] below] and the Buyer shall forthwith notify the Seller of such grant [and in the event that the grant of the Premises Licence is subject to conditions [which are not conditions listed in the schedule]] [which a reasonable buyer would not find acceptable] ('unreasonable conditions') that the Buyer considers the grant of the Premises Licence to be subject to unreasonable conditions]

[(5) In the event that the Seller does not agree that the grant of the Premises Licence is subject to unreasonable conditions he shall inform the Buyer of his disagreement within [ ] working days of the Buyer's notification referred to in clause [4] above and such dispute shall be referred to the independent [surveyor] in accordance with clause [ ] of this agreement whose decision as to whether or not the grant of the Premises Licence contains unreasonable conditions shall be final]

(6) If the Premises Licence has not been granted to the Buyer by [ ] ('the Longstop Date') either party may rescind this Agreement by written notice to that effect to the other party whereupon this Agreement shall become null and void but without prejudice to any claim by either party against the other for any antecedent breach of the terms of this Agreement [Provided That in the event that there is an appeal against the Licensing Authority's rejection of the application for the Premises Licence or the conditions

attaching to the Premises Licence which has yet to be determined the Longstop Date shall be extended to [ ] working days after determination of such appeal]

(7) For the purposes of this Agreement the grant of the Premises Licence shall not be deemed to be obtained until the time limits for objectors to appeal against the grant of the Premises Licence have expired or the final disposal of any appeal against such grant

Drafting Note:

(a) Define: 'Premises Licence'; 'Licensing Authority'; 'Completion Date'.

(b) If the option in clause 1 which specifies acceptable conditions is used these will need to be defined in a schedule attached to the agreement.

(c) Clause 5 assumes that there is a dispute resolution clause in the agreement – if not one will need to be drafted. The draftsman will need to identify the independent person who could be an experienced licensing solicitor or surveyor experienced in licensed premises.

(d) Clauses 4 and 5 are drafted with alternative provisions since a buyer may wish to have absolute determination of whether or not conditions attaching to the premises licence are acceptable. A seller may on the other hand wish to have more control or have an objective test of the reasonableness of such conditions.

APPENDIX C4

Contract conditional on issue of provisional statement

(1) This Agreement is conditional upon the issue to the Buyer [or his nominee] of a Provisional Statement for the Property [which is subject only to such conditions as are acceptable to the Buyer [acting reasonably]] [which is subject only to such conditions as are listed in the schedule] [which is subject only to such conditions as would be acceptable to a reasonable buyer]

(2) The Buyer shall [on] [within [ ] working days of] the date of this Agreement apply to the Licensing Authority for the issue of a Provisional Statement and shall use [his best] [all reasonable] endeavours to obtain the issue of the Provisional Statement by the Completion Date [but this obligation shall not extend to the Buyer appealing against any conditions attached to the Provisional Statement] [and this obligation shall extend to the Buyer appealing against any conditions attached to the Provisional Statement if so required by the Seller] and the Buyer shall keep the Seller informed of the progress of the Buyer's application for the Provisional Statement and the decision of the Licensing Authority

(3) The Seller shall use [his best] [all reasonable] endeavours to assist the Buyer to obtain the issue of the Provisional Statement

(4) If the issue of the Provisional Statement has not taken place by the [Completion Date] then completion of the sale and purchase shall take place [on the date of the issue of the Provisional Statement] [within [ ] working days of the issue of the Provisional Statement] [or within [ ] days of a determination that the issue of the Provisional Statement is not subject to unreasonable conditions in accordance with the provisions of clause [5] below] and the Buyer shall forthwith notify the Seller of such issue [and in the event that the issue of the Provisional Statement is subject to conditions [which are not conditions listed in the schedule]] [which a reasonable buyer would not find acceptable] ("unreasonable conditions") that the Buyer considers the issue of the Provisional Statement to be subject to unreasonable conditions]

[(5) In the event that the Seller does not agree that the issue of the Provisional Statement is subject to unreasonable conditions he shall inform the Buyer of his disagreement within [ ] working days of the Buyer's notification referred to in clause [4] above and such dispute shall be referred to the independent [surveyor] [solicitor] in accordance with clause [ ] of this Agreement whose decision as to whether or not the issue of the Provisional Statement contains unreasonable conditions shall be final]

(6) If the Provisional Statement has not been issued to the Buyer by [ ] ('the Longstop Date') either party may rescind this Agreement by written notice to that effect to the other party whereupon this Agreement shall become null and void but without prejudice to any claim by either party against the other for any antecedent breach of the terms of this Agreement [Provided That in the event that there is an appeal against any of the conditions attaching to the Provisional Statement which has yet to be determined the Longstop Date shall be extended to [ ] working days after determination of such appeal]

(7) For the purposes of this Agreement the Provisional Statement shall not be deemed to be issued until the time limits for objectors to appeal against the issue of the Provisional Statement have expired or the final disposal of any appeal against such issue

Drafting Notes:

(a) Define: 'Provisional Statement'; 'Licensing Authority'; 'Completion Date'.

(b) If the option in clause 1 which specifies acceptable conditions is used these will need to be defined in a schedule attached to the agreement.

(c) Clause 5 assumes that there is a dispute resolution clause in the agreement – if not, one will need to be drafted. The draftsman will need to identify the independent person who could be an experienced licensing solicitor or surveyor experienced in licensed premises.

(d) Clauses 4 and 5 are drafted with alternative provisions since a buyer may wish to have absolute determination of whether or not conditions attaching to the provisional statement are acceptable. A seller may on the other hand wish to have more control or have an objective test of the reasonableness of such conditions.

APPENDIX C5

Notice of application for a new premises licence

Licensing Act 2003
Application for a new premises licence

Applicant: [1]
Address: [2]

Details of application: [3]

A copy of the full application can be viewed at the Licensing Authority's address during normal office hours.

Any person wishing to make representations on this application may do so by writing to [4] by [5].

It is an offence knowingly or recklessly to make a false statement in connection with this application, the maximum fine on summary conviction being £5,000.

Drafting notes:

Insert information as set out below.

[1] Name of applicant
[2] Name and postal address of premises
[3] Brief description of application (e.g. application for premises licence to authorise the provision of alcohol and regulated entertainment from Monday-Sunday between the hours of 11am and midnight)
[4] Name and address of Licensing Authority
[5] Date – 28 days from the day after the date the application was given to the Licensing Authority

Index